Practical Wildlife Photography

The Practical Photography Series

Practical Composition in Photography   Axel Brück
Practical Exposure in Photography   Leonard Gaunt
Practical Effects in Photography   Carl Bernard & Karen Norquay
Practical Wildlife Photography   Ken Preston-Mafham

Ken Preston-Mafham

Practical Wildlife Photography

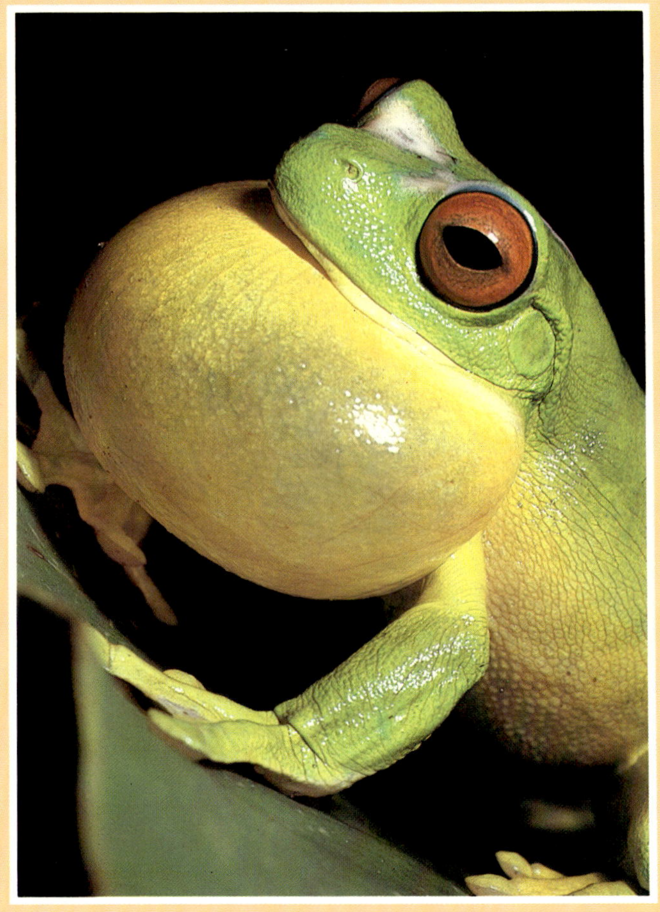

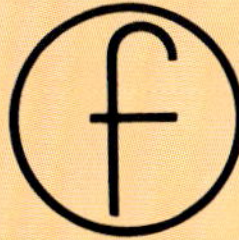

Focal Press London & Boston

Focal Press

is an imprint of the Butterworth Group
which has principal offices in

London, Boston, Durban, Singapore, Sydney, Toronto, Wellington

First published 1982

© Ken Preston-Mafham, 1982

British Library Cataloguing in Publication Data

Preston-Mafham, Kenneth
    Practical wildlife photography. – (The practical series).
    1. Nature photography
    I. Title II. Series
    778.9'3   TR721   80–40792

    ISBN 0-240-51081-X

All photographs appear by courtesy of Premaphotos Wildlife, except those on pages 136 and 145 which are by Mike Wilkes

Typeset by Input Typesetting Ltd, London
Printed in England by Clout & Baker Ltd, Maidstone, Kent

Title page: *Litoria chloris,* Red-eyed treefrog. As mentioned on p. 127, many male frogs are reluctant to call while a light is shone on them. This species was a welcome exception, and would happily blast away with the focusing light only a few inches from its face. The throat vocal-sac is only inflated to its fullest extent for a second or two, so you have to be quick to press the shutter, resisting the temptation to shoot before the sac is fully inflated. Focus on the eye, which must always be in focus, even if the nearest section of the vocal-sac is slightly 'soft'. Queensland sub-tropical rainforest, Australia.

Contents

Introduction

This book has been designed to be of use to those people who already have a knowledge of natural history or photography, as well as to the reader who knows nothing about either. I have made the scope as broad as possible to encompass the maximum amount of information about the natural subjects themselves as well as advice on the specialised photographic techniques involved in much wildlife work.

In the world of plants and animals colour is of supreme importance. Flowers are brightly coloured to attract pollinating insects, male birds use their gaudy plumage to attract a mate and camouflaged insects use drab colours to blend into their surroundings. In view of this pre-eminent position of colour in the natural world most people these days work exclusively on colour materials for all wildlife photography, using mainly colour-slide films which are also the medium normally used for illustrations in books and magazines. I have therefore made no mention in the text of black and white photography and have assumed that anyone reading this book will be intending to use colour-slide films exclusively.

There are many reasons why people take pictures of natural living organisms. Some may do so purely for scientific reasons, placing importance on the accurate recording of colour and shape, or some special aspect of behaviour. Others may want to provide a permanent recollection of a pleasant experience, such as a holiday in East Africa or the Galapagos Islands. An increasing number of people are taking pictures in the expectation of having them published and it is to be hoped that these people are still members of the majority group of photographers who take wildlife pictures simply because they enjoy it.

Throughout the book I have adopted a documentary approach, as I have assumed that the reader wants to produce accurate and sharply focused pictures of plants or animals which show them as clearly and naturally as possible. For this reason I have not referred to the so-called 'mood' type of wildlife pictures, which may often be shot deliberately completely out of focus. However, this is not to say that there is no scope for creative thought in wildlife work, and picture-composition and imagination to create the most pleasing effect possible are as vital here as in any branch of photography.

For me the greatest pleasure in wildlife photography comes from being able to visit unusual and beautiful natural areas in pursuit of my subjects. Any time spent in the field searching for plants and animals can never be wasted, even if no pictures are obtained, and for this reason the emphasis in this book is very much on photography of living organisms in their natural undisturbed state in the wild. I once read an article which began 'Why bother to crawl around on your hands and knees photographing insects in the field when you can photograph them in the comfort of your own home?' The simple answer is because for many people much of the pleasure in natural-history photography comes from leaving the house and searching for living things in pleasant outdoor surroundings. The article to which I refer was illustrated with some really awful studio-shot pictures of insects, and this brings me to my second point. Pictures of plants and animals, especially insects, which are taken in the wild are almost always vastly superior both aesthetically and biologically to the posed and unnatural subjects which we see so often in studio work. I have a collection of over 35,000 colour slides of a large variety of plant and animal life taken around the world, and not one of these pictures has been taken of an organism artificially posed in a studio set-up. The supporters of studio 'wild' life photography ignore the importance of the thrill of achievement which can only come after successfully pitting your wits against a wild creature in its natural habitat. Even now I never cease to feel excited when I receive from the processing laboratory a batch of slides of a subject which was especially difficult to photograph or showed some particularly interesting or unusual aspect of behaviour.

I hope that the reader will be spurred to go out into the field and discover the pleasures of taking genuine wildlife pictures. There are no shortcuts to success. Perhaps more than in any other field of photography, it is necessary to have a thorough knowledge of the subjects before real success can be achieved. Discovering the intricate and sometimes incredible secrets of the lives of insects or the reproductive habits of fungi is one of the most rewarding experiences possible.

Learning about wildlife cannot be hurried, for it requires much reading about the subject as well as many hours spent in the field patiently adding new facts to your growing store of knowledge. As experience is acquired, previously puzzling

aspects of behaviour will be explained, and gradual
understanding of what is being seen will replace confusion. As
your subjects become more familiar it will be increasingly easy
to discover previously unseen species of plants or animals,
perhaps to put a name to them and to predict when they may
mate or lay eggs. At some stage you will realise that specialist
help is needed in many areas, and joining your nearest natural-
history society will be a first step in obtaining expert guidance.

Wildlife photography can be one of the most frustrating
activities possible. It can also be supremely rewarding. On many
occasions in some hot and humid tropical country when the
subjects have all proved totally elusive I have looked helplessly
at the sky and asked myself why on earth I bother with such a
hopeless task. Ten minutes later I have returned to my tent,
filled with a glow of satisfaction after obtaining a set of
beautiful pictures of praying mantids mating or a butterfly laying
eggs. Perhaps it is as well to remember that the photographer
should never become a slave to the camera. It is only too easy
to become dominated by the viewfinder, so that the wonderful
world of living things is seen solely through a rectangular hole a
few centimetres square. It is then simple to fall into the trap of
snapping away at a subject and hurrying on to the next,
without stopping to observe and marvel at what you have been
photographing. If the point is ever reached where a picture is
taken solely because it may be published and earn money, or if
pressing the shutter becomes a boring chore, then it is time to
move on to new fields. Above all wildlife photography should
be an enjoyable experience, and one which will leave you richer
and more humble in spirit.

Many of the pictures in this book have been taken on my
overseas trips, and I should like to thank the following for their
kind assistance. Trinidad: Jack Price, Julius Boos and Matthew
Cock. Papua New Guinea: Dr John Ismay. Kenya: Dr Angus
McCrae. Australia: Dr Roger Kitching and Andy Browne. Borneo
and Java: Ken Proud, WWF. Malaysia: Ken Scriven, WWF. USA:
Dr Pierre Fischer, Ken Heil. I include in my thanks their wives and
families.

For invaluable help in identifications I am grateful to the
following. Peru: Dr Gerardo Lamas. USA: George Yatskievych,
University of Arizona Herbarium. Australia: the State Herbaria of
Queensland and Victoria. Britain: the staff of the British Museum
(Natural History) and the Herbarium, Royal Botanic Gardens,
Kew.

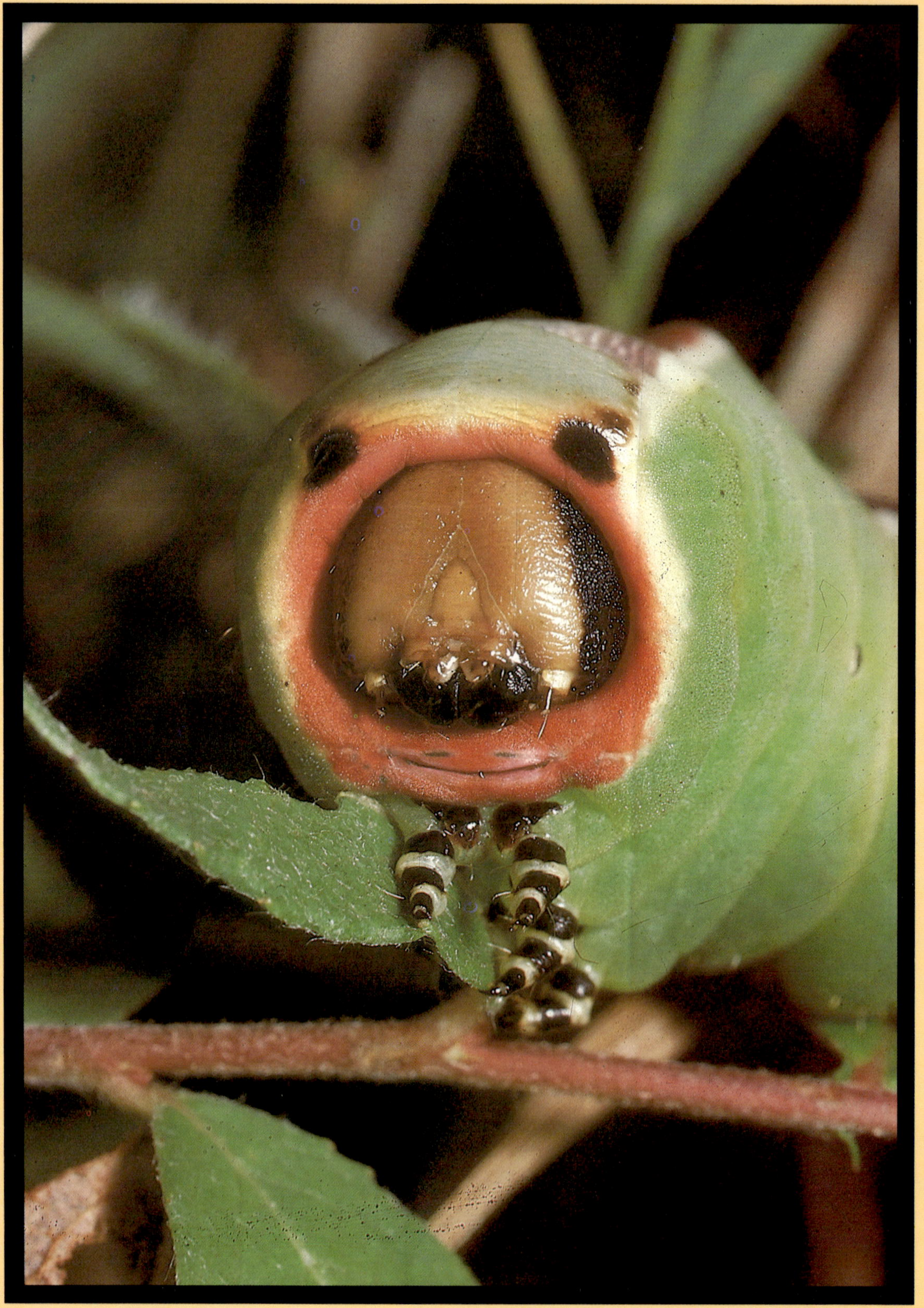

1 Equipment and Technique

Large format cameras with a picture size greater than 6 × 6cm and small format simple cameras with the viewfinder separate from the lens are generally unsuitable for most wildlife work because they lack a wide range of accessories and are difficult to focus on small or distant objects. These days most wildlife photography is undertaken with reflex cameras.

Choosing the camera
Reflex cameras, usually called SLRs (single lens reflex), have the great advantage of showing the photographer exactly what is being recorded on the film. The light passing through the lens strikes a mirror set at 45° from the horizontal and is reflected upwards, into a pentaprism which reflects the image to the magnifying eyepiece and presents it the right way up and laterally correct. The image is focused on a screen and the camera is normally held up to the eye when in use. Some cameras have a waist-level finder which laterally reverses the image when viewed from above. When the shutter is fired the mirror moves automatically out of the way for the exposure to be made. Using SLR cameras, critical focusing is available at all times. The standard lens is detachable and a large range of specialist lenses and accessories is available.

6 × 6cm, 6 × 7cm, 6 × 4.5cm   A number of SLRs are currently manufactured in these larger formats, but they are generally more expensive than 35mm cameras and the range of accessories is less extensive. Running costs are also higher as the film is more expensive. These cameras are fairly heavy and bulky, and may be difficult to hand-hold in the field, requiring the further weight and bulk of a sturdy tripod. The size of negative produced is larger than with 35mm, but this advantage is largely offset because the highest quality fine-resolution Kodachrome films are only available in the smaller format. If the pictures are intended for publication remember that prejudice against 35mm has now almost disappeared. If close-ups of small organisms, eg insects, are your principal objective, the larger format is less suitable (see depth of field below). If you intend mainly to concentrate on large mammals, birds, flowers (other than close-ups of small kinds) or other larger subjects, and you have the cash to spare, a larger format camera may be worthwhile.

35mm SLRs   I find the 35mm format ideal for all my wildlife photography. There is now a huge choice of models and lenses at a range of prices which starts gratifyingly low. Some types, however, are more suited to natural history work than others, so here are some points to consider when choosing a model.

1. *The shutter.* Cameras which have a leaf-shutter mounted inside the lens (TLR) are too limited to be considered for wildlife work. Choose a camera with a focal-plane shutter which runs just in front of the film. This enables a range of accessories to be used. A model with a metal-bladed shutter which synchronises at 1/125 sec with electronic flash is an advantage.

2. *The focusing screen.* The standard screen fitted to most cameras is completely unsuitable for natural history photography. There is usually a central focusing 'aid' consisting of a split-image device or a micro-diaprism. These are useless for any kind of close-up work or with the longer telephoto lenses as they black out. Try to choose a camera which offers interchangeable screens, or with a range of different viewfinders and screens (eg Nikon F3). The best general-purpose screen for all wildlife work is plain ground glass, its main disadvantage being that it is rather dull for focusing in poor light. If you have a camera without a facility for changing screens, you must ignore the central 'aid' and focus instead on the surrounding fresnel area.

3. *Depth of field preview button.* In close-up work it is often useful to be able to check what is going to be in focus by closing down the aperture of the lens before taking the picture. Some cameras have a button for this, but not all, so check.

4. *Light metering.* Most cameras now have a metering system which measures the light actually coming through the lens (TTL). This is not a universal panacea guaranteeing perfect exposure every time, but it can be useful, so check whether your camera has it, especially if you are thinking of buying an older secondhand model. Most cameras these days are 'aperture priority' automatic, where you set the lens aperture manually and the camera selects the shutter speed. These are useless for most wildlife work, because shutter-speed is often vitally important. I use a completely manual Nikon F2A Photomic, and prefer this to any of the so-called 'quicker to use' automatic cameras.

5. *Handling.* Much wildlife photography is undertaken in

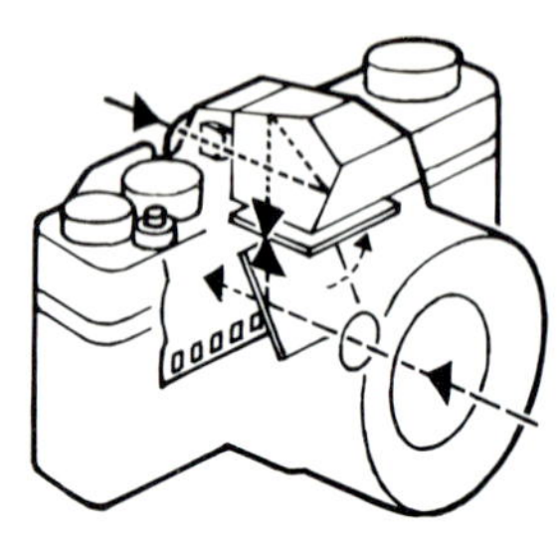

SLR principle. Light entering the lens is reflected up into the viewfinder. At the moment of exposure the mirror flips up and the light passes through the open shutter to the film

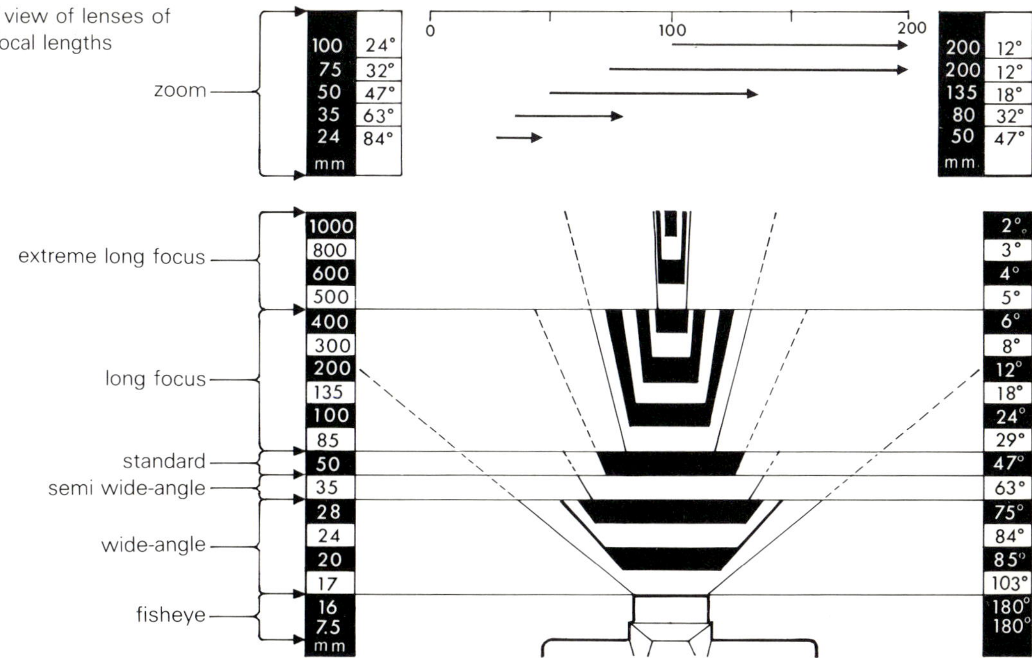

difficult conditions in the field, where speed of working is often vital, so it is important to use a camera which feels really comfortable in your hands and whose controls are easily understood and simple to operate.

Lenses

A camera is just a box for holding film. The quality of the final results (apart from your own skill as a photographer) will be decided mainly by the lens. You can save money by buying a cheap and simple camera body with no 'gadgets', but never try to economise by purchasing a cheap lens, although lenses made by specialist manufacturers such as Tamron and Vivitar are generally cheaper than the camera manufacturers' 'brand' lenses and usually just as good.

Focal length   The focal length of a lens is the distance from the optical centre of the lens to the film-plane when the focus is set at infinity. Most 35mm SLR's are sold with a 'standard' lens of 50mm, giving a field of view similar to that of human vision. On a 6 × 6cm format the standard lens is usually 80mm. Standard lenses are excellent for most purposes, and with suitable accessories can be used for close-ups (see below). *Wide-angle lenses* are used if a wider field of view of shorter focal length is needed, usually 35mm or 28mm. In wildlife work the main uses of wide-angle lenses are for habitat photography, and pictures of large aggregations of animals or flowers. *Telephoto lenses* have a longer focal length (some major manufacturers supply them up to 2000mm) and have a narrower angular field. They bring the subject closer in the same way as a telescope. They are mainly used for photographing distant birds or mammals, and the shorter telephotos are useful for reptiles, amphibians and insects.

Mirror lenses usually have focal lengths of 500mm and 1000mm. Their special form of construction, which reflects the light back and forth inside the lens, makes them smaller and lighter than telephotos of conventional design. However, mirror lenses suffer from the disadvantage of a fixed aperture (usually *f*8 or *f*11) and of being rather less robust than conventional lenses.

Zoom lenses have the ability to vary the focal length within a single lens. A very large number of different designs is now available, offering focal lengths going from wide-angle to short telephoto, 'standard' to medium telephoto or medium to long telephoto. The different combinations are enormous, but a very popular lens seems to be the 70mm (sometimes 80mm) to 200mm (or 210mm). This type of lens has many uses for the wildlife photographer, including birds, mammals, reptiles, amphibians and insects. Some lenses have a built-in 'macro' facility and an image of half life-size is possible without using an accessory. Modern zoom lenses are extremely good, being much lighter and more compact than earlier designs, and with a vastly superior performance. I use a 70-210mm Vivitar Macro-Zoom for a lot of my photography and find the results excellent. The slight fall-off in definition at the edges of the picture which most zoom lenses exhibit is not so important in wildlife work, where the subject rarely extends across the whole frame. When choosing a zoom lens go for a 'one touch' design in which focusing and zooming are incorporated in a single twist-grip, permitting the very rapid operation vital for action photography. Always use a large lens hood with zooms (except for close-ups) as they are very prone to flare in awkward lighting conditions.

Aperture and diaphragm   The aperture expresses the transmitting power or 'speed' of a lens. This is expressed in *f* numbers or stops on the lens barrel, and increases by a factor of 1.4 starting at *f*1. The smaller the *f* number of a lens, the larger the effective diameter. This is called the lens 'speed', and 'fast' 50mm lenses may have a maximum aperture of *f*1.2. The faster the lens the higher the price, and a slower cheaper lens is best for most wildlife work, and is even preferable for close-ups. Closing the aperture by one stop, for example from *f*8 to *f*11, halves the amount of light reaching the film. The aperture is controlled by an iris diaphragm, which by varying the size of the central opening alters the amount of light entering the camera.

Automatic lenses are focused at full aperture, ensuring that the focusing screen is bright and easy to use. When the shutter is triggered the lens automatically closes-down to the preselected aperture.

Preset lenses are also focused at full aperture, but before taking the picture a ring is rotated to close the aperture to the preselected *f* number. Preset lenses are usually time-consuming to operate and of doubtful use for action photography. They are cheaper than automatic lenses, but it is worth paying the extra money for an 'auto' model.

Depth of field The depth of field is the zone of sharp focus available in front of and behind the plane on which the lens has been focused. Changing the aperture also changes the depth of field, and the smaller the *f* number, the larger the zone of sharpness on *both* sides of the plane of focus. The depth of field is constant for a given image magnification, regardless of the focal length of the lens. The depth of field is not equal on both sides of the plane of focus, extending $^2/_3$ beyond and only $^1/_3$ in front, and this must be borne in mind when selecting the focusing point of close-ups. In addition, the greater the reproduction ratio required of the subject, the smaller the depth

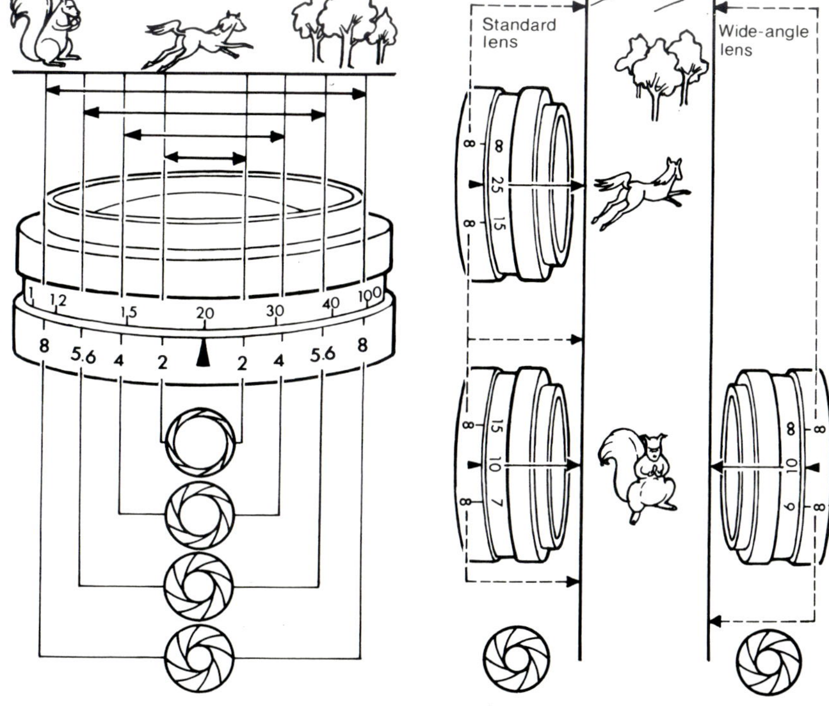

Near right: depth-of-field scale. Small apertures ensure sharpness over greater range of distances than large apertures. Aperture numbers on each side of the focusing index are opposite figures on the distance scale, indicating near and far limits of depth of field. Far right: zone focusing. Standard lens provides two or more useful focusing zones according to the distance-scale setting; wide-angle lens covers a deeper zone at the same aperture

of field becomes, so in close-ups it may become very small (for a life-size or 1:1 image it is 3mm at *f*22). This may be important when you are deciding whether you need a 35mm format or something larger. A small insect such as a ladybird will be just about acceptable at life-size on 35mm, but will need to be 2½ times life-size on a 6 × 6cm format, to avoid appearing as a small spot in the middle of the picture. At this reproduction ratio very little indeed of the ladybird will be in focus, so the whole advantage of a larger format for better image quality is lost, and indeed better quality is obtained on the smaller format.

Flash

Flashbulbs are seldom used now as they can only be used once. However, if you only intend to photograph animals such as badgers at night, it may be worthwhile contemplating a bulb-unit (see Chapter 9).

Electronic flash Most people today work with electronic flash units. These are available in a large variety of sizes and specifications, from large high-powered 'studio' units to tiny pocketable guns the size of a cigarette packet. They all work by producing an instantaneous discharge of electricity in an enclosed glass tube. It is of very short duration, usually 1/1000 sec but may be as short as 1/40,000 sec on computer units or special-purpose equipment. When choosing a flash gun it is best to select a unit which can be operated both off ordinary batteries and rechargeable nickel-cadmium cells. Bird photographers will need a unit which has the flash-heads separate from the battery pack.

Computer flashes have a sensor which measures the light

Syrphus balteatus hoverflies on a Marigold in my garden. A picture like this takes only seconds to achieve; flash.

The guide number of a flash unit is the product of flash distance and lens aperture at which correct exposure is obtained. As the flash distance increases, the lens aperture must be opened wider

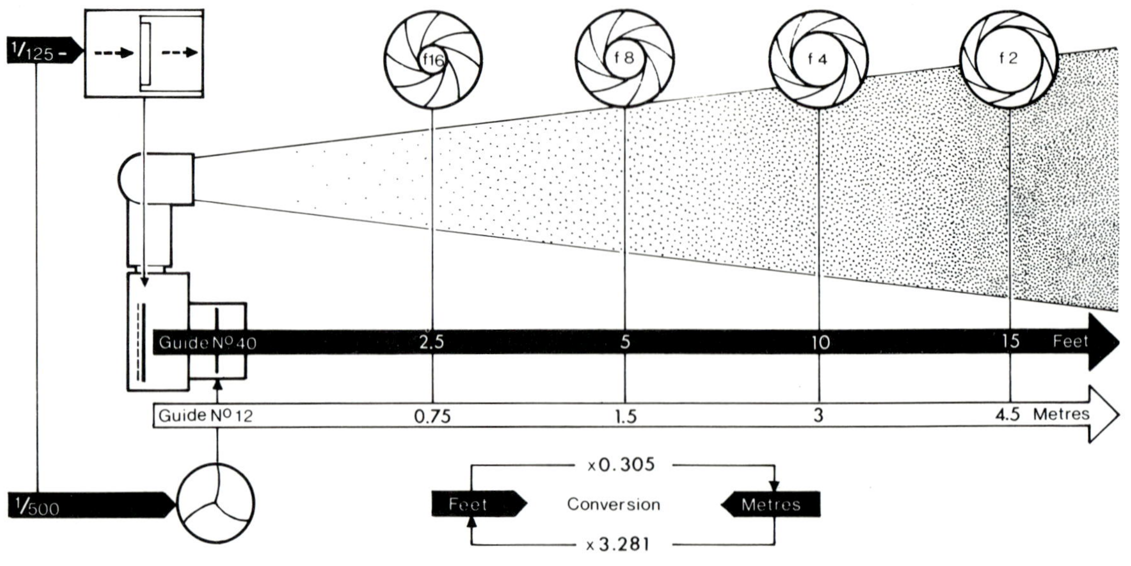

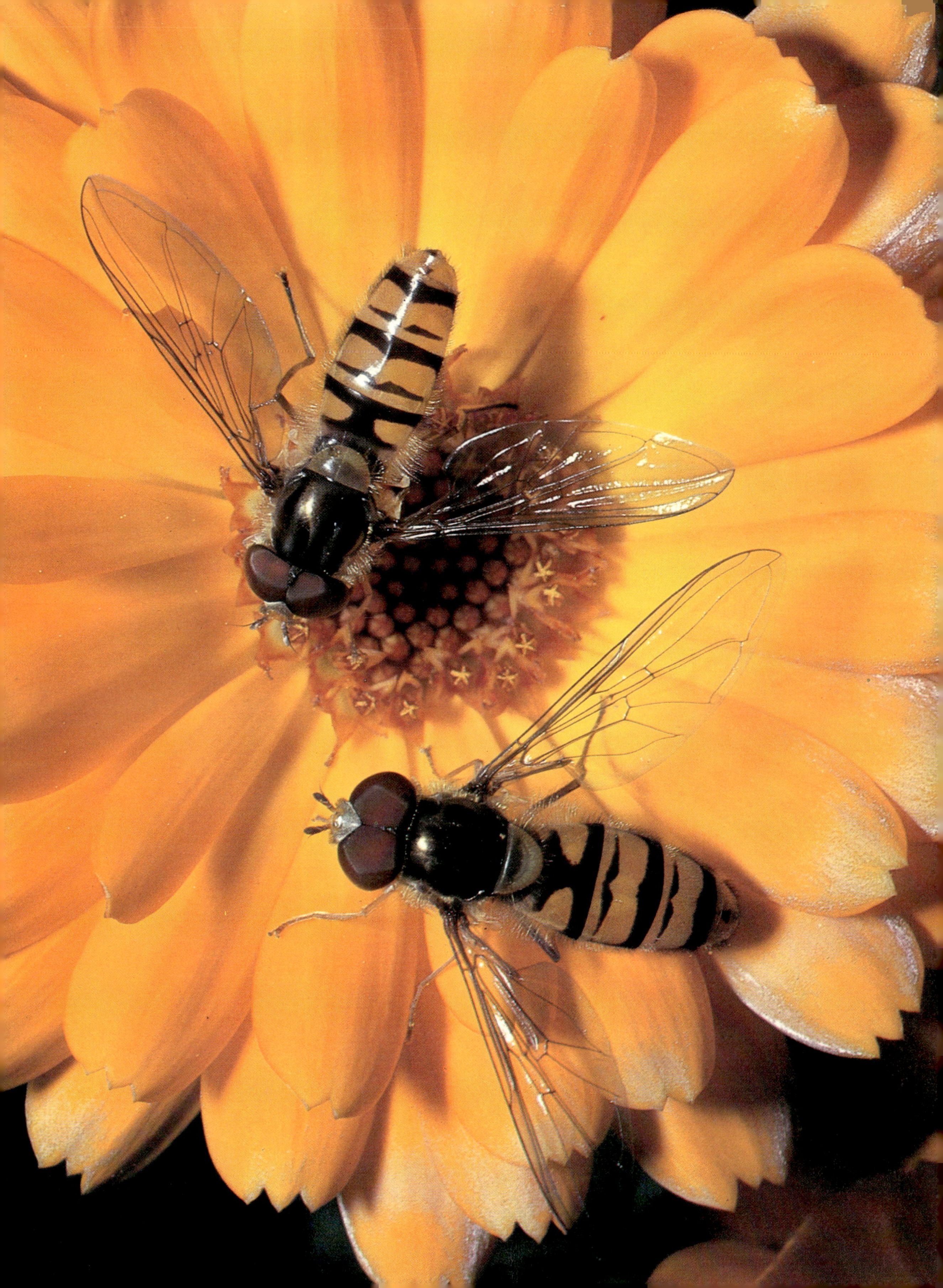

returning from the subject and adjusts the length of the flash duration to give correct exposure. Using the smaller pocketable units will usually mean setting the *f* stop at between *f*4 and *f*8 when using slow colour films, giving insufficient depth of field for most subjects. I prefer a manual unit, as most people 'bracket' their exposures anyway. Remember that the exposure chart on the back of your flashgun is calibrated for correct exposure indoors and will give a corresponding underexposure outside, especially in woodland. Allow at least one or two extra stops when using a gun outside, and check your results for how they compare with the maker's chart. With experience you can build up your own 'corrected' chart, either writing the values on a piece of card attached to the flash, or carrying them in your head as I do.

Ring flash units have a circular discharge tube which fits around the lens. The lighting given is very flat and lacks detail. It can be improved by blanking-off part of the ring with tape. However, the cheapest ring flash costs at least ten times more than my small 'standard' flash, and in my opinion is not worth the money.

Camera supports

For much wildlife photography the best support for your camera is your hands. I have taken colour photographs in all kinds of difficult conditions around the world and have always been glad that I was not hindered by a tripod. A support of some kind is obviously necessary for people who find it difficult to hand-hold a camera without camera shake, although a tripod limits the amount of action photography possible.

However, if you intend to do much bird photography you will definitely need a tripod. Choose a really sturdy model with a smoothly operating pan and tilt head. Never mind the weight, it is the final results which count and there is no point in travelling 'light' only to return with a batch of blurred pictures caused by a wobbly tripod. When photographing flowers or fungi using 35mm equipment a lighter tripod can be used, especially if the exposure is made using a long cable release or the camera's delayed-action mechanism. For subjects where rapid adjustment is more important than smooth tracking, a ball and socket head is preferable to a pan and tilt. Some tripods have a reversible centre-column so that the camera can be used for low subjects near the ground, but the amount of working space between the legs may be rather limited. In this case you may prefer to use a ground spike or miniature tripod, or one of the multi-purpose supports, such as a combistat, which will hold the camera virtually anywhere. A monopod is useful in situations where a tripod would be too difficult to erect. Even if you do not require a support for the camera, one may still be necessary for holding a flash unit to lighten the background.

Film

As mentioned in the introduction, I am assuming that anyone using this book will be principally interested in taking colour slides, although it is, of course, possible to make prints from the transparencies. The main characteristics of different films is their relative sensitivity to light – the film 'speed'. Film speed is usually printed on the film pack and is expressed in figures designated ASA (American Standards Association, now the American National Standards Institute), DIN (Deutsche Industrie Norm) or ISO (International Standards Organisation). Slow films have a low number and are fine grained with a high resolution of fine detail. Fast films have a high number and have larger grain size with poorer resolution.

The type of photography you propose to do largely dictates your choice of film. If close-ups using flash are your chief interest then a slow film is best. I always use Kodachrome 64 rather than Kodachrome 25 for daylight work. It gives excellent results and has that initial extra speed. Action shots of birds or mammals may demand a faster film in order to obtain any pictures at all. Films such as Ektachrome 200 (200 ASA), Ektachrome 400, Fujichrome 400 or 3M 400 are fast and can be 'pushed' by the processing laboratory to even higher speeds. Do not expect Kodachrome-type results from these faster films, which are mainly useful for recording interesting or unusual events which may otherwise be missed.

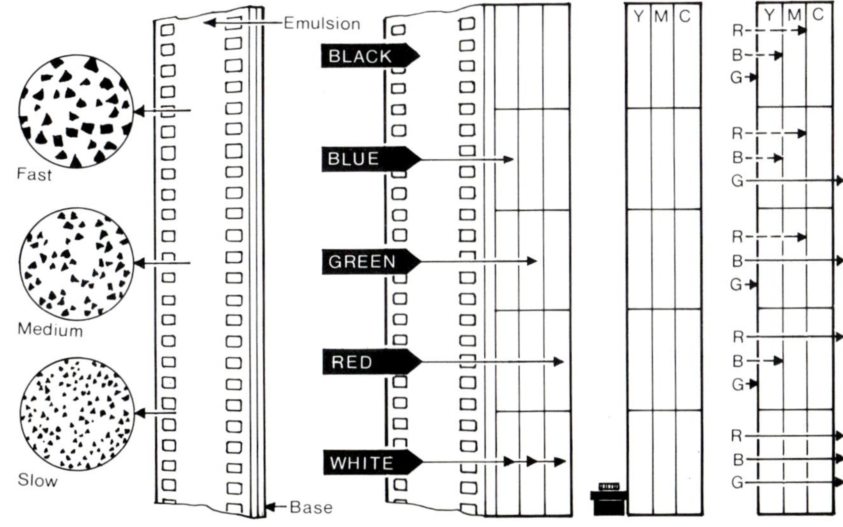

Near right: broadly speaking, faster films need larger grains of light-sensitive material and may produce a noticeably 'grainy' image. Far right: colour film has three emulsion layers of different colour sensitivity, incorporating dyes that are released on development

Once you have settled on a film it really is essential that you stick to it, for complete familiarity with a film is vital for obtaining constant exposure.

Colour films are especially prone to a phenomenon called *reciprocity law failure*. The technicalities behind this need not concern us here, but the results do matter. Colour slide (reversal) films are designed to give satisfactory colour within the normal range of shutter speeds. Longer exposures may entail a severe loss of speed and unacceptable colour changes. For this reason long exposures on these films should be avoided and flash used instead.

When using colour film in hot climates remember that heat affects the emulsion, especially after the film has been exposed in the camera. If processing cannot be carried out quickly, store the films in a cool place, preferably a refrigerator. Never store film in the boot of a car standing in the sun. When motoring always keep the film inside the car, which you will keep as cool as possible for your own comfort. Always reload with film in the shade, even if this is only the shadow cast by your own body.

Equipment for close-ups
Much of the challenge of natural history photography lies in obtaining high-quality close-ups of your subjects, and however good your equipment, there is no substitute for practice and experience.

Supplementary lenses Supplementary lenses are simple additive lenses which screw onto the front of the prime lens. Their power is expressed in dioptres, usually +1, +2 and +3, or combinations of these. Lower powered close-up lenses are cheap and perform adequately if your lens is stopped down to at least *f*11, so that they are excellent for use with flash when apertures of *f*16 are frequently used. However, more powerful close-up lenses perform unacceptably even at small apertures and this restricts their use to larger subjects such as flowers, fungi, amphibians and the largest insects. The main advantage claimed for them is that they do not need any exposure increase (see below) but since flash will be used for real close-ups, this point becomes valueless.

Extension tubes A much better method of getting close-ups is to increase the distance of the prime lens from the film-plane. One way of doing this is to mount the lens on tubes of varying lengths. The greater the extension used, the greater the magnification obtained. With a 50mm lens mounted in the normal position, most sets of tubes allow magnification up to life size. Varying the combination of tubes varies the magnification, which must be decided upon before you start shooting. Automatic tubes retain the automatic aperture on the prime lens and also couple to the TTL metering system of the camera. Tubes are generally more expensive than close-up lenses, but cheaper than bellows or a convertor (see below).

Bellows With a bellows unit a continuously variable magnification is available up to and beyond life-size. However, there are drawbacks. The minimum extension on most bellows units is still considerable, so that they are useless for quite a large and much-used part of the close-up range. The focusing-rack at the bottom of the bellows permanently sticks out at the front. This can be a nuisance, especially when working among grass and vegetation, where I have actually had the bellows knock insect subjects unceremoniously off a leaf. In addition most bellows are not automatic and a complicated z-ring and double cable release will be needed. Lastly, bellows units are usually expensive, and automatic units are *very* expensive. I last used a bellows unit in 1970, and have no intention of returning to them.

Exposure for close-ups Both tubes and bellows require an increase in exposure which is proportional to the length of extension used. Various tables are published for calculating the increase required, but they are generally impractical to use in the field, and better results can be obtained far more quickly by guesswork. With experience your guesses will become increasingly accurate, and in addition most people 'bracket' their exposure either side of what they think is the correct exposure. I never bracket on both sides, but always take one shot at the exposure which I think is correct, and then a second picture with ¾ stop less exposure. This is because for publication purposes a slightly underexposed slide is preferable to one which is slightly overexposed. When using flash the exposure compensation tables are not required anyway, as the increase in exposure due to longer extension is normally balanced by the greater light from holding the flash closer to the subject. In practical terms this means that almost all close-ups with flash can be taken using the same exposure, which will vary for each flash/film combination. In my case I use *f*16/22 for everything from around ¼ life-size to three times life-size. Remember that light-coloured subjects need one stop less exposure than 'normal' subjects.

Macro-convertor Several manufacturers now offer macro-convertors for close-ups. These are inserted between the lens and camera as with bellows and tubes, but rely on an internal

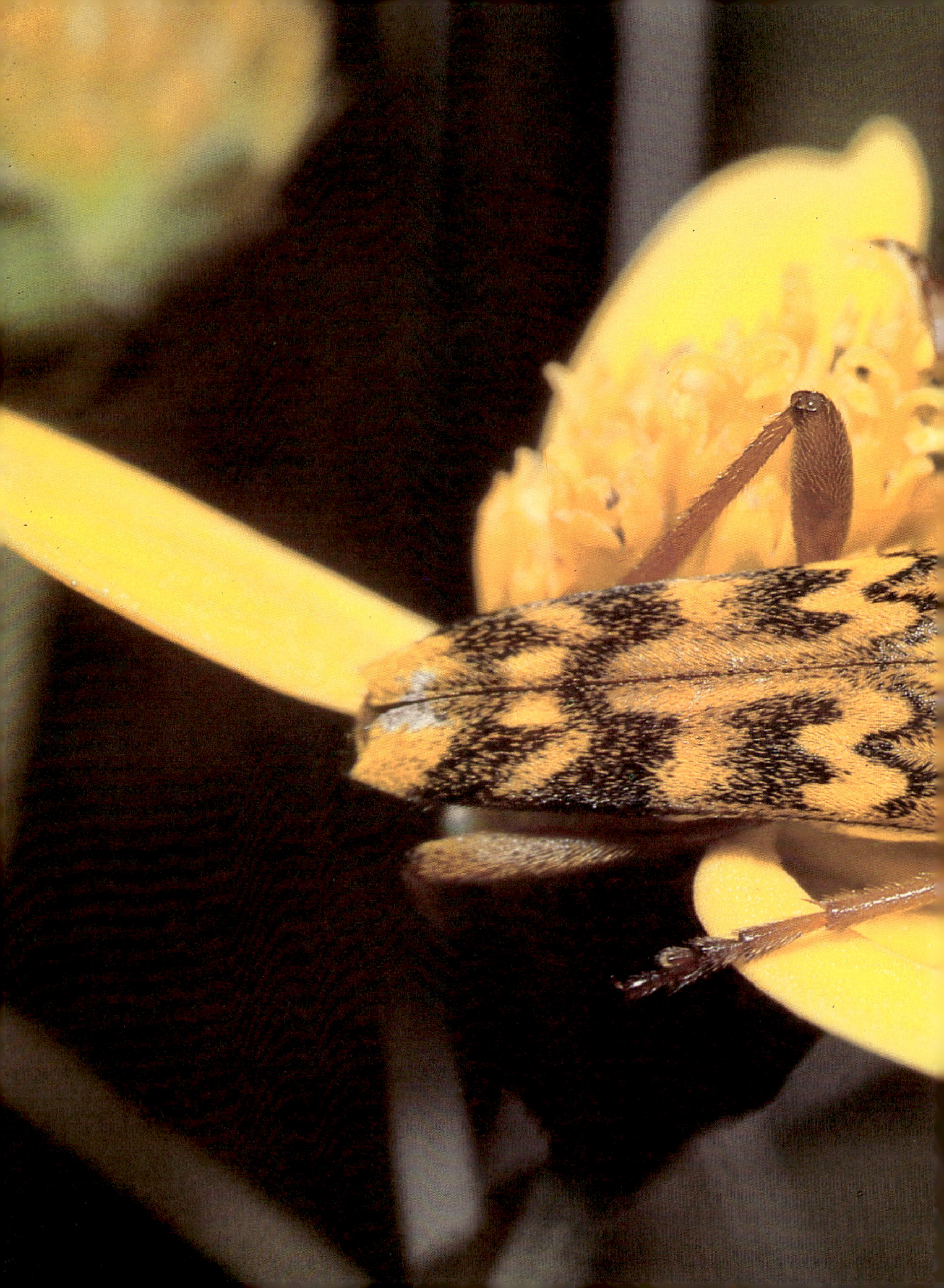

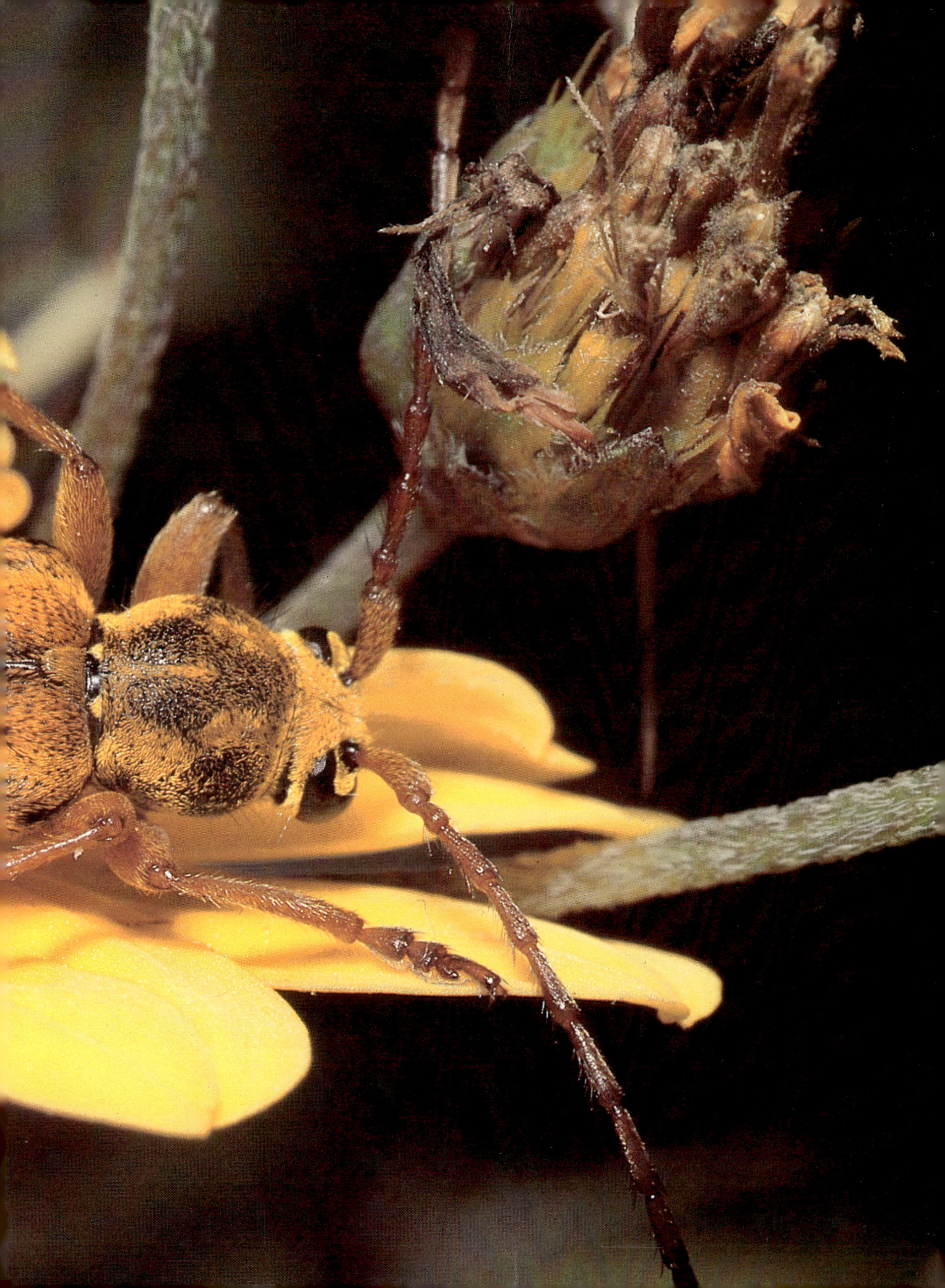

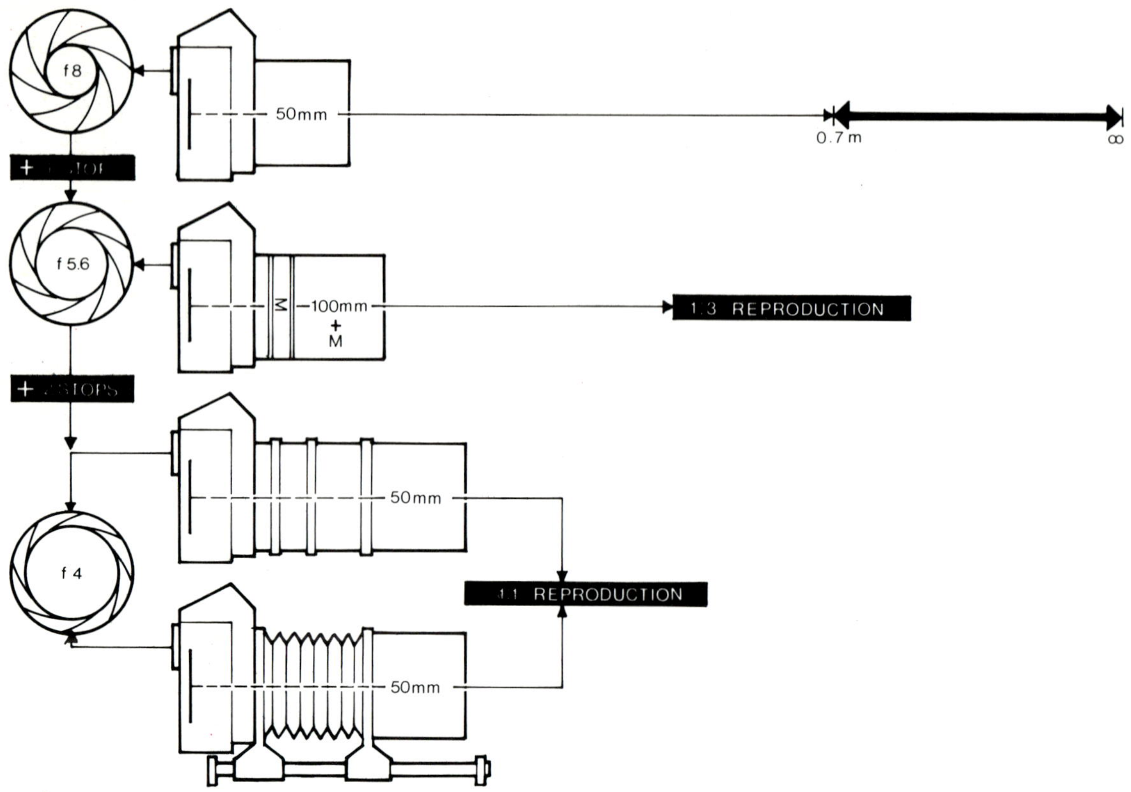

set of sliding lenses to achieve magnification of from 1:25 to 1:1, depending on the make. Convertors are optically precise and are designed to enable your own prime lens to work more efficiently in the close-up range than it will when on tubes or bellows. I have found the small, light Aico Panagor convertor very useful. Focusing is carried out by turning a ring on the convertor, not on the lens. The automatic diaphragm operation and TTL coupling are retained when using this convertor, which was designed for use with 50mm lenses, but also works extremely well with wide-angle and shorter telephoto lenses. A disadvantage is that when you fit the convertor to the camera you lose two stops of lighting, which severely curtails its use in available light. However, for the sort of close-up range offered by the convertor, flash is the main form of lighting, so the loss of stops merely means using a slightly larger flash.

Macro lenses These lenses are specifically designed to give their best resolving power when used close-up, while still giving excellent results up to and including infinity. Most macro lenses have a continuous focusing range from infinity to half life-size (1:2). The addition of a single automatic ring increases this to 1:1. Some lenses can focus down to life-size without the added ring, and it seems to me a great pity that all macro lenses do

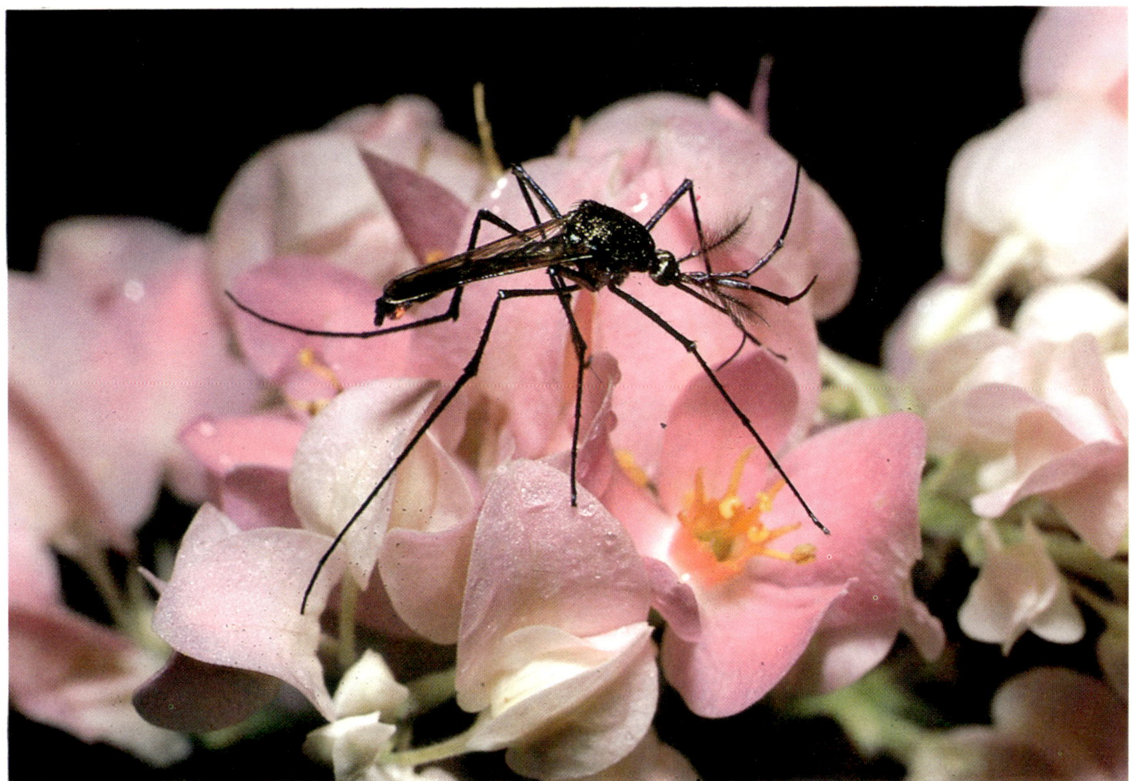

Toxorhynchites species, a mosquito. Even the females of these mosquitoes feed on flowers, and do not suck blood. Photographed in Trinidad, using 55mm lens reversed on 90mm of extension, single flash. A very small subject, requiring extremely accurate focusing (done from a standing position with back bent) and care to ensure that the whole insect appears against the pink flower, as it would otherwise disappear into the dark background.

not have this exceedingly useful facility. Most macro lenses stop down to *f*22 or *f*32 to obtain the maximum depth of field in close-ups. 'Standard' macro lenses usually have focal lengths of 50mm or 55mm, but there are tele-macros available of 80mm or 100mm focal length. These increase the working distance but are less useful for smaller subjects because of the additional amount of extension they require (double in the 100mm).

Reversing the lens   If magnifications greater than 1:1 are required, definition can be improved by mounting the lens with its front element facing the camera (this also applies to macro lenses). The automatic diaphragm and TTL functions of the lens are then lost, and manual operation is required via a double cable release, although I use the plunger on the Nikon E2 ring by pressing it with one finger, making depth of field preview very simple.

Choosing the equipment

Much will depend on what you can afford and whether or not the camera feels right. Most makes these days are adequate for the task, so shop around until you find something which really suits you. There is, however, one point to remember. Beginners are often overimpressed by the claims made by the manufacturers and retailers of optical equipment. Do not forget that the most complex (and therefore often the most expensive) item of equipment is not necessarily the best for the job which *you* require it to perform. Much equipment has more value as a status symbol than as a means of obtaining good photographs at reasonable cost. Another problem may be the urge to amass a vast collection of different 'gadgets' without which you feel that you cannot adequately perform your photographic tasks. This often leads to more interest in 'gadgetry' than in photography and the subjects themselves. Some wildlife photographers seem to feel that you simply cannot be capable of taking good close-up pictures without having complicated tripods, multiple flashes and cable releases sticking out in all directions.

In the field I always work with the minimum of equipment. I carry a single Nikon F2 with a 55mm Micro-Nikkor, a set of tubes and reversal ring and the cheapest and smallest electronic flash available. In the tropics I always carry a 70–210mm macro zoom in one pocket and a slightly larger flash in the other, using them to take, for example, butterflies and lizards. Sometimes I carry a small bracket on which to mount the larger flash, but at other times I hold it in one hand, as I do the smaller unit. Unencumbered by clumsy superfluous equipment I have managed to sweat through steamy jungles and scramble up steep mountainsides around the world, concentrating on actually obtaining good wildlife photographs. Infatuation with equipment is an easy trap. Do not fall into it.

Using the equipment
Before venturing into the field in search of subjects you should first familiarise yourself thoroughly with your equipment, so that handling it becomes second nature. If your knowledge of natural history is rather hazy, or better in some areas than others, some concentrated reading of relevant books will make finding and understanding your subjects much easier. If you intend to use extension tubes, experiment with different combinations, so that you will know which to use when you spot an interesting small animal in the field. There is no substitute for experience, and as your equipment and subjects become more familiar, your pictures should show a corresponding increase in quality.

Choosing the lighting
Some people tend to be over-dogmatic concerning lighting. There are 'purists' who maintain that available light is the only 'natural' form of lighting, and that any form of flash gives

artificial colours and 'unnatural' results. This argument
conveniently ignores the fact that photography is by its very
nature basically a chemical process, and that different makes
and batches of film give very different colours. Also we do not
'see' the world in the same way as a camera and film 'see' it.
Our eyes record an imperfect image which is heavily 'corrected'
by the brain. For this reason no photograph can reproduce a
scene exactly as we see it. This is even more relevant in close-
ups, where the inability of our eyes to resolve images clearly at
close quarters makes any argument about 'naturalness' totally
irrelevant. In contrasting light conditions the brain tends to
even-out the light and dark areas, something which the camera
cannot do, so once again 'natural' pictures do not look anything
like the scene we remember.

No doubt arguments about lighting will go on for ever, but
do not listen to anyone who is dogmatic about any one form of
illumination. What really matters is whether or not the final
photograph is a good one and shows the subject in a way which
satisfies *you*.

Using available light   Cameras with TTL metering measure the
light reflected from the subject. They work on an averaging
principle, and centre-weighted meters which are biased towards
a reading off the central area of the screen are now very
popular. This allows more precise readings of a selected subject
area and gives more balanced exposures. All TTL systems are
prone to incorrect readings in difficult lighting conditions, eg
against the light. Many professionals still use a hand-held meter.
These can measure the incident light, which is the light actually
falling on the subjects. Generally speaking, whatever method is
used, it pays to bracket your exposure to be sure of at least
some perfect results.

Using flash   Having acquired a new flash unit the only way to
ensure correct exposures is to take an experimental set of
pictures, making careful notes of the exposures against which to
calibrate the flash for future use. The worst place for mounting
a flash is on the camera, so the modern trend towards 'hot-shoe'
contacts only is to be deplored, like much else in modern
camera design. 'On-camera' flash gives flat lighting, lacking in
modelling and concealing interesting surface-details on small
subjects. I always hold the flash in my left hand, using my wrist
to direct the light exactly where I want it. If you find this
difficult use a bracket with a ball and socket head, which
enables you to adjust the angle of lighting at will. Some people
do not like the shadows *sometimes* caused by a single-flash
working and use a white-card reflector or second smaller flash

to fill-in, sometimes even using a third flash to light the background. This sacrifices a great deal of mobility and I find it rather impractical.

The power of light decreases inversely as the square of the distance; this is called the inverse square law. In practice it means that when using flash for close-ups the subject is adequately lit but the flash then rapidly fades giving an under-exposed background. In isolated subjects, such as insects on flowerheads, the background may be totally black. Some writers give the impression that this is a problem with every single close-up taken with flash. This is not so, and it is in fact a very minor problem, which in almost every instance can be solved by careful selection of the subject and its background. Some people use bright blue cards as backgrounds for insects, but to me this just makes the pictures look dreadfully artificial.

When using flash at, say, 1/60 sec (the maximum sync speed with electronic flash for a specific camera) on a sunny day, any movement of the subject will result in a ghost-image as both daylight and flash exposures are made on the same frame (for solutions to this see Chapter 3).

For many subjects, especially flowers, a compromise between available light and flash is often preferable, and this 'fill-in' flash frequently gives the most pleasing results, particularly in contrasty light conditions. I set the camera to underexpose by half a stop on the meter, and then fill in the rest using flash. Some people work in reverse, using daylight as the main lighting and flash held further away than normal to give a less powerful fill-in effect.

For subjects with low relief such as lichens and liverworts, try holding the unit near the level of the subject and directing the light across its surface to emphasize small details (grazed flash).

Focusing for close-ups
Difficulty in focusing accurately is a common problem for many beginners to close-up photography. Their first problem is actually locating the subject in the viewfinder. This can be annoyingly difficult at first and may require a great deal of practice before you become proficient. I always felt a complete fool when repeated attempts to locate an insect on a leaf through the viewfinder ended several inches to one side, so it is better to practise this without anyone watching you, which just makes things worse.

When working close-up, the lens is normally set on infinity (unless it is a macro lens), and focusing is performed by moving

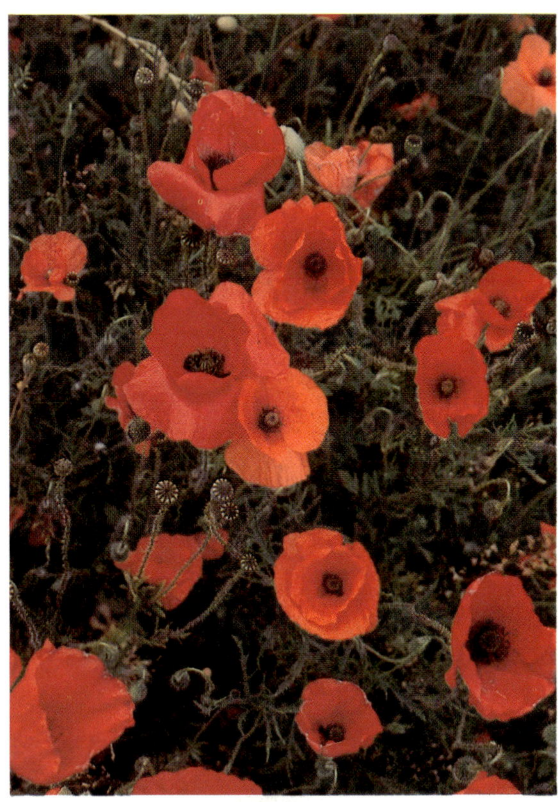

Papaver rhoeas, Corn Poppy, growing on a roadside in the Cotswolds, England. Taken on a dull day using fill-in flash.

the whole camera towards the subject until it is brought into sharp focus on the screen. With subjects such as insects it may be difficult at first to decide exactly where to focus, remembering the small depth of field available. This varies according to the angle of approach, but it is vital that the eyes, if they are in the picture, should be in focus. Constant practice is the only way of perfecting close-up focusing, and with experience it is possible to focus accurately under extremely dull and difficult conditions.

Hand-holding for close-ups
Hand holding is the key to successful close-up work on subjects such as insects. It is an acquired knack, although some people can do it straight away, while others never manage it, even after much practice. Even those with a steady hand will find it easier if the elbows can be rested on the ground, the knees or pressed into the stomach. Learning to stand and brace the body to maximum effect is also vital, and with practice accurate close-ups can be taken from very awkward positions.

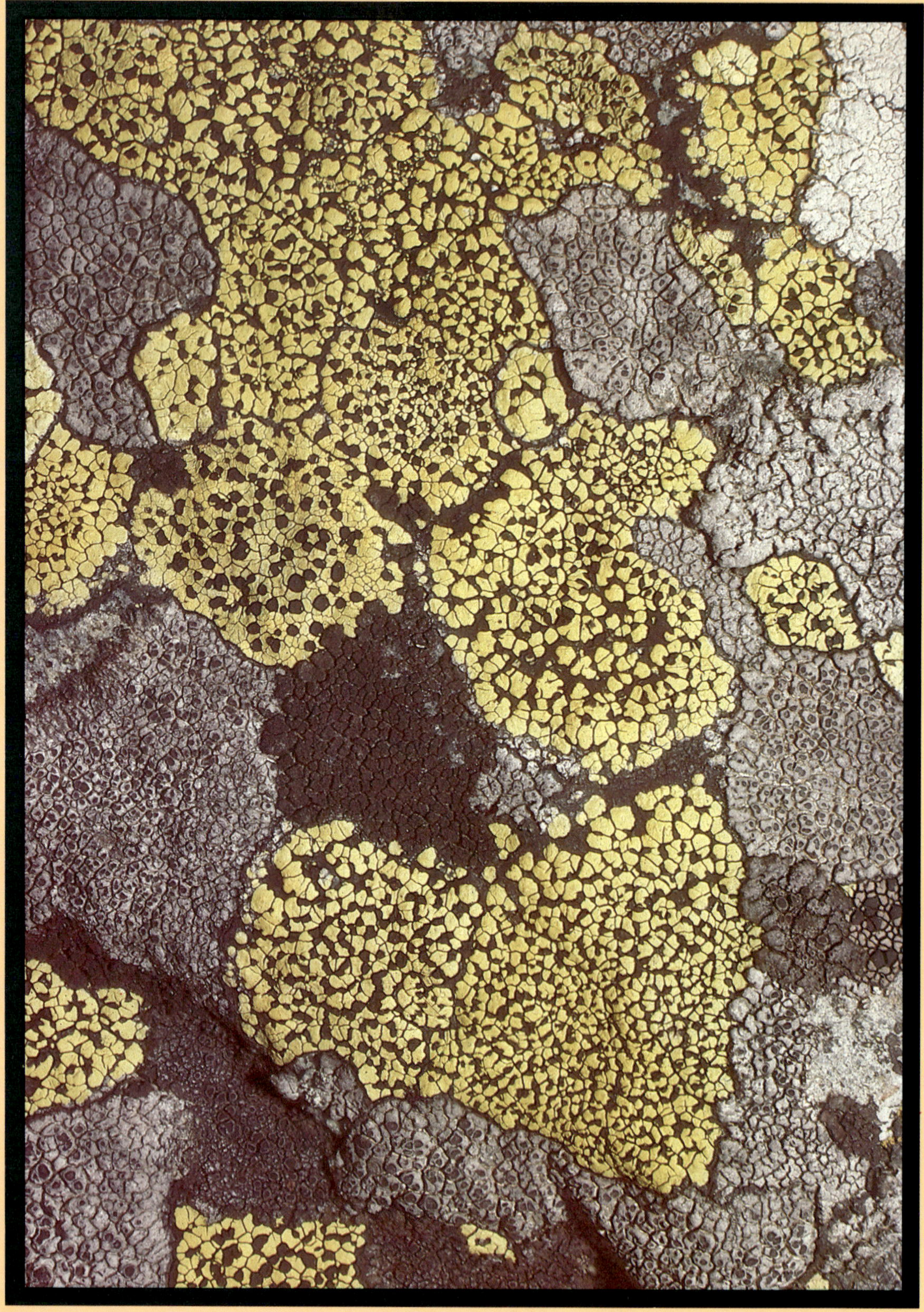

2 Flowerless Plants

Clubmosses, horsetails and ferns are a very ancient group of plants which, in common with the flowering plants, possess fibrous (vascular) tissue.

CLUBMOSSES

Clubmosses are a characteristic group of usually low-growing plants which are much more robust than true mosses. They prefer wet districts and are most easily found on damp, rocky areas on mountainsides. Many species bear at the tips of their stems, or sometimes in twos or threes at the ends of long stalks, cones containing spores. Species growing in tropical rain forest may be very luxuriant, and can be several feet high, although most are prostrate. Some tropical *Selaginella* species are covered in a beautiful metallic bluish sheen.

Photographing clubmosses

The techniques and equipment required to photograph clubmosses is, in general, adequate for the rest of the plants in this chapter and for those described in Chapters 3 and 4. I hand hold the camera for all my pictures, but many people prefer to use some form of support. For low-growing plants like clubmosses and true mosses a ground spike or miniature tripod is ideal, or something like the Combistat mentioned in Chapter 1. In many instances you can rest your elbows on your knees or on the ground, which makes hand holding very easy, especially when using flash. Extension tubes or bellows are needed for close-ups of small mosses or for fine details on ferns, and take a lens-reversal kit for close-ups of moss capsules. A single small flashgun is ideal, or a larger unit if it can be held further back than the camera. I use a 55mm macro lens for all my plant shots, although a wide-angle lens may be useful for ferns in cramped spots.

A supply of small envelopes for collecting mosses and lichens and a notebook and pencil for making notes on exposures are also essential.

For low-growing subjects I normally kneel on the ground

and focus the camera by hand, holding the flashgun in my left hand and directing the light from slightly above the subject to give a reasonably natural effect. Clubmoss plants bearing cones are best for portraits, and remember to take some close-ups of the cones themselves. Close-ups of the stems emphasise their regular shape.

HORSETAILS

This ancient group of plants comprise only some 23 species, all belonging to the genus *Equisetum*. Horsetails are cosmopolitan, growing in swamps, meadows, forests, sandy wastes and along roads and railway embankments. The usually erect stems are jointed and from the bases of the joints there usually arise more or less regular whorls of ribbed and jointed green branches. Some species, such as the Water Horsetail (*Equisetum limosum*), bear fertile cones at the tips of some of the green stems. Others, like the Common Horsetail (*E. arvense*), bear their cones on separate, fatter pale brown unbranched stems which appear early in the year and then wither as the green barren stems appear. The cones are covered in numerous hexagonal scales under which the spores are borne. Each spore-bearing scale resembles a minute star-like 'flower' and makes an interesting close-up.

Photographing horsetails

Plants growing in masses in open spots look very good taken by available light, especially against the sky, which emphasizes their graceful outlines. In young green stems the whorled branches are closely adpressed to the stem, opening out as the plant develops, thus making an interesting series or single side-by-side shot. Close-ups of the stem-sheaths showing the spoke-like arrangement of branches are interesting, as are close-ups with reversed lens of the star-like scales on the cones. Flash helps to give the depth of field required for close-in working. I always use my small flash for this.

FERNS

The largest group of modern pteridophytes is the ferns, a worldwide group containing around 7,000 species. Ferns tend to prefer moist shady places, and reach their peak of abundance in the tropics, where rain forests may boast everything from tree-ferns over 10m high to tiny filmy ferns which look more like mosses.

Right: *Equisetum telmateia*, Giant Horsetail. Close-up, using single flash, of a barren stem showing the sheaths and whorls of jointed green branches. Growing on a disused railway line in the Cotswold Hills, England.

Far right: *Salvinia rotundifolia*. This is a water fern which carpets ponds, photographed in Trinidad, showing the interesting shape and texture of the fronds; flash.

Near right: *Cnemidaria spectabilis*. This is an ally of the tree-ferns, a large fern, photographed in the Northern Range in Trinidad. I lay on my back beneath the large frond and held the camera above me to focus; flash. Note the wavy lines of dark sori.

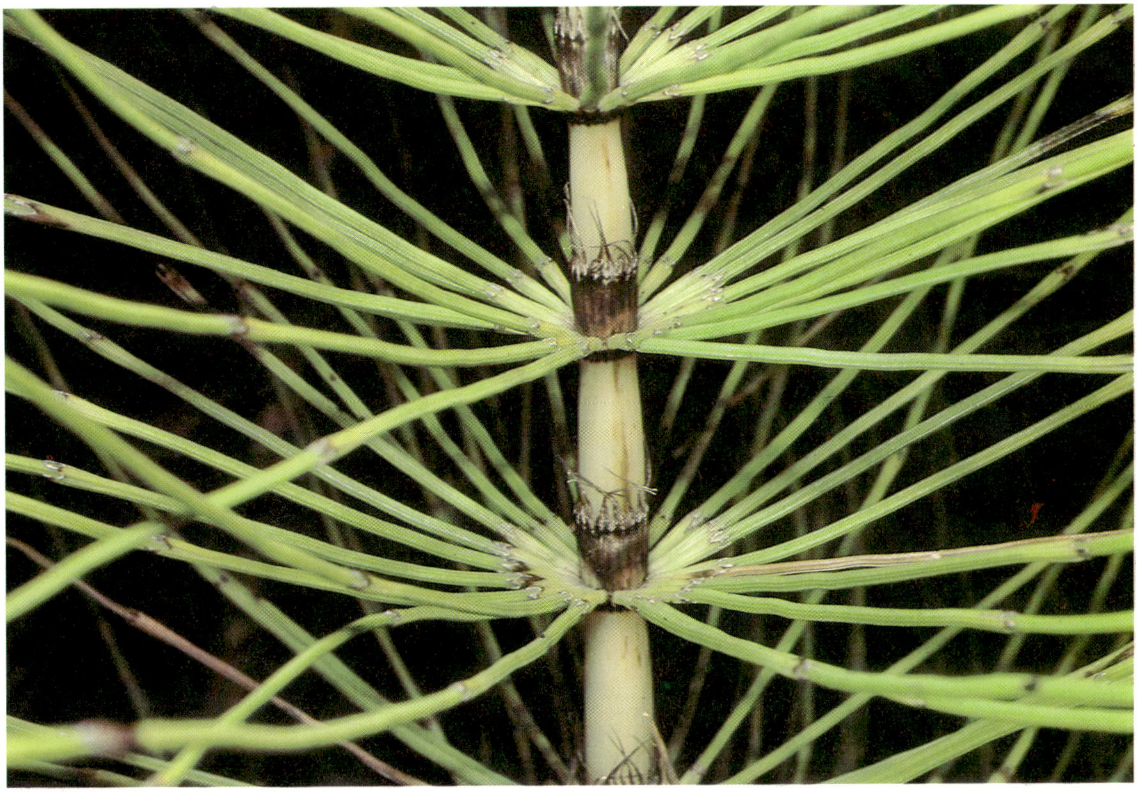

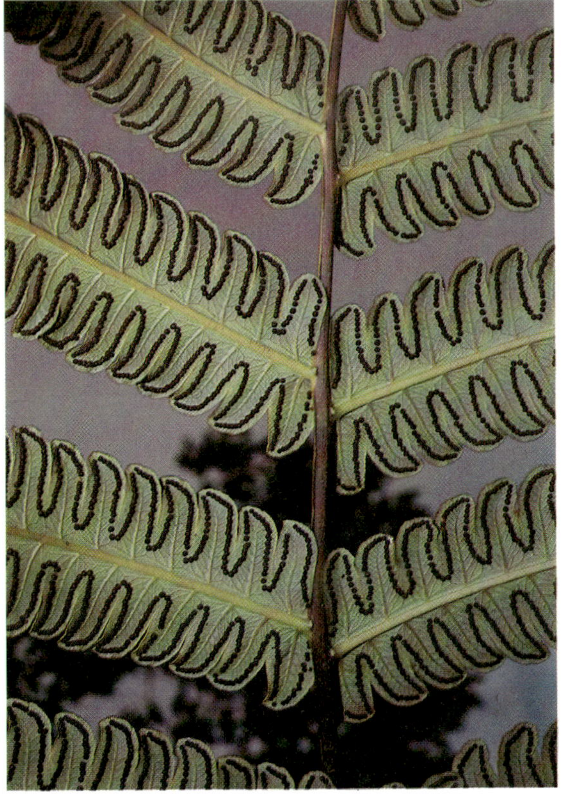

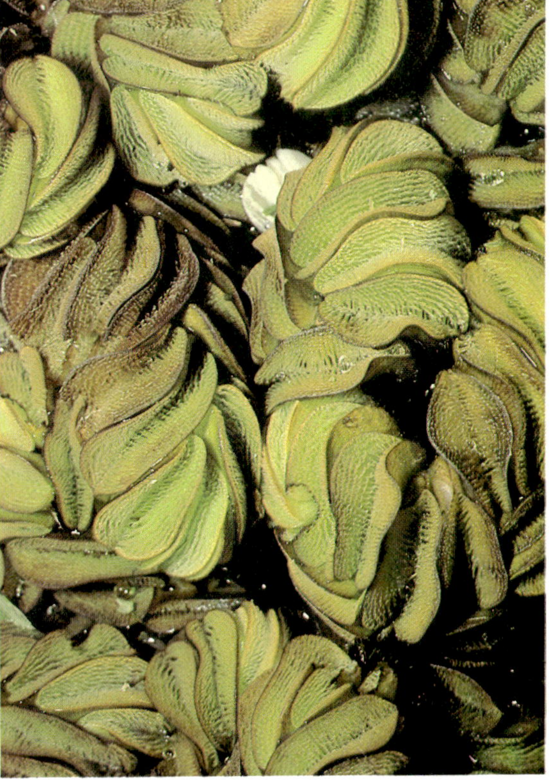

Unlike horsetails, ferns do not produce their spores inside a cone. Instead they are contained in minute cases which are grouped together in raised heaps called sori. Some ferns have naked sori, but usually each sorus is covered in a flap-like membrane called an indusium, the shape of which varies according to the species. In most ferns the sori are borne on the undersides of the normal leaves, but there are exceptions. The splendid Royal Fern (*Osmunda regalis*) has the narrow upper branches of some of the central leaves densely covered on both sides with rich brown spore cases which superficially resemble spikes of tiny brown flowers.

Upon germination the spores give rise to a tiny short-lived plant called a prothallus which bears reproductive organs. This finally leads to a new fern plant, and tiny plantlets can often be found on shady banks growing out of the minute prothalli.

Finding ferns

In temperate countries, damp rocky woodlands and mountain sides are richest in both numbers and species of ferns. However, ferns are by no means absent from drier places, and a number of xerophytic species grow in profusion with succulent cactus plants in the mountains of Mexico. Some species are aquatic, such as the very pretty moss-like Water Fern (*Azolla filiculoides*) whose blue-green overlapping stems may completely cover the surface of a pond or ditch.

Early spring is the best time to start looking for the brown shaggy mass of decayed leaves that is the remains of last year's plants. Arising from among this will be the new year's growth of young fronds, which in bud are tightly folded and usually covered in an attractive felty coat of brown or silvery scales. In unfolding from the bud the leaves uncoil from the base towards the apex and continue to grow until they reach full size.

Later in the summer ferns are easier to find and some species, such as Bracken (*Pteridium aquilinum*), may be the dominant form of vegetation over large areas. An oak wood liberally sprinkled with the graceful arching fronds of the Lady Fern (*Athyrium felix-femina*) or one of the Shield Ferns (*Polystichum* spp) is a lovely sight. Not all ferns grow on the ground or in one type of woodland. A favoured man-made habitat is provided by old walls. Species found on walls usually include one or more species of the delicate little Spleenworts (*Asplenium* spp), Rusty-Back (*Ceterach officinarum*) and one or more kinds of Polypody (*Polypodium* spp). Polypodies and some other ferns also grow in trees, and in humid woodlands may clothe the spreading boughs of gnarled old oaks.

Photographing ferns

Spring is the time to photograph the unfolding fronds. Lighting
is less of a problem than it would be later in the summer
because of the lack of leafy canopy, and the gentle spring
daylight is excellent for the pastel shades of the young fronds.
The coiled leaves with their felty coating make excellent close-
ups. It is best to use fill-in flash, which is also useful for
reducing the dense shadows caused by the low position of the
sun at this early season. Backlighting highlights the scales on the
stems, and a small flash fills in frontal details if desired.
Backlighting is excellent for pictures a little later in the year
when the pastel green fronds are fully expanded but still fresh.
Gentle sunlight streaming through the transluscent fronds
emphasizes their beautiful shape and the attractive way the
stems arch from a single rootstock. Choose ferns growing on
sloping ground, as it is then simple to select a low viewpoint
looking upwards, with the light shining directly through the
leaves. Unless you want an 'artistic' effect, be careful not to
include the sun, as it often causes flare.

Many of the most beautiful ferns have large graceful
spreading clusters of leaves, pinnately divided into many small
leaflets, usually growing on the ground in woodland, which may
be very gloomy even on a sunny summer's day. Here a tripod is
useful and a wide-angle lens may be necessary for the larger
spreading species when there is little free space around them. If
you have no tripod you can use a fairly slow shutter-speed and
brace your body against a tree or rock. Even at slow speeds you
may still need a wide aperture in the gloomier woodlands,
especially when using high quality but slow colour films such as
Kodachrome. The use of a wide aperture helps to isolate the

Sunshine in woods: if
readings from sky plus
foliage and from tree
trunks are within a six-
stop range, adequate
exposure should be
obtained by adding three
or four stops to the close-
up reading from the trees

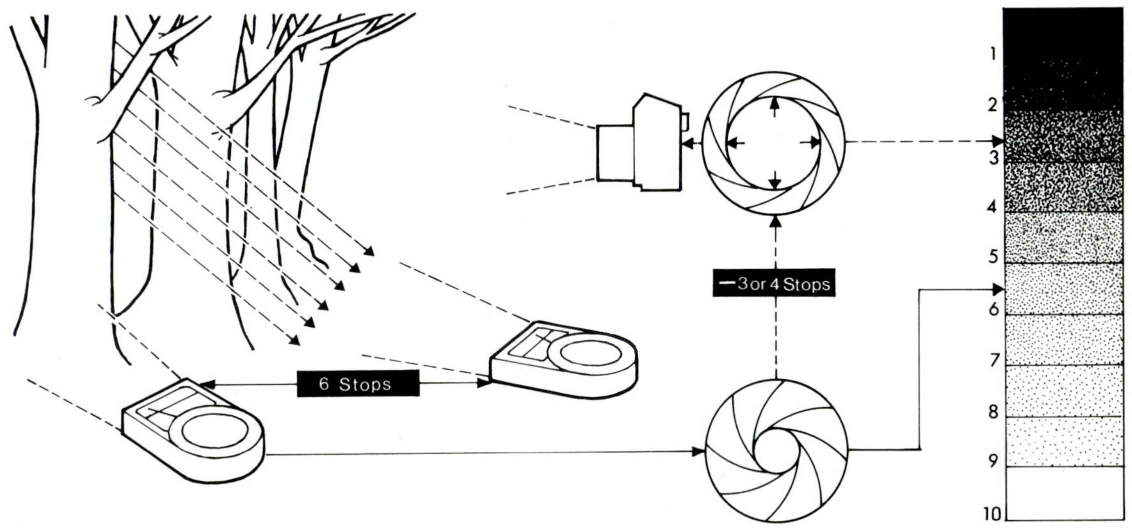

plant from its surroundings by throwing the background out of focus. Unfortunately this may mean that much of the subject itself is out of focus, because spreading ferns require a large depth of field.

Even with adequate available light there may still be problems. In the blotchy, contrasty half-light of a woodland, with the ground-cover predominantly shades of green, your green fern may 'disappear'. I have taken available light shots of ferns which seemed to stand-out perfectly well among the other plants, yet the final slides were useless as the subject was almost invisible, with heavy shadows concealing most of the detail. I now always use flash, which gives adequate depth of field and makes the plant much easier to see, however severe the lighting contrasts. Flash will help to isolate the plant by giving it more exposure than the background. Fill-in flash is also useful for ferns if the available light gives a good depth of field.

The shape of fern fronds varies enormously, so take advantage of this by studying each species and exploring its photographic possibilities. The lovely Maidenhair Ferns (*Adiantum* spp) have masses of elegant fan-shaped leaves which are often 2–3 pinnate and set alternately along wiry black stems. The Filmy Ferns of the family *Hymenophyllaceae* often cluster densely on rocks, screes or bark, and have thin leaves reminiscent of some seaweeds. The Holly Fern (*Polystichum lonchitis*), a tufted species found on mountain sides, has leathery elongated fronds, the leaflets edged with spiny teeth. Fern fronds can be pictured in their entirety and then the structural details in close-up.

From midsummer onwards start turning over fern leaves to look for the sori, the arrangement of which varies greatly from species to species. The common Polypodies lack an indusium, and the sori are very conspicuous yellow or brown blobs on the pale undersides of fronds. The spore-heaps of the lady fern have toothed covers and form rather elongated lines, while those of the shield ferns have roundish covers and are situated on veins which run beyond them to the leaf-margin. Some of the tropical ferns have small globular sori in particularly elegant S-shaped rows.

Photographing sori may mean picking part of a frond and laying it on the ground for photography, although many kinds can be photographed *in situ*. I usually take at least three shots. One shows the whole of the top third of the frond with its arrangement of sori. The next shows a number of leaflets with the sori in greater detail and the last is a reversed-lens close-up of a few groups of sori. I use a single electronic flash and graze the light across the leaf so that the spore heaps stand out in relief. Take care with your exposure, because the underside of fern fronds is usually much paler than the top, and I always give either a ¾ stop or a whole stop less exposure.

Identifying ferns
With a little experience ferns of temperate regions are not too difficult to identify as long as care is taken in distinguishing between closely related species. Being vascular plants they are usually included in floras and in handbooks on flowering plants. Always attempt identification in the field, and only collect and press a single frond if all else fails. Fern plants should not be dug up and removed from their natural habitat. Not only is this usually illegal, but it may also render some species locally extinct.

BRYOPHYTES

This group includes the liverworts and mosses, and with 20,000 species constitutes a major division of the plant kingdom. In the British Isles there are over 600 species of mosses and 300 of liverworts, in comparison with some 1500 species of flowering plants. Bryophytes are small, often inconspicuous green plants most species of which live on land, although usually in rather damp places. Some have a flattened body called a thallus, but most have developed simple stems and leaves, although they lack true roots.

Although less obviously attractive to photograph than flowering plants, bryophytes have the advantage of being at their best from November until April, when flowering plants are mostly dormant and there are few other natural-history subjects available to photograph. Bryophytes are also very widely distributed, and can be found in almost any habitat from coastal sand dunes to mountain tops, or country woodlands to the walls of town gardens. The best place to search is probably in a damp rocky woodland with a stream running through it and abundant ancient trees.

Many wildlife photographers have probably never regarded bryophytes as worth photographing, having merely trampled them unthinkingly underfoot while searching for more 'glamorous' subjects. However, the many different shapes and colours of the stems among mosses and liverworts and the frequently rather quaint appearance of their reproductive structures, together with their availability during the winter, make them an extremely interesting group in their own right.

The liverworts or *Hepaticae* are primitive land plants, most of which grow in the presence of ample moisture on soil, rock or trees. The vegetative body is usually more or less prostrate, and is either thalloid or leafy. Many of the commonest species have a very wide distribution.

A typical thalloid species is *Marchantia polymorpha* whose shiny dark green ribbon-like thalli sometimes carpet the ground. Dotted over the thallus there are usually a large number of tiny cup-shaped objects which contain minute clusters of cells called gemmae. These break away to form new plants in a form of asexual reproduction. The plant is, however, at its finest when in a fertile state, for then the thallus is covered in structures resembling tiny umbrellas. These are the reproductive organs which are borne on separate male and female plants. The umbrella is a simple disc-shape on the male plant, but on the female it has nine rays, from the underside of which the spores are released.

Lunularia cruciata is a smaller species which is very common indeed and may be a troublesome weed, covering the soil in flowerpots. If you examine the plant closely you will see numerous curved ridges of tissue protecting little piles of gemmae, hence the plant's common name of Crescent Cup Liverwort.

Most liverworts are of the leafy kind, and many may be confused with mosses. The stems and leaves are often a delicate transluscent pale green and grow massed together. The 'fruiting' structures usually consist of a white stalk surmounted by a shiny black knob, which splits into a star-shape to release the spores. Many leafy liverworts look alike, and are generally less interesting than the thalloid varieties.

Photographing liverworts
Most liverworts grow in damp shady spots, so flash is usually essential. The shining lobed leaves of the thalloid kinds make interesting patterns. Take close-ups of gemmae-cups using grazed flash so that they stand out in relief from the shiny pale green thallus. Stop down a little more than normal for these pale subjects. Distant shots of fertile liverworts showing the massed 'fruits' are very rewarding, and also close-ups of individual fruiting structures from the side. I usually take top shots looking down on the spoked 'umbrellas' and side shots to show the stalk. A single flash is all that is needed for photographing these plants.

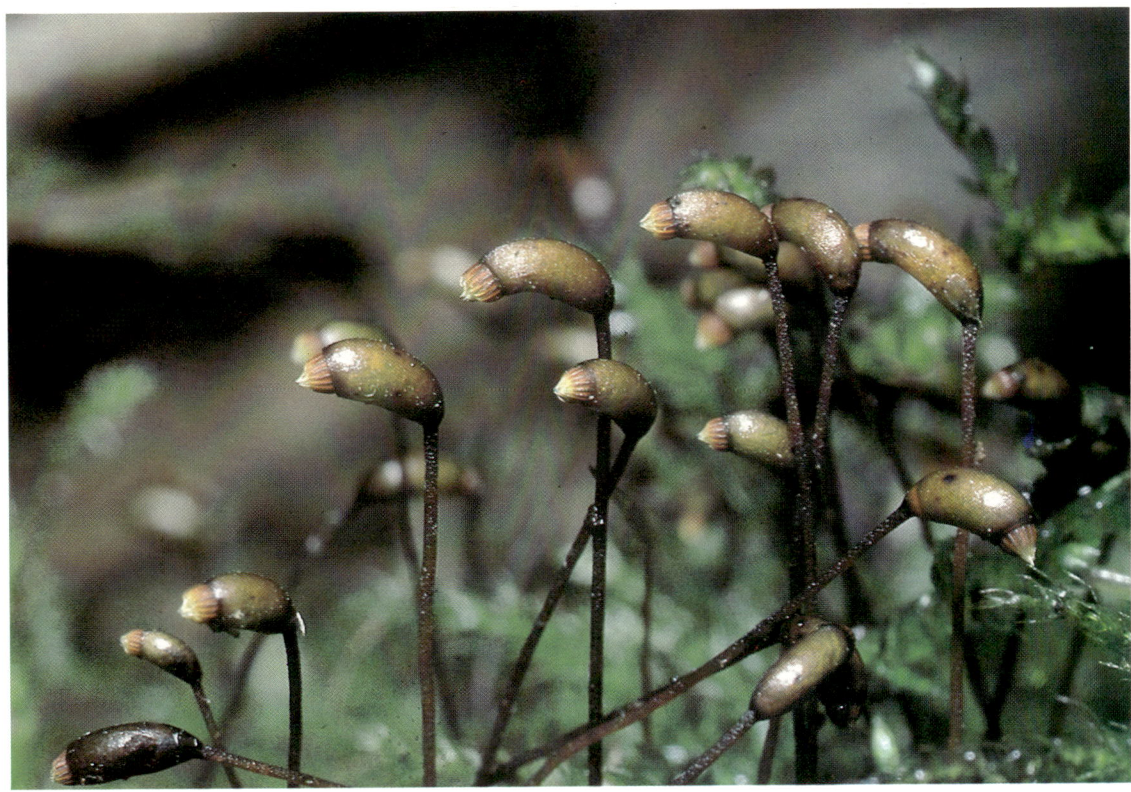

MOSSES

The mosses, with 14,000 species, constitute a larger and more advanced group than the liverworts. They are of wider distribution and live under a greater variety of conditions, including habitats with a long dry period. Mosses are conspicuously leafy and some kinds may be mistaken for tiny delicate ferns.

Reproduction in mosses is extremely interesting. The female organ, the archegonium, is normally inconspicuous, as is the male organ (antheridium) in most mosses. In some species, however, the antheridia attain a large size and may resemble miniature 'flowers'. The spores are contained in capsules which are usually borne at the tip of stalks called setae. Some mosses rarely produce capsules, although others are always abundantly fertile.

Broadly speaking, mosses can be separated into two groups, the acrocarps or cushion mosses and the pleurocarps or feather mosses. Cushion mosses normally consist of a number of mainly upright stems clustered closely together, with their spore capsules at the tip of each stem. Feather mosses are mainly prostrate, forming intricate mats of numerous branched stems,

with the setae and capsules in a lateral position. This may seem
rather complicated, but it is really very easy to distinguish
between the two kinds with some certainty, and indeeed to
recognise the more distinctive species in the field.

Cushion mosses

Sterile cushion mosses seldom make tempting subjects, usually
appearing as rather featureless green mounds, although some
species have a more attractive star-like arrangement of leaves
and more openly-spaced stems. The genus *Tortula* contains a
number of small mosses common on walls in towns. Some
species have long silvery hair-points on the leaves which look
star-like when seen in close-up. Some common species of
Grimmia which also grow on walls have even longer hair-points
which give the plant an overall silvery appearance. These mosses
are frequently very fertile. *Tortula muralis* is often topped by
forests of capsules on red setae and is a good subject on which
to practice photographing mosses, as it is so accessible.

The genus *Polytrichum* contains more robust mosses which
may carpet large areas of ground in woods, or on moors and
heaths. The pronounced star-like arrangement of the dark green
openly-spaced stems is very attractive. In addition these mosses
often produce masses of conspicuous flower-like antheridia and
plentiful capsules. The antheridia of *P. juniperinum*, called
Squirrel-tail Moss in the USA, are like little red stars studding
the dark green of the plant, which often covers recently burnt
heathland. *P. formosum* may form a luxuriant soft green carpet
in oak woods. The antheridia are pale green and the capsules,
which are borne on long setae, are protected when young by a
loosely-fitting cap or calyptra.

Feather mosses

Unlike cushion mosses most feather mosses are more attractive
when sterile and few of them produce really spectacular displays
of capsules. Many feather mosses are beautifully fern-like, for
example the widespread *Thuidium tamariscinum* and
Hylocomium splendens, a striking species with yellowish leaves
contrasting nicely with red stems. The very common
Pseudoscleropodium purum has shiny concave leaves which
tightly clasp the blunt-tipped stems, giving them a fat, rounded
appearance. These three species often grow intermixed and a
single picture can show the great differences in colour, shape
and texture. Many feather mosses grow in dense carpets on
rocks, grassy banks and on the trunks and larger branches of
trees, so that finding them is usually very simple.

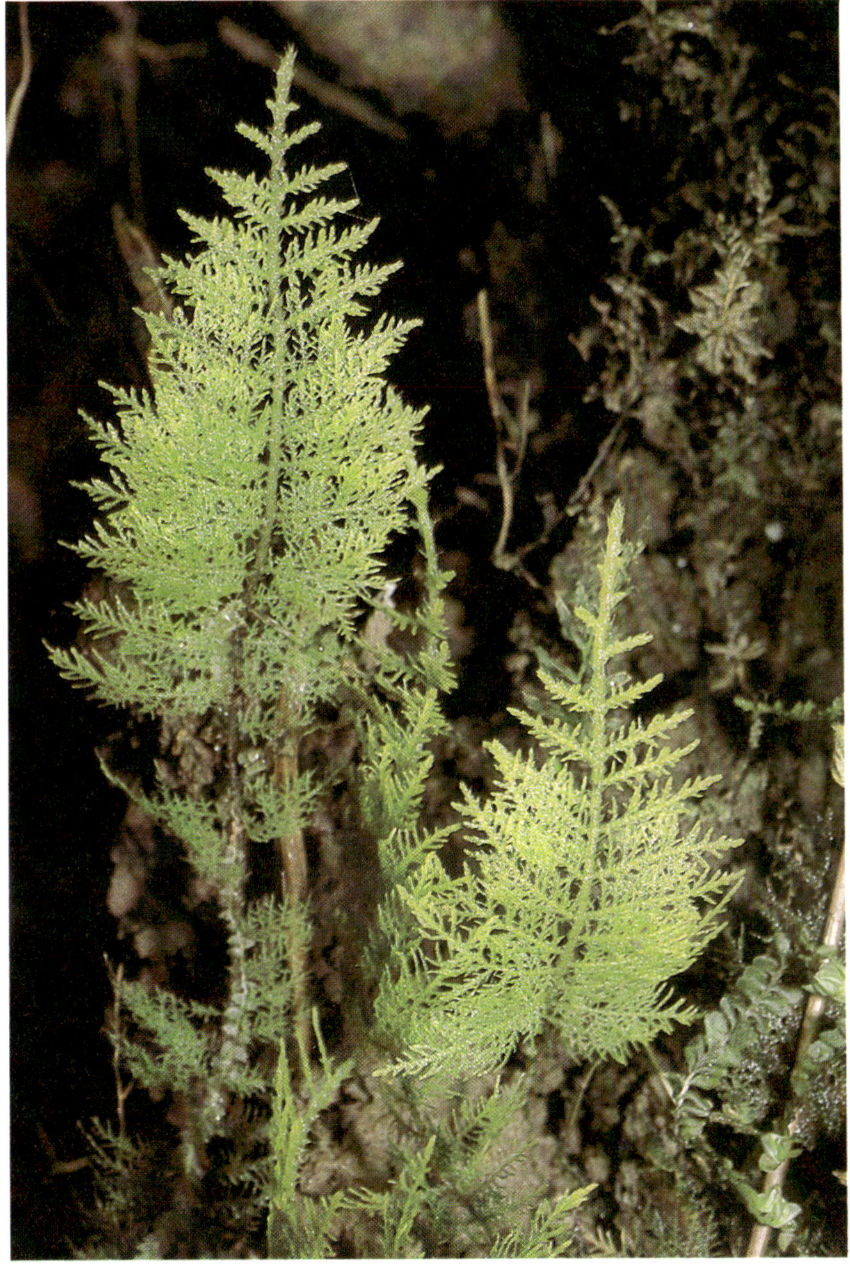

Thuidium tamariscinum, a feather moss. Two fronds arching out from a vertical bank above a stream in shady woodland in the Cotswolds. One of the pictures taken on the snowy winter's day mentioned in the text. Each frond is about 45mm long. This moss is very widespread in woodland and on limestone grassland, where it may look deceptively like a diminutive fern. Single flash held above.

Photographing mosses

In good habitats several species can be found growing together, and these can be photographed from a distance so that the different shapes and textures can be compared. Generally speaking, however, mosses are best considered as close-up subjects, for only then can the intricate tracery and varied shades of yellow, green and red of the stems be appreciated, as well as the detailed structure of antheridia and capsules.

Pictures of mosses are often taken on dull winter days in shady spots where electronic flash must be the main form of lighting, although species in more open habitats and large cushions in woodlands can be photographed using available light. On a cold March afternoon with snow scudding down from a leaden sky I photographed over 50 species of mosses out of a total of 73 species growing along 100 metres of woodland river in the Cotswold Hills in England. Only the use of flash enabled me to work quickly and obtain consistently good results.

For most bryophytes I hold the flash above and to the left, varying the angle to suit the subject. As mosses are very low-growing there are seldom any of the problems associated with flash and dark backgrounds. Using flash also gives plenty of depth of field when photographing masses of capsules. I usually take three pictures of cushion mosses with capsules. One shows the whole plant, the second concentrates on the capsules and setae and the last uses reversed-lens with lots of extension for close-ups of the capsules themselves.

When photographing feather mosses you will be looking chiefly for plants with attractively shaped stems. Where these cover the ground or a tree trunk, it is tempting to focus right in the centre of a mass of stems. This is often a mistake, as they tend to blend into each other, and the picture lacks scale and 'shape'. I usually select stems at the edge of the main plant where they creep over the rock or wood. For fern-like species look for single stems emphasising the beautiful lacy appearance.

Mosses are generally best photographed during damp weather as they shrivel and look completely different when dry, although this can make an interesting series of pictures, particularly with feather mosses. For most photography try not to select a really wet day after rain, as the film of water on the stems produces distracting highlights and may even completely mask the delicate branching. If you find a habitat rich in mosses, search for places where cushion mosses grow next to feather mosses, so that a single picture will show the difference. Bryophytes are among the easiest of all natural subjects, the main problems being to select interesting viewpoints for feather mosses (which comes with experience) and kneeling on the wet ground in cold winter weather (try taking a kneeling-mat).

Collecting and identifying bryophytes
Bryophytes can be collected for identification later at home. Place a small piece of the plant together with any capsules in a small envelope. Mark this with the place and date of collection,

Cladonia fimbriata, a very common lichen, showing the 'pixie-cups' of a plant growing under pines on a slag-heap in the Forest of Dean, England. Taken on a very cold and dull day in November, using single grazed flash.

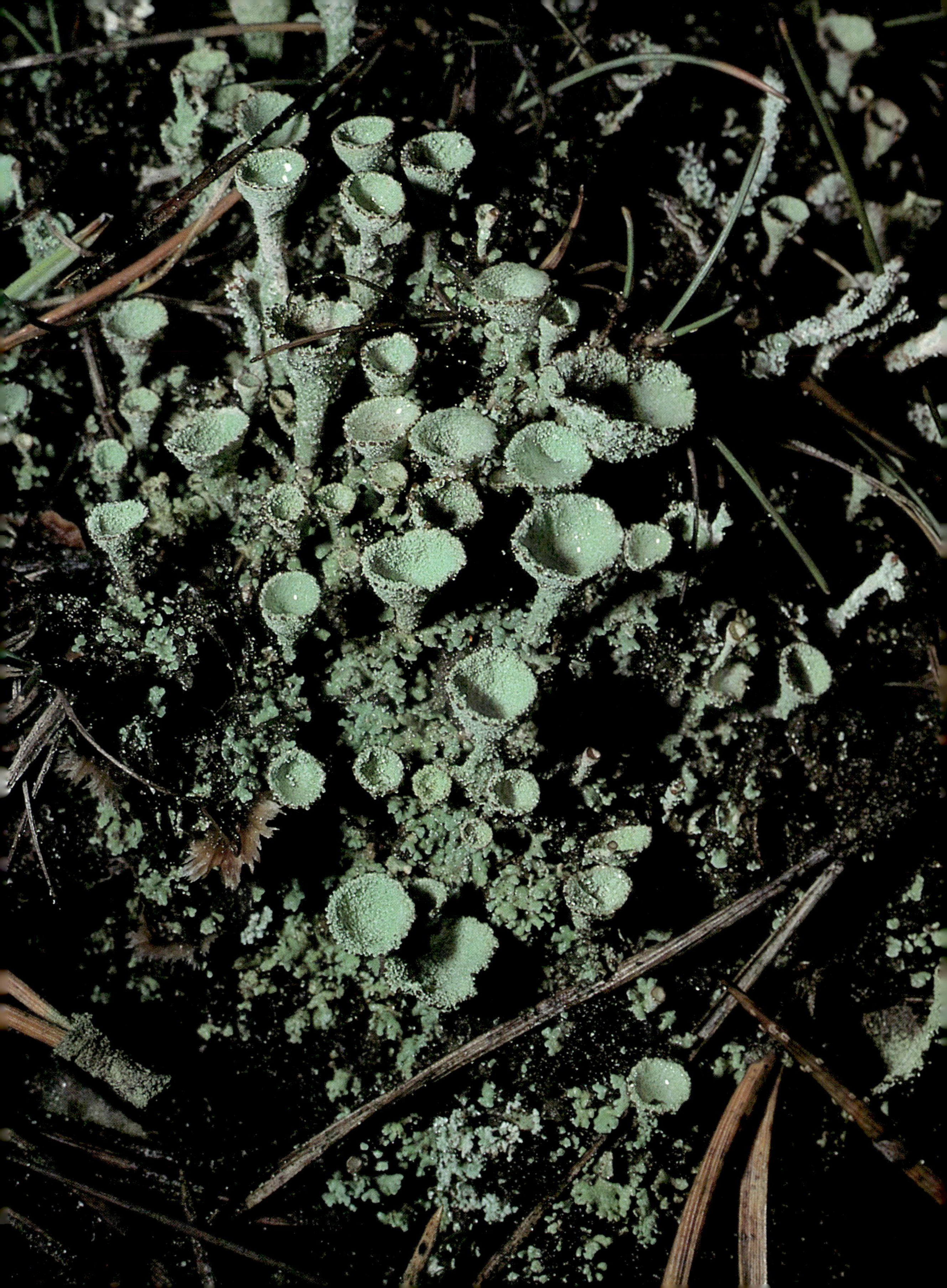

the habitat, exactly where the moss was growing ie on an oak tree, on a limestock rock, etc, your name and type of film and frame-numbers. At first you may find it difficult to match a moss specimen to a picture, so careful cross-referencing is vital.

Some bryophytes can be identified quickly and easily, but accurate identification usually involves the use of a book containing an identification key and the extensive use of a microscope. Identification of bryophytes frequently depends on characteristics in the cells of the leaves, and these are only visible under high magnification.

LICHENS

Lichens are dual organisms, consisting of a fungus, to which the plant owes its shape and form, living in intimate association with an alga which, like all green plants, can use the light energy from the sun to manufacture food from simple materials. By living together in this way these completely different kinds of plant are able to produce a more elaborate structure with a longer life-span than either could manage alone.

Lichens may be divided into three types: branched or fruticose; leafy or foliose; encrusting or crustose. The leafy kinds are often very abundant, the grey-green *Hypogymnia physodes* sometimes completely clothing the branches and twigs of trees. Species of *Parmelia* are known as dog lichens. They are mostly large, flat greyish or brownish leaf-like plants with broad shining lobes, often creeping on the surface of the ground where they may be mistaken for liverworts. Typical fruticose lichens are the Old Man's Beard lichens (*Usnea* spp), with their long branched greyish threads hanging in streamers from trees. Much more widespread but far less conspicuous are the encrusting lichens, which mostly grow on rocks, trees and such man-made habitats as fenceposts, walls and gravestones. Many kinds are not very obvious, as they appear only as lighter areas on the substrate. All lichens are very sensitive to air pollution and the best place to look for them is on unpolluted mountains in humid highland areas. A few species are smoke-tolerant and live even in the centres of large cities.

Some species of lichen are rarely fertile but when fruit-bodies (apothecia) are produced, the variety of shapes and colours is fascinating. Several very common and widespread species of *Cladonia* can often be found covered in tiny elongated cup-shaped structures, usually called 'pixie-cups'. Around their edges they may also bear apothecia, which are smooth and may be brilliant scarlet. Many lichens produce tiny plate-like apothecia, often of a different colour from the plant. They are usually grouped around the centre of the plant, and are often seen on the flattened species which grow on tree trunks and rocks. Even without apothecia, many lichens are worth photographing, notably the antler-like fruticose kinds which grow on the ground, pendant branching species on trees and the colourful rosettes and mosaics often found on rocks in upland areas. Although typical of rather humid areas, lichens are not restricted to these habitats, and many varieties occur in the Mexican and South American deserts, even growing densely on the trunks and branches of large cacti.

Photographing lichens

Plants on rocks in the open can be photographed using available light and a tripod. Available light is especially suited to the flatter lichens with apothecia, as it gives an unrivalled three-dimensional effect. For plants in darker spots, or on dull days, I always use flash, using grazed lighting for flattened plants. This is especially important for showing flat plate-like apothecia in relief. I always take the whole plant or several together, and then close-ups of any apothecia. Close-ups of the smaller kinds need reversed lens and a lot of extension. Close-ups of the intricate branching of fruticose species are also of interest. Look out for several species of different colours growing together on bark or rocks, as the crazy-paving effect makes a lovely picture.

Collecting and identifying lichens

Identification is often not easy. Collect small pieces of the plants and follow the procedure for mosses. On no account should any pieces be removed from large specimen plants. Always try and collect from a plant which is imperfect or damaged. Even with specimens, accurate identification may be impossible for the beginner and expert help will probably be necessary.

Finally, a general word about studio photography. All the plants in this chapter are extremely easy to photograph in the wild, and bryophytes and lichens are perhaps the easiest of all natural history subjects. I therefore see no need to collect the plants for photography later in the studio. Such photography is pointless and to be condemned, first because studio pictures are ecologically and biologically less rewarding and second because large amounts of the plant have to be collected and this is vandalism towards our natural flora.

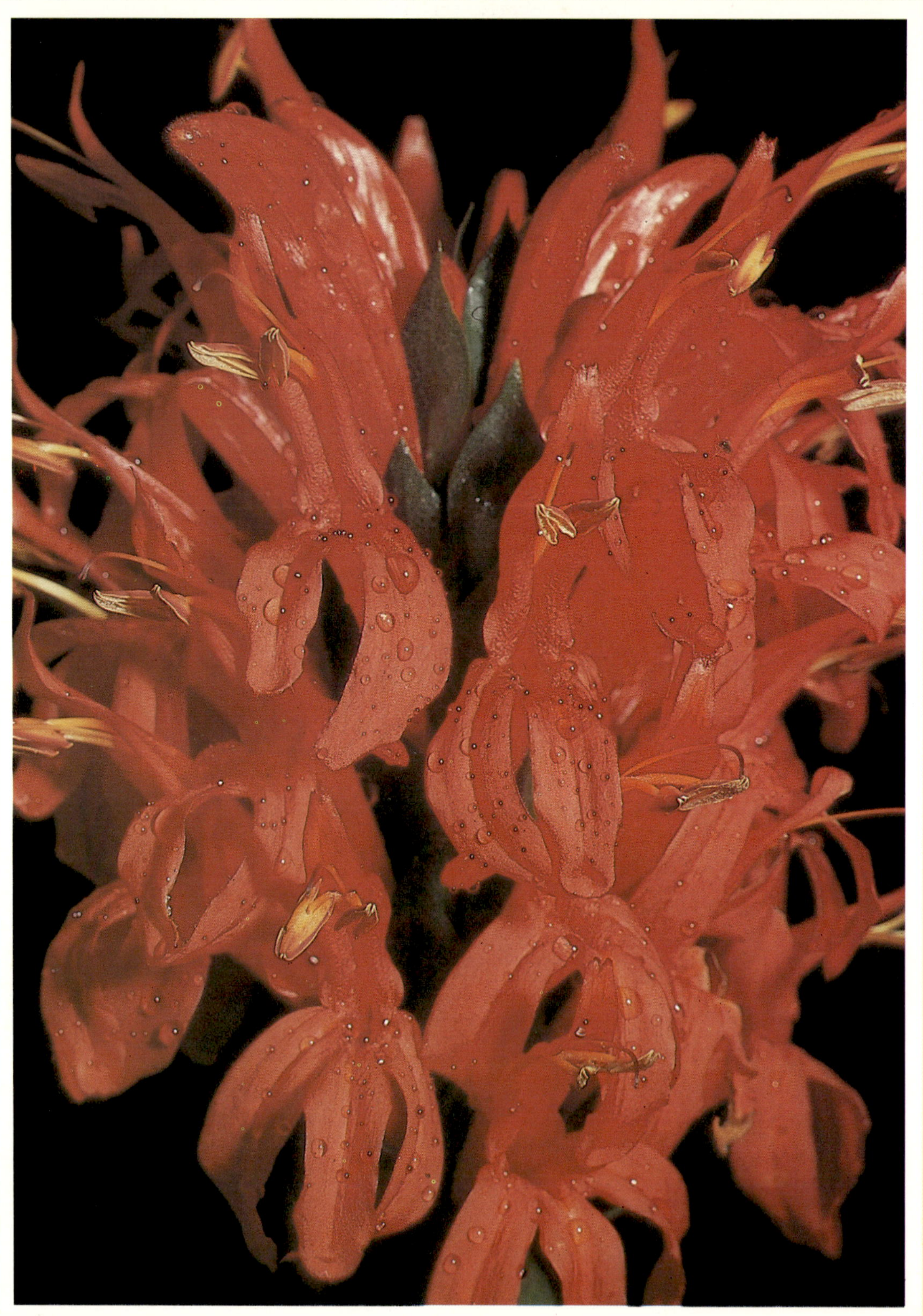

3 Flowering Plants

Flowering plants are the dominant life-form over most of the earth's land surface, occurring in most types of habitat, so it is not surprising that they are a popular subject for photography. Nevertheless, it is still a challenge to find and photograph to a high standard plants as diverse as a tiny duckweed, the size of a full-stop, to a mighty forest tree several hundred feet high. Between these extremes are the majority of medium-sized plants most frequently chosen as subjects. Despite their obvious attractions as colourful and static subjects, outstanding photographs of flowers are difficult to achieve, perhaps because their very simplicity as subjects invites a casual approach leading to indifferent pictures. Equipment for flower photography is fairly basic and is similar to that described in Chapter 2.

WOODLANDS

Woodlands and forests still cover large areas of the earth, although man's depredations reduce it each year. In temperate countries woodlands often consist of stands of a single species of tree, for example oak, birch or pine, with perhaps a few subordinate species intermixed. Tropical rain forests are quite different, and many kinds of tree grow together, with no single species predominant.

Temperate deciduous forests are very seasonal. Flowering, coming into leaf and fruiting of the trees and their associated flora occur in a set order restricted to a few months of the year. The same events in a tropical rain forest may occur in different species throughout the year, so that the forest always looks green, and flowers and fruits can be found at all seasons.

Photographing trees

Trees usually occur naturally in large aggregations, and when standing alone have usually been planted by man. These single specimens are often the best for photography, for only then can the full shape be appreciated and the tree seen as a whole rather than as part of a confusing mass. The shape may vary greatly depending on the habitat. A lone beech tree has a squat broad trunk with the arching branches reaching low down towards the ground, whereas the same species in dense woodland has a tall slim trunk and a small head of more spindly branches perched at the top, where the light can reach the leaves. Isolated oaks develop a broad crown of a very characteristic shape, but are taller and slimmer in woodland. Most trees develop an easily recognisable shape when well-grown in isolation, making identification possible even from a distance and in the absence of leaves or fruit.

Single trees   Open parkland is the best place to find good specimens of single trees, for there will be less chance of ugly intrusions such as telephone wires and traffic. Select a specimen with the typical shape of the species. Avoid trees in leaf which have some dead branches, unless you want to show how disease attacks living trees. Walk around your chosen specimen and assess the background from each angle. Avoid distracting backgrounds with buildings or scattered smaller trees, or one into which your specimen may merge, such as a nearby woodland edge. The sky usually makes the best backdrop, but watch out for electricity pylons which seem to be everywhere. Avoid using a 'white' glaring sky on very hot sunny days.

Take a series of pictures throughout the year, showing the bare outline in winter, the soft green leafing-out in spring, the deep green rounded fullness of summer and the muted tints of autumn. In North America, fall is the best time for tree photography, for then woodlands of maple and aspen become a blaze of yellow and red. Choose your lighting according to what you want to show. Backlighting gives a silhouette showing the general shape of the tree, frontal lighting shows the overall texture and colouring.

Tree bark varies greatly from species to species. It may be either smooth and fine-grained, or deeply-furrowed or shredding off in strips. Winter is the best time for close-ups of the bark, as the absence of leaves exposes the trunk to the gentle winter sunlight. Sidelighting is best as it reveals the texture of the bark to the greatest advantage.

Trees in forests and woodlands   It is not easy to show a single tree and its shape when growing crowded with others and also to show the general character of a forest. Selecting an interesting viewpoint in apparently uniform woodland takes much care and patience, plus some imagination if a muddled picture is to be avoided. Sometimes, of course, uniformity may actually be required, as when portraying the regimented rows and bare ground of a commercial conifer plantation. Usually, however, it is better to choose a viewpoint which shows the habit of the tree concerned.

Take a series of photographs throughout the year, showing the serried ranks of trunks in midwinter, perhaps with driven snow forming conspicuous lines down them; the pastel shades of the fresh springtime canopy; the densely shaded deep green of summer and the varied hues of autumn. A wide-angle lens is invaluable for all tree photography, but especially so in woodlands. A particularly effective series can be made by lying on your back and looking upwards into the canopy from the same spot at different times of the year in various types of woodland. This will show the development and loss of the leaves, and the density of the final canopy. You can either choose an open spot between trees to show the whole area of interlacing branches, or else place the camera and wide-angle as low as possible at the base of a tree and take a set of pictures looking up the length of the trunk, with the branches spread out above. In really dense woods, such as aspen groves, a short telephoto can replace the wide-angle to foreshorten the viewpoint and emphasise the crowding of the silvery barked trunks. Pictures can also show the effect of man's management of woodlands, such as coppicing of hazel or hornbeam. A path or track through a wood is often the best place for a picture, giving added scale and depth, particularly if a human figure is included.

Photography of woodlands can be tricky, as the lighting is frequently very patchy and may consist mainly of sunlight shafting to the ground in more open spots. Take several pictures on bracketed exposures, especially if shooting against the light. This is a very effective method in woodlands. When taking pictures upwards into the canopy ensure that you give sufficient exposure to show the colour of the leaves, as the bright sky shining through can often fool a TTL meter into giving you a silhouette. I use a hand-held meter to take several readings rapidly over areas of varying intensity, making the final decision myself as to correct exposure.

Close-ups of trees It is necessary to get in close for portraits of the buds, leaves, flowers and fruits of trees. Contrary to the advice given in some other books, this can almost always be accomplished without difficulty *in situ*. It should seldom be necessary to remove any part of a tree (or any flowering plant) in order to take it home for studio photography. It is also usually illegal to do this and is always damaging to the tree.

Buds and leaves In temperate countries midwinter is the time to search for the protective devices employed by trees to shield

Overleaf: *Fagus sylvatica*, European beech tree. A series to show the development and loss of the leaves, taken looking up the trunks of a double-trunked tree, using a 28mm wide-angle lens. Series taken over several years in Buckholt Wood Nature Reserve, Cotswolds, England.

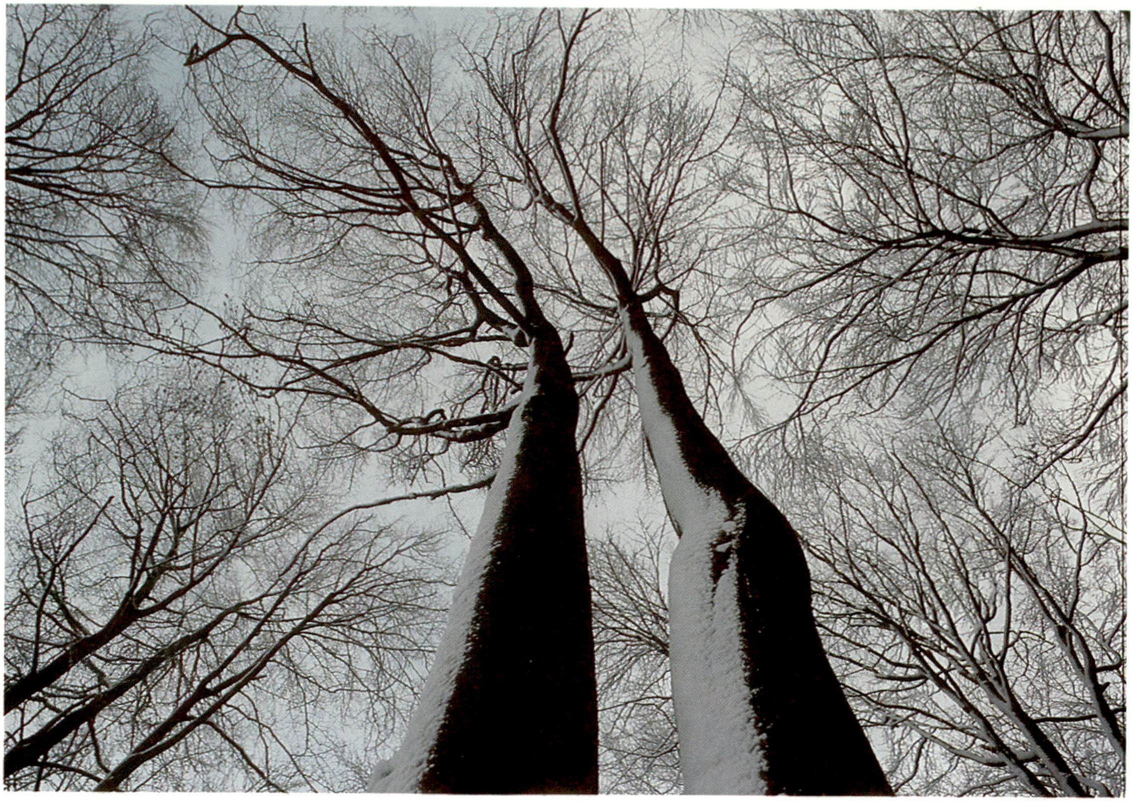

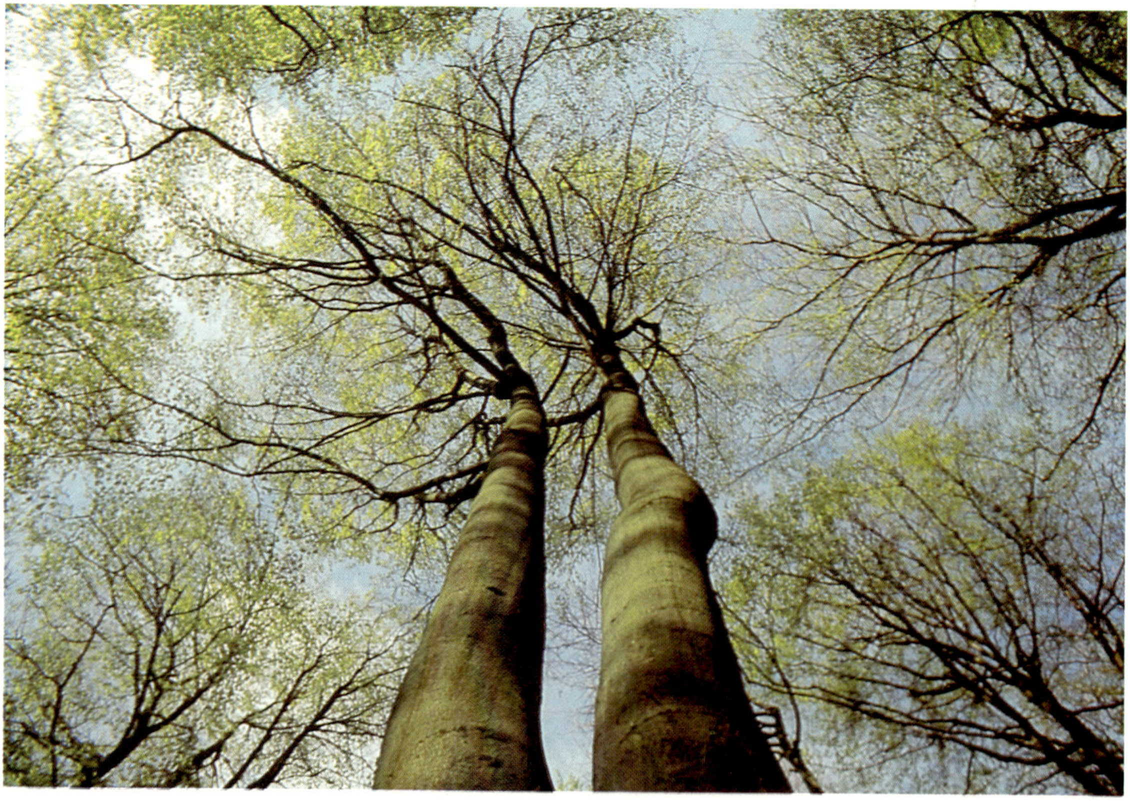

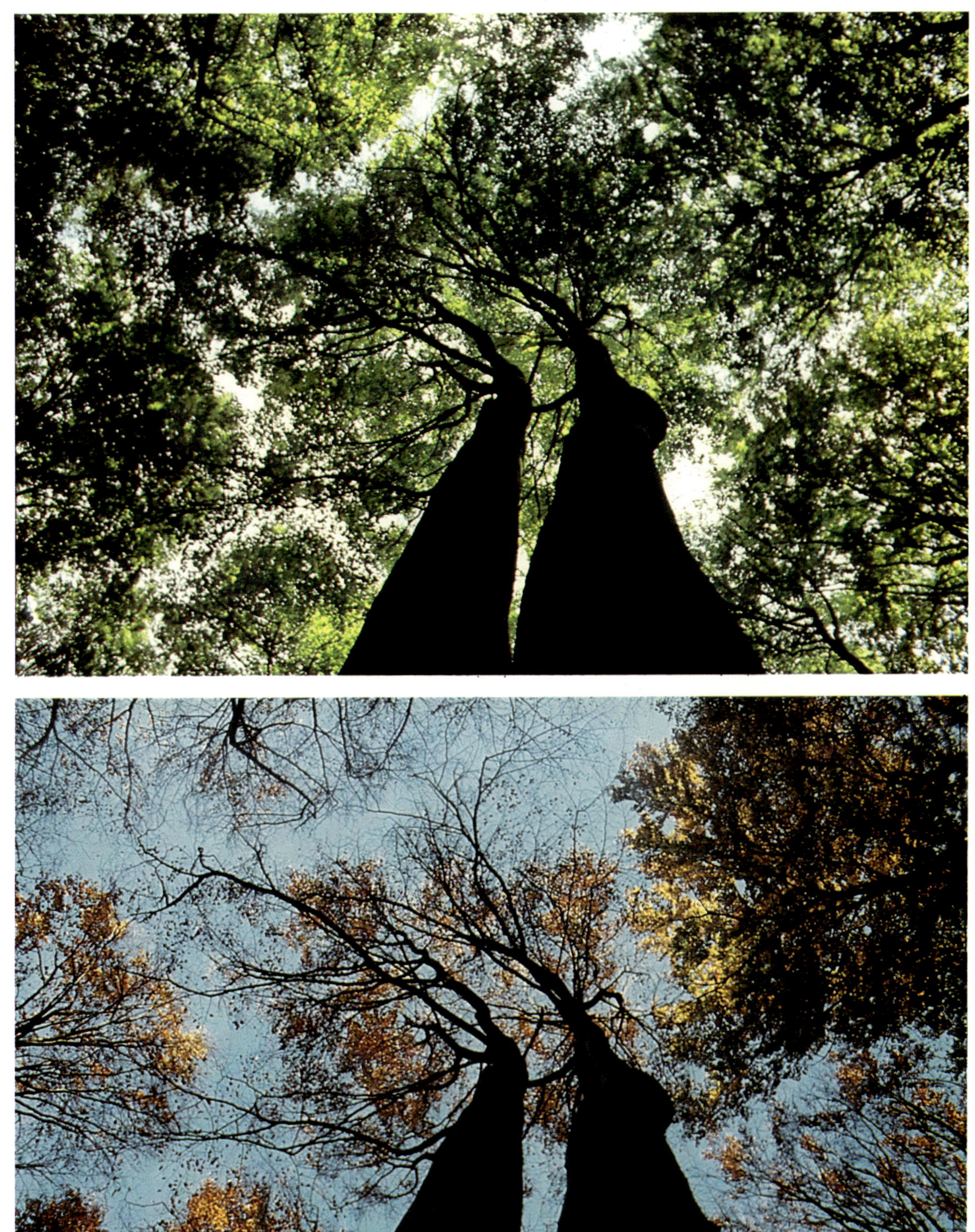

their delicate buds from the frost. Some species have strong sticky scales, others have woolly or felty coverings. The Ash (*Fraxinus excelsior*) has characteristic matt black scales, for example, and many other trees can be identified in winter from their buds alone. Groups of buds or twigs can be photographed against the sky using the gentle winter sun, but an electronic flash improves clarity for close-ups showing single buds. Wind-shake is always a problem, so it pays to be patient and pick the moment when there is least, or no, movement. Daylight can cause a blurred secondary ghost image when the principal light source is flash (see p. 28).

Backlighting is most attractive for the fresh green leaves as they break from the buds in spring and can be used for close-ups as well as clusters of leaves. Do vary your approach and use frontal lighting as well, perhaps using flash to highlight detail. Springtime is also best for close-ups of fully developed leaves, as later in the summer they darken and lose their pastel tints. They can also become damaged by insects and weather and sooty from a mould which grows on aphid honeydew. In autumn, leaves will look especially vivid and colourful when photographed against the light.

Flowers on trees   Sooner or later all trees will flower, although the quantity of blooms produced varies greatly from year to year, and some tropical trees flower at very irregular intervals. The flowers may be pollinated by wind or by animals, usually insects, birds and bats. The male flowers of wind-pollinated or anemophilous trees are usually cylindrical and pendant and are called catkins. The female flowers of many trees are often very tiny and inconspicuous. Solitary wind-pollinated flowers may look fairly drab, but large masses may be more appealing, and a male Black Poplar (*Populus nigra*) covered in a halo of reddish catkins is a fine sight. The male flowers of Scots Pine (*Pinus sylvestris*) are borne on conspicuous yellowish spikes at the tips of the branches, and produce prodigious amounts of pollen which can cause severe hay fever. Male catkins often ripen and release their pollen very rapidly, after which they quickly shrivel, so observe your subject closely. If the male and female flowers occur on the same tree try to find them growing together so that a single photograph can show their differences. Incidentally, remember not to look for autumn fruits on male trees!

Flowers which are visited by pollinating animals are usually conspicuous and brightly coloured, and may also be scented. Bat-pollinated flowers, such as those of the African baobab tree and several American columnar cacti, have fleshy white flowers with numerous exposed stamens and a strong odour. Bird-pollinated flowers are often brightly coloured, while those visited by insects are of various types. When in full flower, animal-pollinated trees may be a blaze of colour, especially some tropical kinds, but even temperate species such as the Horse Chestnut (*Aesculus hippocastanum*) or laburnum may be an attractive spectacle.

Larger flowers can easily be photographed *in situ* using available light, preferably with fill-in flash, while flash alone can be used for small flowers. Smaller branches which are out of reach can be hooked down and tied to a stake driven into the ground while pictures are taken, but be careful not to over-bend the branches and risk breaking them. A stepladder is a useful piece of equipment, particularly for flowers or fruits which are just out of reach. Really high-growing flowers can be photographed using a telephoto lens, but the picture quality is generally less satisfactory.

Backgrounds for flowers on trees are largely dictated by conditions and taste. The use of flash on dull days renders the flowers in sharp relief against a dark background, which is excellent for emphasising the shape of catkins. Flash can also be used to advantage for photographing flowers against a blue sky, slight underexposure of the sky renders it darker than normal, thus highlighting the flowers. On sunny days, whether or not flash is used, the leafy branches of the tree itself provide a natural background as well as showing general details of the leaves, which, if possible, should always be included in any picture. In general be flexible, adapting your techniques to the prevailing conditions and the nature of your subject.

Fruits of trees   The abundance of fruits generally corresponds to the quantity of flowers in springtime, so after a poor showing of flowers it is useless to plan an intensive period of photography for autumn fruits.

Some fruits appear very early in the year, and it is interesting to record their development. The pink wind-pollinated flowers of Elm (*Ulmus* spp) are soon followed by lovely fresh green keys, which develop along with the leaves. Ash keys are one of the 'helicopter' types of fruit which twirl to the ground. Keys of maple and ash also rapidly follow the flowers, those of maple darkening to an attractive reddish hue in autumn. The shape and colour of the fruits of any plant will give a clue to the method of dispersal. As well as the 'helicopter' seeds there are windblown 'parachute' seeds, which are produced in huge quantities by willows. Many trees produce heavy crops of berries which are brightly coloured to attract the

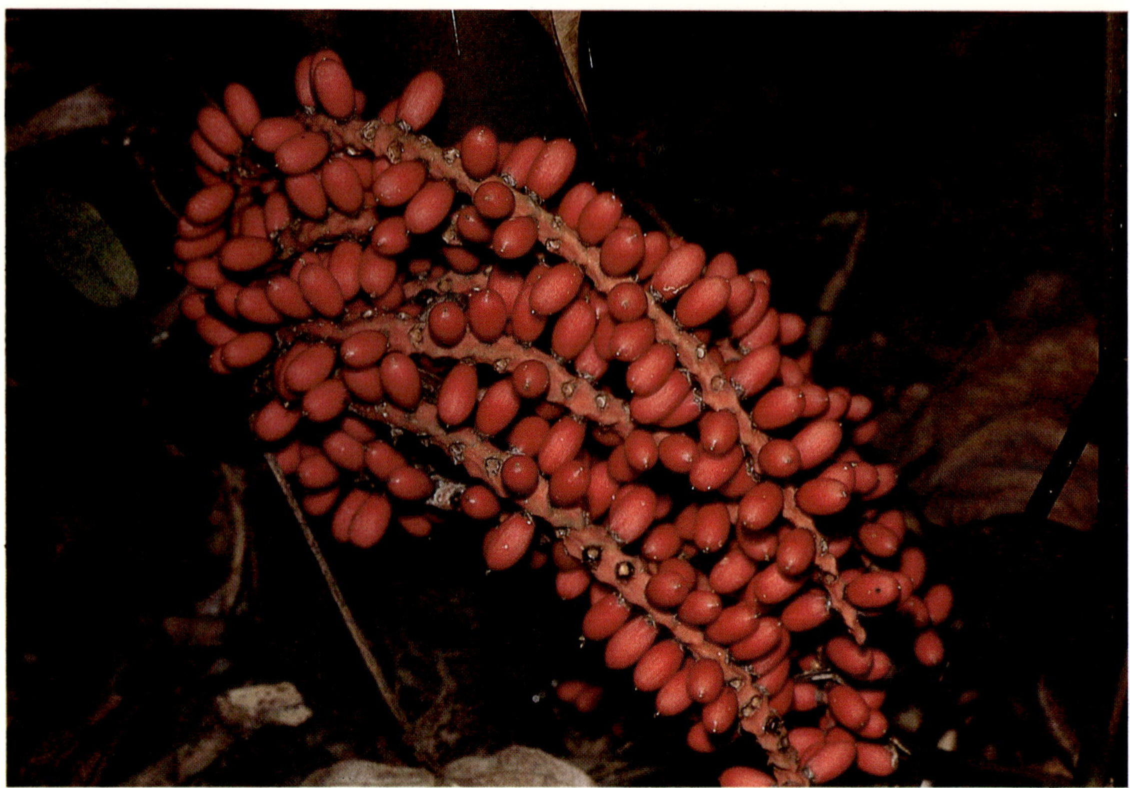

birds which eat them and spread the seeds widely. Many of the red or orange fruits preferred by birds have a very shiny surface. I have read much advice about how to eliminate this shine from photographs. This is ridiculous, as the shine is an intrinsic part of the fruit's self-advertisement and so should not be eliminated to make a 'better' picture. The same applies to naturally shiny leaves, which should never be rubbed with plasticine or anything else to make them appear artificially matt.

The many kinds of colourful fruit make autumn a good season for photography. Some of the most attractive of my pictures were taken using sidelit flash against a slightly underexposed blue sky. Ultra close-ups can reveal small details on fruits, such as fine downy coatings, which are invisible to the naked eye. Keep an eye open in winter for snow on red fruits, as this always looks effective.

The seeds of some trees, such as beech and chestnut, develop inside a tough shell and are then released to fall to the ground, either because the shell splits or a lid opens to release them. (The lid of the brazil nut and its relatives is 6in broad, has a large spike on it, weighs nearly a pound and makes photography in parts of South America decidedly risky.) Take two sets of pictures, one showing the developing fruits on the

Pinanga species, a small palm in dark forest in Sarawak on the island of Borneo. The red fruits develop in clusters at the base of the tree, a habit which is fairly common in the tropics. Taken with single flash. I had to watch out all the time for a tame and very inquisitive and boisterous orang-utan which wanted to play games with my camera!

trees, and another showing the nuts which have fallen to the ground beneath the tree. Pictures of seeds on the woodland floor should, if possible, show the type of tree from which they fell. Show a beech nut near its case upon a carpet of dead beech leaves, perhaps next to a seedling plant. The cones of conifers look attractive after they have fallen and are easier to photograph than when at a great height on the trees. Damage to cones by rodents and squirrels should be recorded. I use flash for all my woodland close-ups, as there are certain disadvantages to using available light (see below).

Woodland flowers

In all flower photography timing is very important to ensure success, and local floras should be consulted for the flowering times of plants in your area. Remember that rising altitude delays flowering times, so that a plant in flower in April in a valley may not flower until a month later on a nearby mountain. Spring is the best season for photographing woodland flowers. This is when the best displays occur, the plants flowering before the dense summer canopy shuts out most of the light. There are of course exceptions to this, and woodlands should be visited throughout the summer. Saprophytic plants, such as the Yellow Bird's Nest (*Monotropa* spp), use a fungus in their roots to manufacture food and lack chlorophyll so that they can flower in the very darkest parts of a wood.

Springtime in woodlands can be very spectacular, and in England I always look forward to the massed displays of Bluebells (*Endymion non-scriptus*) and Wild Daffodils (*Narcissus pseudonarcissus*) which give an overall blue or yellow tinge to the woodland floor. Plenty of light reaches the ground at this time so that photography is much simplified and tripods or flash should seldom be necessary, unless you prefer them.

As a general rule I take three sets of pictures of any plant. The first set is always rather distant, showing a plant or group of plants in their habitat. I then move in for a shot of a single plant more or less filling the frame, and then go in even closer for detailed shots of individual flowers. Gregarious plants should always be shown as such if possible.

As a general piece of advice for all plant photography it is better not to photograph the first specimen which you find. Excitement at discovering a rare or much-prized species often leads to an over-enthusiastic wish to get the first pictures 'in the can'. This is often a mistake, for the first plant to be discovered rarely proves to be the finest example. Having found a locality for a particular species take your time and search carefully for the best plant to photograph. This should be a representative specimen in fine condition. It should preferably be in a position for a good composition, so look carefully at the background from all angles before making your final choice. If necessary take several pictures from different viewpoints and the final result will simplify your decision next time. Sometimes your choice may be dictated by the lighting. Plants spotlit by sunlight shafting through the canopy always give a picture 'mood'.

Lighting for woodland flowers   Having chosen your plant, photography can begin. For taller species a low viewpoint is very effective, showing the nature of the woodland in which the plant is growing. A really low viewpoint sets the plant against the mottled out-of-focus background of the canopy. In this case use flash, so that the canopy is slightly underexposed and the light shining through does not swamp your subject. This brings us to the main problem with woodland photography: lighting. As the light filters down through the dense canopy of leaves it acquires a decidedly green tinge. We do not notice this because our brains act as a filter, and a pink flower in woodland looks to us just as pink as it should. Film cannot do this and records everything with a bias towards green. Photographic filters are not a solution to the problem, and the long exposures on a tripod, so frequently required in dull woodlands, simply make matters worse and introduce the additional problems of reciprocity law failure.

The simple solution is to use flash, but this has its own drawbacks. When used in woodland, flash invariably produces a very dark background, showing nothing of the plant's habitat. Plants close to a background should therefore be chosen, or else a second flash can be mounted on a tripod behind and to one side of the subject and used to light the background. Alternatively, mount the camera on a tripod, use a slow shutter-speed to record at least some detail in the background, and render the main subject clear and free of green casts by lighting with flash. Of course, if you want your plants to appear in relief, dark backgrounds with flash are perfect and are easy to find. *Never* pick or uproot any wild plant to set next to another for a 'manufactured' picture. Always search carefully for naturally occurring compositions, as this is one of the challenges of successful nature photography.

Surprisingly perhaps, tropical rain forests are usually very unrewarding places for the plant photographer. Little light reaches the ground and most of the finest flowers, such as

Right: *Lathraea squamaria*, Toothwort. A parasite, growing on the roots of hazel. Taken to show the trunk of the host behind, plus some leaves of *Adoxa moschatelliana*, Town Hall Clock. In the Cotswolds, England; single flash.

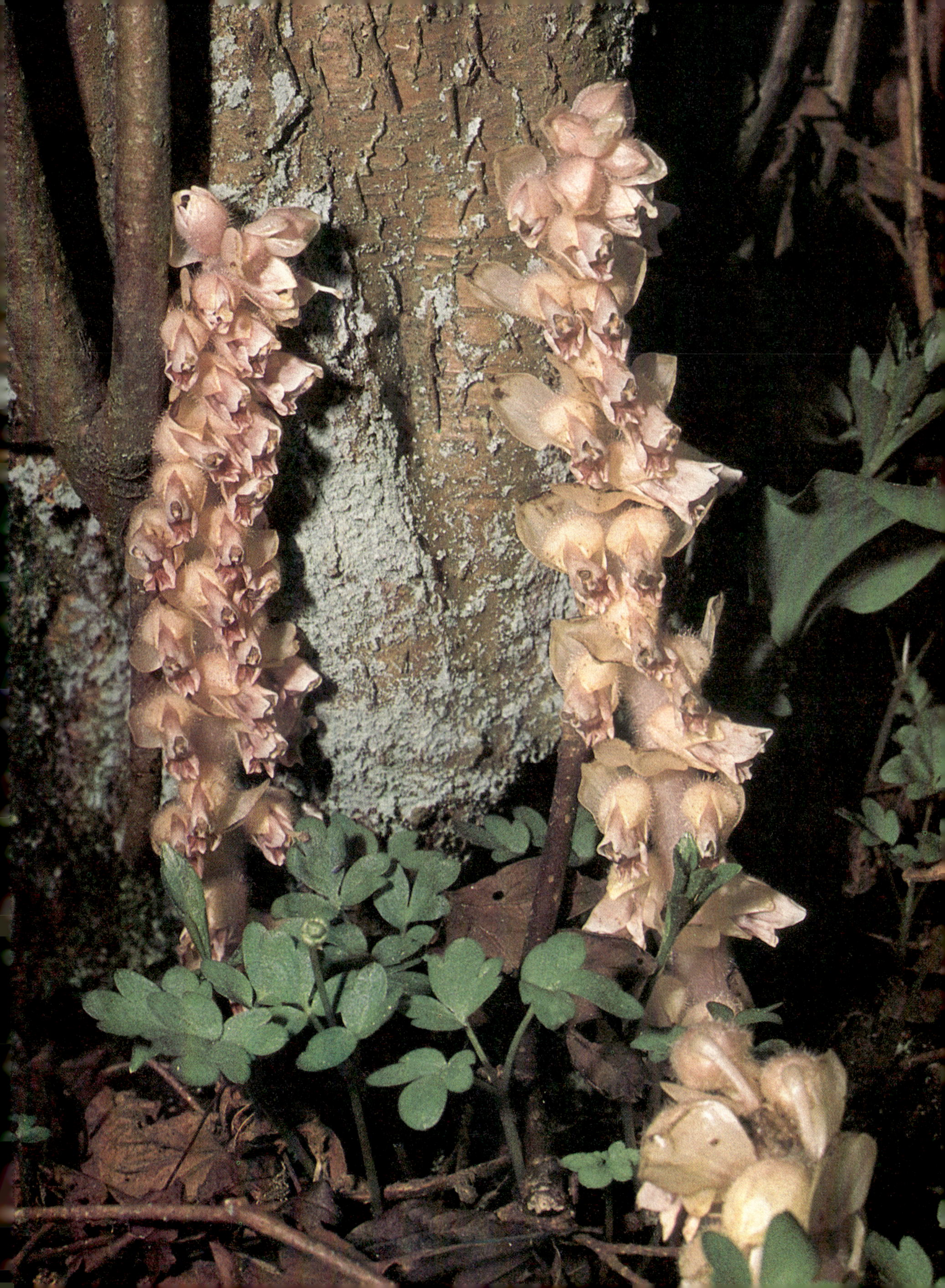

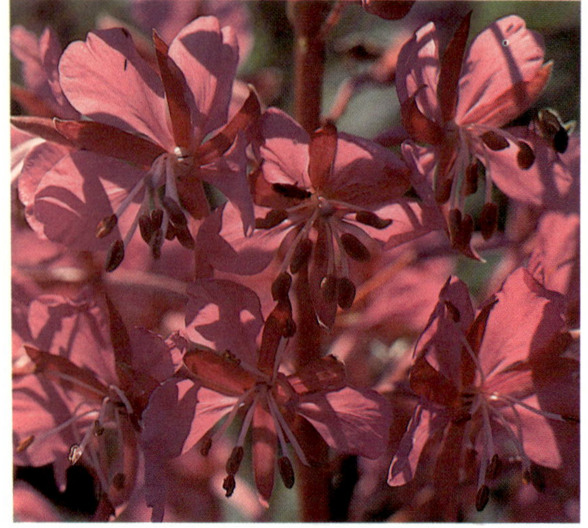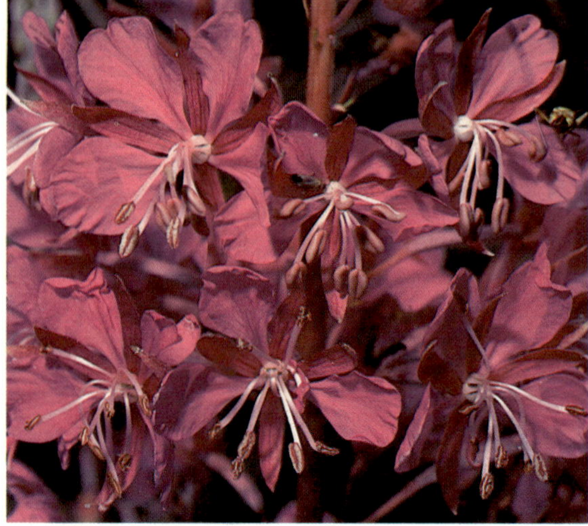

Chamaenerion angustifolium, Rose-bay Willowherb, Warwickshire, England. This pair shows the enormous difference which may be possible between a picture taken by available light and the same subject taken using flash. Left: taken using natural sunlight filtering through the flowers. While making a pleasing picture, the side lighting makes the flowers look rather confused so this picture is less useful for botanical identification. Right: taken using a small electronic flashgun held above and to one side. The lighting is far more uniform and botanical details are clearly rendered. The darker background could have been lightened by using a diffuser on the front of the flash, the resulting depth of field being only slightly shallower and of little import. Both shots were hand-held.

orchids, grow high up on the branches of the trees themselves, so these forests often offer few opportunities for photographing the rich flora.

GRASSLANDS

Flowers of grassland and scrub
Like forests, grasslands have been gradually encroached upon for agriculture, industry and housing, and even the once vast tall-grass prairies of the USA are now reduced to scattered remnants. In Britain and Europe, lowland grasslands are usually subject to constant agricultural disturbance, and the best habitats for wild flowers are on the chalk and limestone hills and on mountains (see below). Scrub is a frequent result of forest clearance and is often maintained as such by the effects of grazing animals which prevent the regeneration of forest. Scrub may contain plants typical of either grassland or woodland, as well as a few of its own particular plants.

Lowland grasslands seldom have the spectacular displays of wild flowers seen on mountains, in deserts and some woodlands, but an English meadow filled with thousands of the dainty flowers of Green Winged Orchid (*Orchis morio*) or

58

yellow Cowslips (*Primula veris*) is a lovely sight. Even a yellow
sea composed of thousands of such common flowers as Meadow
Buttercup (*Ranunculus acris*) or Dandelions (*Taraxacum
officinale*) is a welcome relief from the uniform green of
intensive cereal production.

Lighting for grassland flowers   As grasslands are open places,
lighting generally presents few problems. Available light is
usually sufficient except on very dull days, and there are no
problems with colour casts. However, in more open grasslands
wind is far more of a problem than in sheltered forest and may
in fact be the biggest headache for the flower photographer.
There are a number of solutions to the wind-shake problem. A
fast film (eg 200 ASA) can be used with daylight so that a fast,
movement-stopping shutter speed is possible. This is impractical
for those standardising on one type of high quality but slow
colour film such as Kodachrome. With these slower films a high
shutter speed requires a large aperture and resulting small depth
of field. This can be used to advantage to isolate flowers from
their background, but is not a method which I favour, as at any
aperture wider than about *f*8 it is impossible to obtain a really
adequate depth of field for the main subject, especially if this is
a broad flower head, such as an umbel.

Another method of stopping wind-shake is to use flash. This
is ineffective if your camera synchronises with flash at only 1/30
sec, but may just about work at 1/60 sec and may be very
worthwhile at the 1/125 sec of some metal focal plane shutters.
When using flash with daylight on a moving subject, two
distinct images may appear on the film – one from the main
light source (the flash) and a secondary 'ghost' image caused by
the reduced daylight exposure. At higher shutter speeds, the
proportion of daylight may be so reduced that the ghost image
disappears leaving only that left by the flash.

Unfortunately because the shutter speeds used with flash
stop the wind-shake by reducing the amount of available light
striking the film, they also result in an ever-darkening
background, unless there is vegetation growing close behind
your subject. If you really need an adequately lit background,
then you must either be very patient and wait for that split
second when the wind drops, or else use a wind break. Both of
these methods are rather time-consuming and not for the
impatient. A good windbreak can be made of clear polythene
attached to stakes which are driven into the ground, but it is
one more piece of gear to carry and I always make it an
important rule to carry as little as possible with me in the field.
Another solution is to use a second flash to light the

background, as in woodland photography. The method you choose will probably depend on which you have found to be the most convenient and practical. I always take at least some pictures by flash, even if I have also used available light, as I find that the depth of field is invariably much greater with flash, the colours are constant, important botanical details are not concealed by shadows and the whole flower is crystal clear and sharp. However, flash may give very unsatisfactory results with highly-saturated yellow flowers and certain blue varieties.

Backgrounds Plants are often closely surrounded by grasses and perhaps other plants, so a little 'gardening' may be required. Never trim off all the grass around the plant using scissors. The cut ends look ugly and the plants appear, incorrectly, to be growing isolated in an area of short grass among longer vegetation. The closer stems should be gently bent away from the plant, breaking them off only if absolutely necessary. View the subject through the camera and check that no grasses or other stems go *across* the picture behind or to one side of the subject. This always looks very ugly among the predominantly vertical stems. Horizontal stems look more obvious if you use the depth of field preview button to stop down to the taking aperture. The resultant increase in depth of field behind the subject reveals any intrusions in the background, such as diagonal grasses or twigs, tree branches or more brightly coloured flowers which may swamp your subject. If possible include some blue sky, but try not to let the horizon cut right across the centre of the plant. If the subject is gregarious, take a low viewpoint and show the flowers dotted among the grasses and receding into the distance. A wide-angle lens does this most effectively. Unfortunately, some purple or pink flowers which appear very conspicuous in groups may disappear into the grassland when seen on a slide.

In areas of intensive agriculture wild flowers of grasslands may be restricted to roadsides. It is sometimes advisable to include a piece of the road or a wall in the picture to show how the plant has taken advantage of the only available habitat.

What to photograph in grasslands

Although grasses themselves are usually considered drab subjects, close-ups can look good. The conspicuous drooping anthers of some kinds are bright yellow or deep maroon, and look very attractive against a blue sky. Grasslands and scrub also offer good opportunities for studying and photographing methods of pollination and seed dispersal, particularly if hedgerows are included. In plants such as Mallows (*Malva* spp)

Right: *Chamaenerion angustifolium*, Rose-bay Willowherb. Taken on the disused railway line next to my home in Warwickshire, England, specifically to show how the long pods split lengthwise to release the parachute seeds which are blown away. Taken from an awkward position standing with knees bent to get the sky behind (which shows through as grey between the seeds) on a dull very windy day; single flash.

Right: *Tamus communis*, black bryony berries. I looked for a plant which was growing with the abundant wind-dispersed seed-heads of Traveller's Joy, *Clematis vitalba*, and chose this one which was climbing along a dead branch. Photographed in the Cotswolds on a sunny afternoon, using fill-in flash, from a crouching position in an awkward spot between the dead tree and a large thorny rose-bush.

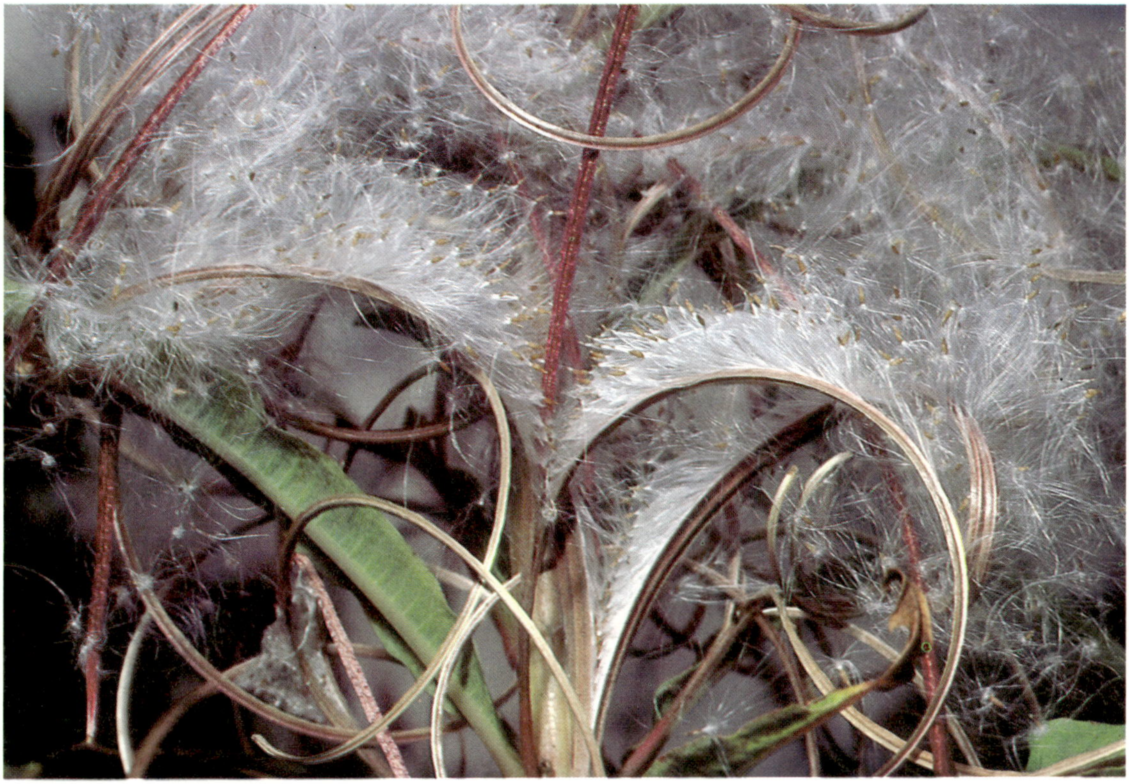

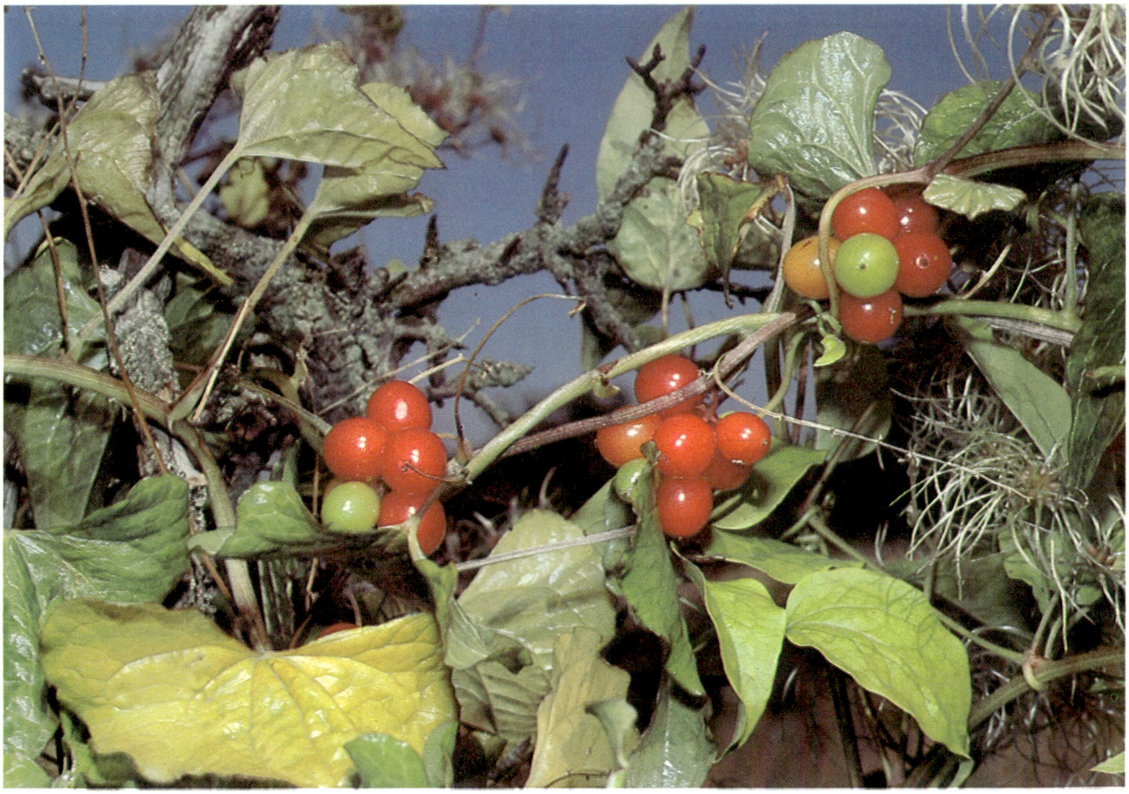

the pollen-bearing male anthers ripen first, followed by the female stigma which only becomes receptive after the anthers have shed their pollen and started to wither. This is one of the many ways in which plants prevent self-pollination.

Seed dispersal is similarly varied, as previously mentioned. Thistles and their relatives have downy heads of small seeds with feathery silver parachutes which are dispersed by the wind. These can be photographed *in situ* as a complete head, and then again with a few removed to show how they blow away. If the stem is rigidly staked, it is possible to blow gently on the seed head and record the seeds actually in flight. If this is done in low ambient light, electronic flash effectively freezes the movement. Silvery thistle-heads also look very pretty backlit by available light against a blue sky, as the sun gives a highlight around the feathery seed head. Cranesbills (*Geranium* spp) catapult their seeds away from the fruit, and pictures should be taken before and after this has happened. Scrubland is often rich in plants such as Hawthorn (*Crataegus* spp), wild roses, Blackberries (*Rubus fruticosus*) and Black Bryony (*Tamus communis*). All have attractively coloured berries which make an interesting series of pictures showing ripening from green through orange to deep red or even black. Sometimes berries in all stages can be found on one stem. Look for spots where plants such as roses with orange hips grow with Old Man's Beard (*Clematis vitalba*) with its parachute fruits, and take a single picture showing these different methods of dispersal.

Blackberries, roses and many other plants have stems with thorns which are often curved and attractively shaped and coloured. These make good close-ups, especially against a blue sky or black background.

Mountain flowers

There are few greater pleasures than hunting for the myriads of lovely wild flowers which grow amid the magnificent scenery of the Alps or Pyrenees in Europe or the Rockies in the USA, and mountains are my own favourite habitat. From the melting of the snows in spring and throughout the summer the display of wild flowers is rivalled only by that seen in certain deserts after plentiful rains. Many of the world's most beautiful wild flowers grow in mountain areas, where the diversity of species is great. Tropical mountains usually lack the magnificent floral shows of temperate areas, but have many peculiarities of their own. Mountains such as Elgon in Kenya boast giant groundsels and

Right: *Puya raimondii*. Taken at about 14,000 ft in the Andes with 28mm Nikkor wide-angle lens. Non-flowering plants used as foreground for flowering plant, which is 20–25 ft high. Plants grow for many years, flower and then die.

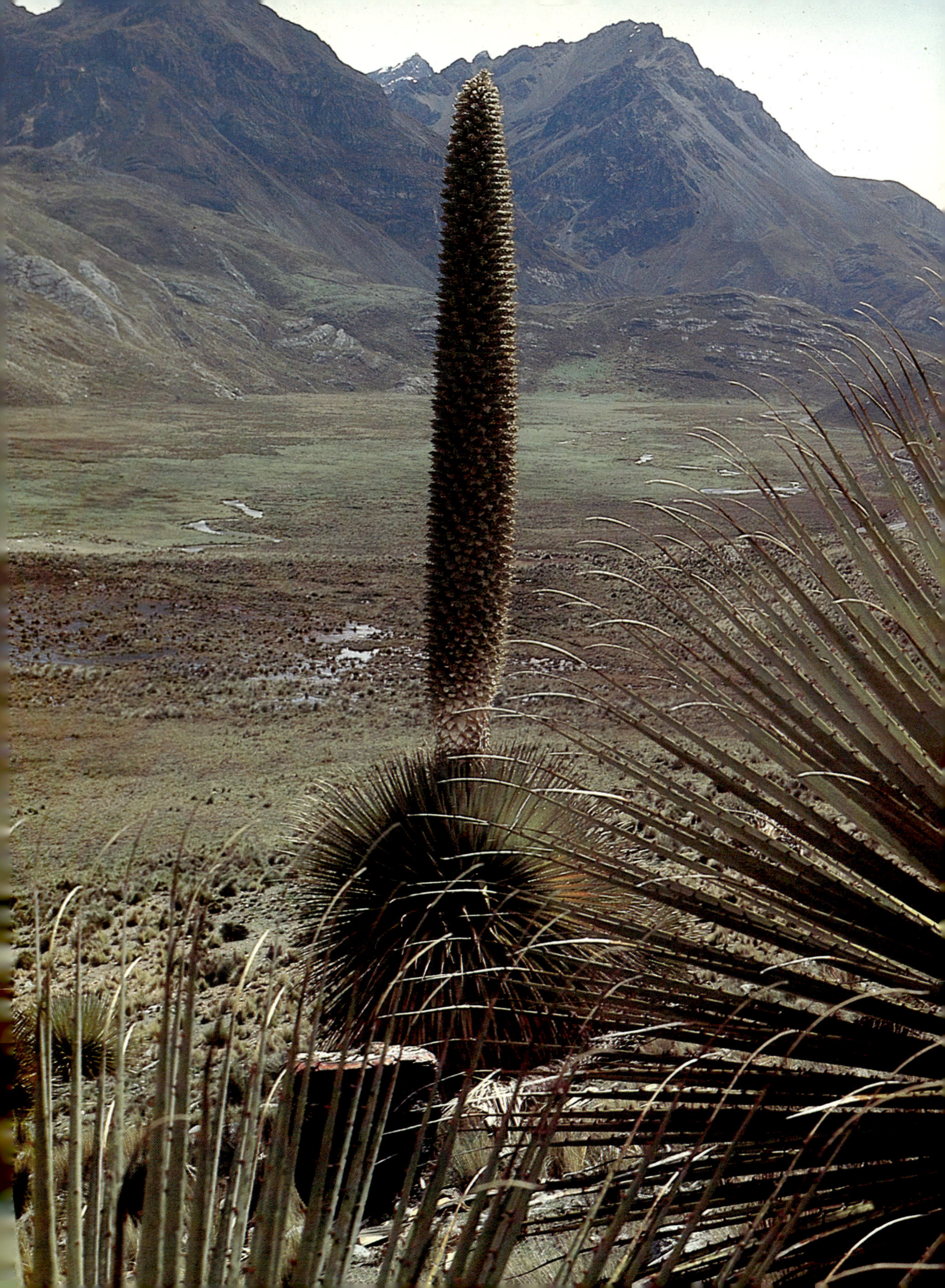

lobelias, Kinabalu in Borneo has numerous weird pitcher plants and the Andes have the wonderful spiky-leaved *Puya raimondii*. Geographical isolation has left many mountains with store-houses of plants found nowhere else, and it is always a thrill to see and photograph these local endemics.

Many mountains are so rich in plants during the summer months that finding them is no problem. Many kinds, however, grow only in restricted areas or habitats, so if you want a certain species it may require considerable patience to find it. Grassy mountain slopes are often tinted with masses of irises, daffodils or penstemons, mixed with numerous other shorter flowers. Higher up and on rocky outcrops more dwarfed varieties occur, closely hugging the rocks in retreat from the wind and insolation at these higher altitudes. Small close-growing plants which form mats include many saxifrages, which are wide-spread in mountains of the north temperate zone.

Photographing mountain flowers
Even during summer, mountains may have prolonged bouts of dull rainy weather, and tropical mountains are often wet throughout the year. Always carry a flash for use in bad conditions, which may strike very suddenly as clouds swirl across the peaks. Available light in the clear mountain air gives excellent results on bright days, although I still tend to use fill-in flash for many pictures. Wind is often a problem, and my previous remarks are relevant, especially those concerning carrying the minimum of gear. Working at high altitudes on steep slopes can be very exhausting, and even a single 35mm camera and small flash can start to feel very heavy after a few hours. If you intend to spend more than a few days in high mountains, give yourself time to acclimatise, and avoid rushing around on the first day. This will also enable you to get an idea of which plants are in flower, and to select the best specimens. This is especially important on mountains, for many plants only grow between specific altitudinal limits. The plants at the upper and lower edges of these are often poorer specimens than those growing in the optimum conditions in between the limits of the species' range. If you are climbing a mountain, therefore, and come across a few specimens of a new plant, delay photography until you have scouted around higher up, where you will probably find better specimens growing.

Photographing plants in mountains provides superb opportunities for really interesting and spectacular backgrounds, which are both attractive and show the habitat. Select a low viewpoint for your subject to show the mountains rising

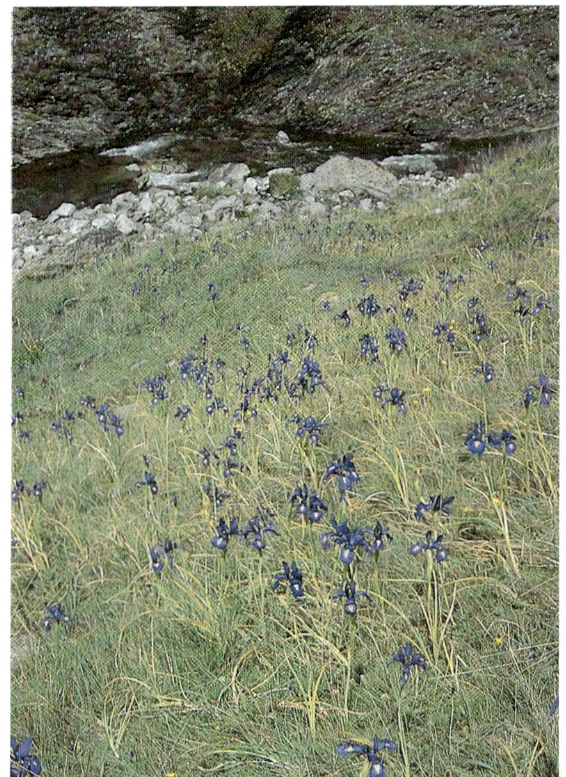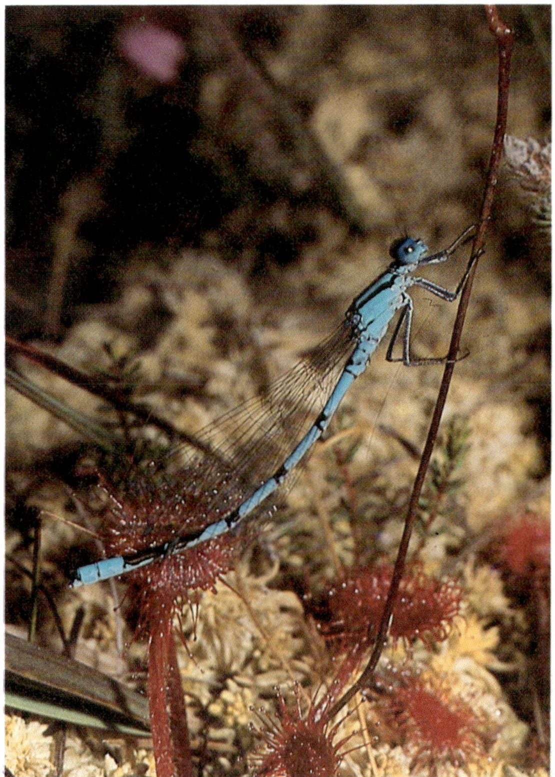

Above left: *Iris xiphioides*, Pyrenean Iris, photographed near the Col de Portelet in the Pyrenees, France.

Above right: *Drosera rotundifolia*, Common Sundew. Shows a leaf of the sundew holding on to the tip of the abdomen of a Common Blue Damselfly male *Enallagma cyathigerum* (also found in USA), which is climbing up the flower-stem in a fruitless effort to pull itself free. Photographed using flash on a sphagnum bog in Dorset, England. Knelt on the wet moss to focus.

beyond, or snowy screes and a clear blue sky. Use a wide-angle lens for the drifts of colourful larger flowers on the slopes, and rock faces with their array of mat-like plants. Close-ups of prostrate plants are easier, as they are not liable to wind-shake and can easily be taken without flash.

The magnificence of the blooms may blind you to interesting biological details of the plants themselves. For example, the very large Pyrenean Saxifrage (*Saxifraga longifolia*) has very striking rosettes of leaves which are silvery grey and covered in a strange rime of calcium deposits. The Pitcher Plant (*Nepenthes villosa*) of Mount Kinabalu, has large reddish pitchers with an elegant convoluted rim – excellent for close-ups.

PLANTS OF WETLANDS

I am including in this section plants which at some period of the year grow wholly or partially submerged in water, or which prefer permanently water-logged soils. The various kinds of wetlands may each have a very different set of associated plants. Those species growing in a sphagnum bog in a valley, for example, will have little in common with the plants in a marsh on nearby chalk hills.

Bog plants

Bogs are characterised by acidic waters and the frequent abundance of sphagnum mosses which may coalesce to form a floating mat – the well-known quaking bog. The associated plants are often highly specialised, the most interesting being the various kinds of insectivorous plants such as Sundews (Droseraceae), venus fly traps and pitcher plants. Sundew leaves are usually reddish and bear numerous tentacles tipped with a globular sticky droplet. The leaf gradually bends around to envelop and digest any insect which becomes ensnared. Venus fly traps capture insects in a spring-loaded 'gin-trap'.

Photographing bog plants   Bogs are an uncomfortable habitat for photography. The surface usually undulates in a most unsettling manner, and a careless step may plunge you into deep water below. Always step carefully, trying to put your feet on the larger tussocks of wiry sedges and rushes. Never take risks to reach an especially attractive plant, it is not worth endangering your equipment or your life. Be prepared for an unpleasantly wet session. Photographing the prostrate leaves of insectivorous plants on sopping sphagnum is best done by kneeling on the moss, which leads to a pool of water forming around each knee. A tripod saves you kneeling, but must have broad rubber feet which will not penetrate the sphagnum. Flash gives the best results for the smaller plants, and enables you to work rapidly in difficult conditions, so that you spend less time trampling on this rather sensitive habitat. Flash also highlights nicely the sticky blobs on sundew tentacles, and is indispensable for obtaining a close-up series of the leaf catching an insect.

Some bog plants have striking flowers, such as the yellow Bog Asphodel (*Narthecium ossiphragum*) with its furry orange anthers, and the beautiful strawberry-red flowers of Marsh Cinquefoil (*Potentilla palustris*). The conspicuous red fruits of Cranberries (*Vaccinium* spp) sometimes carpet the sphagnum, and can be treated in the same way as other prostrate plants.

Plants of marshes and freshwater margins

Marshes do not have such acidic waters as bogs, and lack the dense growth of sphagnum. Marshes may occur on poorly drained hillsides, along river valleys or over extensive areas of low-lying land. Many marsh plants are also common along the margins of ponds, lakes and rivers. Waterside plants tend to have thicker, more hollow stems than those on land, and generally flower later in the season. Most of the general remarks already made also apply to these plants. Specimens in flower on the margin of a river or lake should be taken from a viewpoint with the water as a natural backdrop. When photographing riverside plants, ensure that the opposite bank does not make an ugly line across the picture. Looking along the river is better. Marsh plants often grow in a very dense clutter of large-stemmed vegetation, so be prepared for some careful and thoughtful gardening. If you use a tripod remember that the legs are going to get wet and muddy. A short telephoto lens is useful for pictures of plants on the opposite bank, with the water providing an attractive and natural foreground. Waterlilies and other floating plants often grow well away from the bank, so a telephoto may be essential for pictures of their flowers, while a wide-angle portrays the mass of floating leaves.

Marshes in the hollows between coastal sand dunes are often exceptionally rich in flowers, particularly orchids, which may cover the ground in certain areas. Always beware of trampling too many plants in your enthusiasm. Man is constantly draining and filling wetland habitats, but is also creating new ones in the form of sand- and gravel-pits. These are colonised by a fascinating succession of plants, beginning with weeds typical of disturbed ground and ending with typical marsh vegetation. Recording such a development makes an interesting and valuable project spread over many years.

Salt marshes occur on the coast and up tidal rivers, sometimes for a surprising distance. The plants are often highly modified to tolerate immersion in saline water. Plants such as Glassworts (*Salicornia* spp) have rounded fleshy stems lacking in obvious leaves. Large areas of this and related plants look very uninviting, but the stems make good close-ups, especially when they turn red. Salt marshes are transformed into areas of considerable beauty when large quantities of Sea Lavenders (*Limonium* spp) or sea asters are in flower.

Taking pictures on salt marshes can be a very muddy business, so take care of yourself and your equipment. The mud oftens looks deceptively firm until you step on it and just keep sinking. Ensure that you know the times of the tides, and beware of being overtaken and cut off by water which rises with amazing speed on these low flat areas.

DESERT PLANTS

In the right season deserts have a wonderful display of wild flowers. True desert, where rain almost never fails and vegetation is virtually absent, occurs over large areas of North Africa and the Middle East, and also in parts of North America and western South America. Elsewhere a vegetational type called semi-desert and scrub is usually found, which may be amazingly rich in both plant and animal life. For example, areas in the arid-looking deserts of the south west USA or Mexico are far richer in most kinds of wildlife than the British Isles with their abundant rain and green mantle of plants.

After heavy and lasting rains, many deserts are transformed into gardens of colourful wild flowers, which may completely cover the ground over large areas. Arizona is renowned for its spring parade of showy desert blooms, and excellent examples of the photography of desert flowers can be found in the magazine *Arizona Highways*. The deserts of southern Africa are also notable for their spring flowers, and the arid lands of Western Australia support one of the most unusual and beautiful floras on earth. Even the coastal deserts of Chile may become carpeted with wild flowers after rains which may only occur at intervals of many years.

Stimulated by abundant rainfall, desert annuals must complete their life-cycles very rapidly before the heat and drought of summer wither them. You must therefore plan your photography very carefully, as a couple of weeks could make a vital difference. If you plan to visit a desert area in springtime, check beforehand with someone living in the area to see how advanced the flowers are and whether it is a good year.

In addition to the unpredictable desert annuals there is a host of perennial plants, many of which have very showy flowers which can be relied upon to appear even in dry years. The best known of these are the cacti with their interesting succulent bodies adapted for storing water and resisting drought. Giant candelabra cacti, such as the Saguaro (*Carnegia gigantea*) in Arizona and many more kinds throughout the Americas, make magnificent portraits against desert skies or the setting sun. Take forests of Organ Pipe cacti using a wide-angle lens to emphasise the crowded fluted stems. Cactus spines are extremely effective in close-up, varying greatly in colour and shape. The Arizona Rainbow Hedgehog (*Echinocereus pectinatus* var *rigidissimus*) has a close-fitting comb-like (pectinate) arrangement of spines which are pink when young and become yellow with age. These spines make an excellent 'pattern' close-up and are also biologically interesting. The Sand-dollar Cactus (*Astrophytum asterias*) of Texas looks like a spineless sea-urchin. In the Big Bend area of Texas grows the strange Living Rock Cactus (*Ariocarpus fissuratus*) which looks like the rock in which it grows. Other kinds of living rock cacti occur in Mexico, the commonest being *Ariocarpus retusus* which closely mimicks limestone rocks.

Right: *Neolloydia conoidea* cactus with pink flowers next to a Living Rock Cactus, *Ariocarpus retusus*. Photographed in the Chihuahuan desert near the large city of San Luis Potosi in Mexico. The *Ariocarpus* is about 3½ in across. Taken on a very dull day, overcast, with occasional heavy rain, using flash.

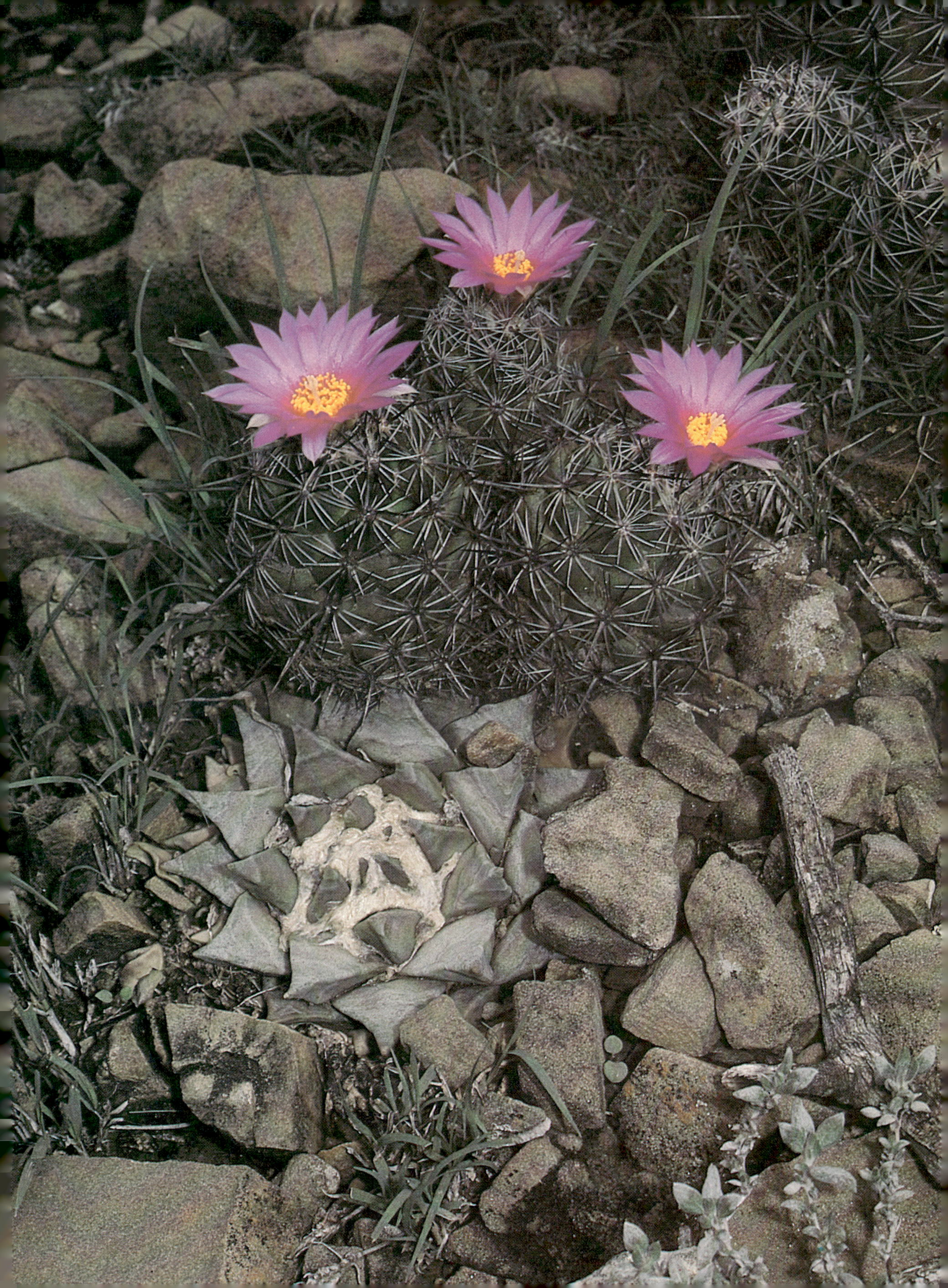

The most famous of these mimickry plants are the *Lithops* or Living Stones from South Africa. These occur in various shades of rust red, grey, violet, green and pink, and closely resemble the stones in their desert habitat.

Photographing desert plants   When taking pictures in desert areas your own welfare should be your primary concern – the camera equipment comes second. Make sure that you have plenty of liquids with you, wear a hat and do not spend too long in hot sunlight in pursuit of photographs. Wear long trousers of a thick material and leather boots to protect against the desert plants which are often very hostile. The notorious American Jumping Cholla cacti have barbed spines, and the whole of one section from a stem easily becomes attached to a trouser leg. This is an effective if painful method of dispersal.

Never leave camera equipment or film in the sun, as it will soon become very overheated, even when in a reflective aluminium case. Carry as little gear as possibe, for deserts can be very tiring, and some of the best areas are at quite high altitudes, especially in the Americas, so take it easy. Do not stray too far from a road in your pursuit of rare or exciting plants. By crossing just one more ridge while searching for a still finer specimen you may lose sight of your car. It is then easy to become disoriented and lost. Being lost in a desert is to be avoided at all costs, and may be fatal.

The desert sun is often harsh and directly overhead in a glaring sky. The available light is therefore often very contrasty, an effect which is accentuated by reflections from rocks and sand. Try to obtain as many pictures as possible before the sun becomes too high. I used fill-in flash for most of my pictures of desert plants, and was very pleased with the natural-looking results. Wind-shake is not a problem with the thick-stemmed perennials such as cacti, but may be a problem for less rigid flowers. Many desert areas are blessed with spectacular scenery, so choose your background with this in mind.

IDENTIFYING WILD FLOWERS

In Britain there is a manageable number of species of wild flowers (about 1500) so that with a little practice it is possible to identify most of them in the field with the aid of the numerous handbooks which are available. The more 'difficult' members of the British flora are the grasses and sedges, which fortunately are less photogenic. Luckily the most attractive plants are often the easiest to identify. European countries, such as France, Spain and Greece, have much richer floras, so

70

identification can present problems. The USA has a very large number of flowering plants and although those of a limited area can be easily learned using handbooks, anyone who travels widely in search of plants may have some difficulty in naming them all. The situation in the tropics varies from country to country, but it is generally impossible to identify more than a few plants in the field, at least without considerable experience. Tropical floras are often very imperfectly known and catalogued, with new species constantly being described.

If you have tried to identify a plant in the field and have failed, as a last resort you may have to collect the specimen. A specimen should only be taken if the plant is abundant in the area, or if it is intended for scientific study. Only take one plant, and never take any plant which you suspect may be rare or endangered. Many countries have a list of species which it is illegal to pick or uproot, and in some countries it is against the law to collect *any* wild plant or animal without a permit. Also remember that you should never pick flowers growing on nature reserves, or in national or state parks or reserves. If you are satisfied that you are acting correctly the plant should be carefully picked, taking as much of it as possible to show the maximum amount of detail. It should then be pressed between sheets of absorbent paper – newspaper will do if nothing else is available. Carefully arrange the plant on the paper to show the shape of the leaves and flowers, and take some fruits if they are present. Whenever possible use a proper herbarium plant-press. Attach a label to *each* specimen with the following information: place and date of collection, giving the locality as accurately as possible; type of habitat in which found; collector's name; a local name if you know it (especially relevant in the tropics); finally your own reference number, preferably cross-referenced to the film and frame numbers.

The specimens should then be presented to an expert, with a slide of the living plant if possible. Remember that professional botanists are highly skilled and very busy people and their valuable time has to be repaid in some way. You can do this by presenting a well-pressed adequately documented collection of plants with slides to match. These may then make a valuable contribution to the botanical knowledge of the area in question. It is *not* sufficient merely to present an expert with a collection of colour slides in the hope that they can be named to species. Plant identification normally requires careful examination of small details, which may be invisible on a photograph, and experts can seldom spare the time to examine slides unaccompanied by pressed voucher material.

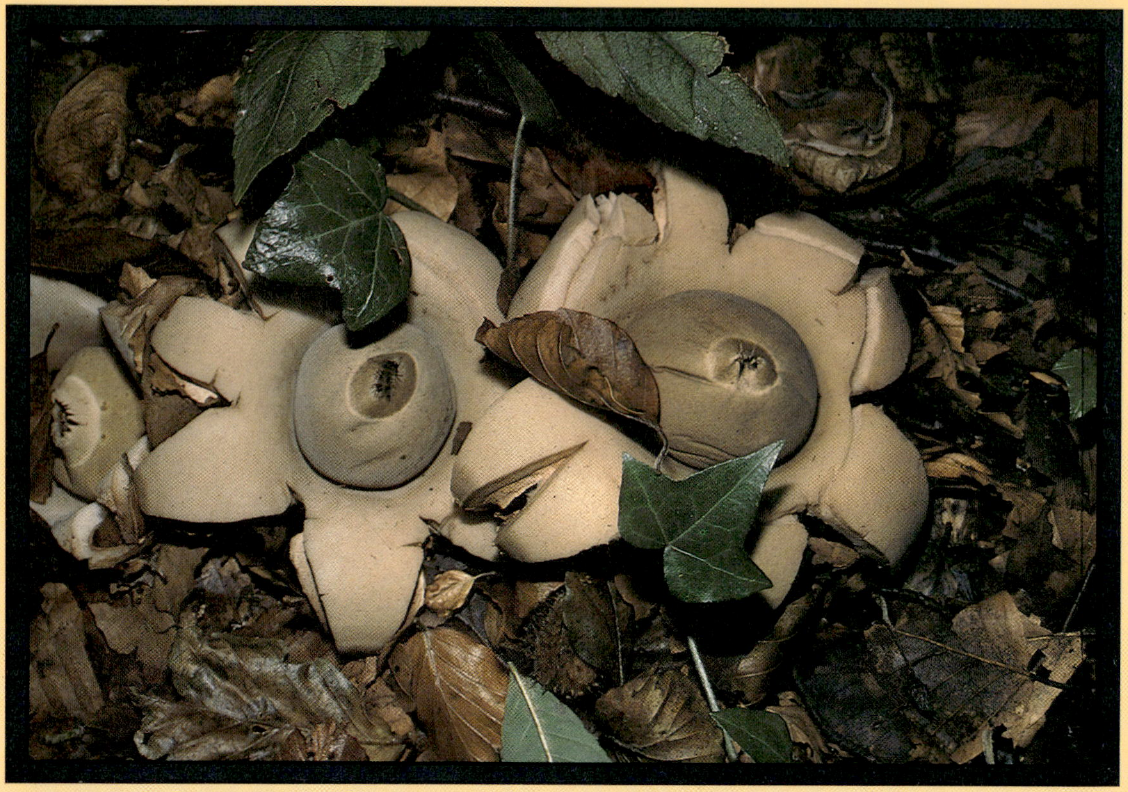

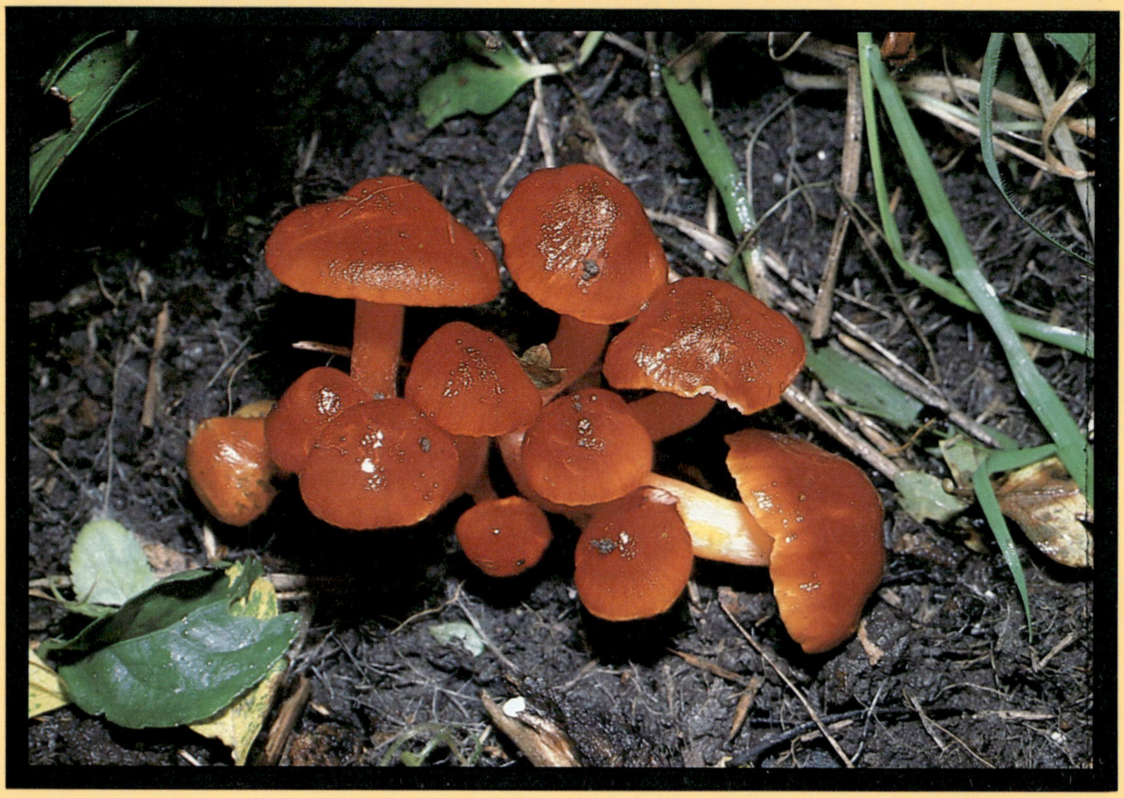

4 Fungi

Fungi form a large and important group within the vegetable kingdom. In Britain there are at least 3000 species with a reasonably large fruiting body, in addition to many small or microscopic kinds. All fungi lack the green chlorophyll of flowering plants, mosses, algae etc, and are therefore unable to utilise the energy from sunlight to synthesize their food. Instead, fungi have to live as parasites on living organisms or as saprophytes on their dead remains. Food intake is via the mycelium, which consists of a cobweb-like weft of minute tubes called hyphae, which are usually buried in the soil, under rotting leaves or in the body of the host. The toadstools, bracket-fungi, puffballs etc are the visible fruiting bodies produced by the invisible mycelium, and their purpose is to produce spores which upon germination give rise to a new mycelium. Yeasts and rusts are examples of the huge number of small or microscopic fungi, many of which are harmful disease organisms. Here I shall deal solely with fungi having single fruiting bodies easily visible to the naked eye, and use the term 'fungus' to refer to the fruiting body rather than the mycelium.

Although some fungi can be found throughout the year, the appearance of many is strictly seasonal, and in temperate areas the best time is autumn, with numbers peaking in September, October and early November if there are no early hard frosts. Spring is the main season for cup fungi, morels and St George's Mushroom *Calocybe (=Tricholoma) gambosa*, while the larger bracket fungi such as *Polyporus, Daedalea* and *Trametes* have perennial fruiting bodies. Temperature and moisture are very important in determining the abundance of the autumnal flush, which after a prolonged drought may fail to appear. Plentiful rain in late summer, followed by a period of warm weather, usually results in the appearance of large numbers of fungi.

Types of fungi
The most frequently seen fungi are the 'agarics' or cap fungi, commonly known as toadstools. Agarics generally have an upright stem or stipe, surmounted by a circular cap, beneath which are produced the spores. These may be released from

between gills or teeth, or from pores on the underside of the
cap. The colour of the cap varies greatly, making fungi very
attractive subjects. Of other kinds of fungi, most cup fungi grow
on the ground and often have a rather convoluted rim to the
cup. The fertile heads of false morels are more or less saddle-
shaped or folded, while the morels have caps with honeycomb-
like pits. Fairy clubs are usually densely branched, resembling
some corals, and chanterelles are funnel-shaped. The majority of
brackets grow on dead wood, where they may attain a very
large size. Puffballs and earth stars are mainly ground-living; the
spores are held in a more or less globular container, and are
released through a pore at the top. The Jew's Ear (*Hirneola
auricula-judae*) is a curious gelatinous fungus growing on dead
wood. The spores of the fascinating little bird's nest fungi are
contained in several greyish 'eggs' at the bottom of a miniature
'nest'. This necessarily brief resumé gives some idea of the vast
variety of shapes produced by fungi, varying in size from large
brackets several feet across to tiny bird's nest fungi only 2mm
wide. Photographing such diverse single organisms, whether
growing singly or in groups, obviously requires several different
approaches, some of which are suggested below.

Woodland fungi
The majority of fungi are found in woodland, and many of
them are restricted to specific types, such as beech, oak or
conifer woods. This is because the fungi are attached to the
living roots of the trees in a give-and-take relationship known as
a mycorrhiza. Certain species can only live with a specific host
tree. Thus *Suillus grevillei (=Boletus elegans)* seems only to
grow under larches, and Fly Agaric (*Amanita muscaria*) grows
mainly under birches but sometimes with pine. It would be
useless to look for these species in a beech wood, which has its
own typical species, such as the pink-capped *Russula mairei*,
which are found nowhere else. When on a fungus foray visit
woods of various types and on different soils to be sure of
finding a comprehensive variety of fungi. Although often
generally distributed throughout a wood, fungi may be more
common in one or two definite areas, which look no different
from other parts of the wood but are for some reason especially
favoured. Most of the larger agarics, brackets and puffballs are
quite easy to spot, particularly in a good year, but smaller types
such as bird's nest fungi may only be found after a careful
search of dead wood in suitable localities.
Selecting the viewpoint   As suggested in the chapter on flowers,
take your time and select typical specimens before commencing

your photography. The colour of the cap may change with age, so to be representative you must photograph specimens of different ages, especially if they can be found growing together. Young agarics can often be seen pushing up from beneath a carpet of moss or pine needles, which form a little 'hat' on the developing fungus. A picture of this shows how the fruit body grows upwards from the underground mycelium. The caps of some ink-caps, such as *Coprinus micaceus*, auto-digest as they mature, disseminating the spores in a black inky ooze. The caps become ragged and unattractive, but should be photographed as they show the specialised habits of these fungi, especially when old dissolving caps occur beside young fresh specimens.

Before commencing photography a certain amount of gardening may be necessary. As fungi do not need light, the fruit bodies often appear in rather inaccessible places. Deep shady spots under masses of other vegetation are popular, and the cap may be concealed under dead leaves. These must be carefully removed, along with any impeding plant stems.

Unlike flowering plants, fungi are seldom tall enough to permit a low viewpoint showing the woodland behind and this can normally only be achieved when photographing groups of fungi. So some attempt should be made to depict the habitat. *Tricholomopsis rutilans* is an attractive cap-fungus with a deep purplish scaly cap and a yellow stipe, which grows on conifer stumps. A pine cone or a few pine needles scattered near and on the plants improves the picture, as do oak leaves or acorns for species occurring in oak woods.

Agarics, with their broad cap overhanging a central stem, present special problems. If possible both the front of the cap and the central stem should be in focus and this requires great depth of field. In addition, the colour of the cap must be visible. This demands a viewpoint from slightly overhead, which conceals the spore-releasing mechanism on the underside of the cap, ie teeth, gills or pores. Some photographers overcome this by picking one or two specimens and laying them next to the specimen to be photographed, with the undersides of their caps facing the camera. This always looks very artificial and if repeated too frequently produces boring pictures. It may also have the very undesirable effect of making it appear that solitary species are growing gregariously, something to be avoided in the pursuit of biological accuracy. The best solution is simply to take two pictures, one from a low viewpoint looking upwards to show the underside of the cap, the other from above to show the colour. Alternatively, careful searching may reveal groups where older specimens have rather turned-up

edges to the caps, showing the underside. Where these occur
next to younger specimens, a single picture can reveal all
necessary details.

As they expand, some fungi such as *Boletus* exude large
amounts of water in the form of droplets, which sometimes
form a ring around the underside of the cap. A low viewpoint
shows these well. In addition to photographing whole plants,
take some close-ups showing the underside of the cap in greater
detail. You will need to pick the fungus but this does not harm
the mycelium, which will continue to 'fruit'. Close-ups are easy
to obtain in the field, and there is no need to take the plants
back to the studio as some people suggest. Simply lay the
specimen on the ground or a log with the underside of the cap
uppermost. I always use a hand-held camera but a miniature or
standard tripod can equally well be used. If possible it is best to
avoid focusing on a spot directly in the centre of the mass of
gills or pores, as the picture will lack scale and it may not be
obvious what is being portrayed. I usually select the area where
the stipe joins the cap, or where the edges of specimens growing
together overlap. The spongy yellowish pores of some *Boletus*
species often bruise black or blue when touched, so handle them
carefully if you want to show an unmarked specimen. However,
bruising is sometimes a diagnostic character, and you may wish
to bruise the pores deliberately to show the change of colour.

Bracket fungi are usually found on trees, both living and
dead, and on fallen logs and stumps. Looking up at the
undersides of brackets against the sky makes a dramatic and
instructive picture, but if possible take another picture showing
the colour and texture of the top. A telephoto lens can be used
for specimens growing out of reach, but wherever practical get
close, perhaps with the aid of a lightweight ladder.

Cup fungi, morels, puffballs, earth stars and fairy clubs are
all easier to photograph than agarics, as it is usually possible to
convey all the necessary information in a single picture.

The agarics decay fast and must be photographed quickly
once they are found. Decaying agarics sometimes have other
fungi growing on them, such as the silvery *Nyctalis parasitica*
which clusters on the stems and gills of rotting *Russula*. These
make excellent close-ups, if you can bear to put your nose close
to the rotting *Russula*, which can smell particularly nauseating.
A furry coating of moulds can often be found on rotting fungi,
providing excellent opportunities for close-ups of this large
group, to which penicillin belongs. Stink-horn fungi, such as
Phallus impudicus, can be tracked-down by their smell, for the
honeycombed head is covered in a blackish-olive foetid spore-

mass. This is usually covered in a host of flies, which eat and disseminate the spores. Photograph the flies busily feeding and then frighten them away and show the complete fungus.

Lighting for woodland fungi The colours of the caps of agarics often show only subtle differences between species. It is therefore important to establish a 'standard' of lighting for these and indeed for most fungi, in which colour is usually very important. As mentioned already, sunlight filtering down through the trees casts a greenish hue onto anything below. Because of the pale and delicate colouring, fungi are especially affected by this, and also by the blotchy contrasting effect of mixed light and shadow. I use flash for all my pictures of fungi, regardless of the available light, in order to achieve constant accuracy of colour rendering. Coming from above, sunlight fails to illuminate evenly the stems of agarics, whose broad caps make efficient sunshades. The powerful illumination provided by flash gives sufficient depth of field to enable both stem and cap of agarics to be in sharp focus. Although most fungi prefer shady spots in woodlands, dark backgrounds are less of a problem than with flowering plants. This is because many fungi are of low stature, so the background of dead leaves is relatively close and usually receives a portion of the light from the flash. If problems arise, position a slave unit to light the background. This can also be a useful method of lighting the caps of agarics when a small unit is being used frontally to light the stems.

Using electronic flash, it is possible to photograph a large number of species in a relatively short time. This may be important, for many fungi are decidedly ephemeral; as more than 100 species may be found in a single wood on one visit, speed of working is obviously an advantage. Electronic flash also simplifies close-up work in the field, showing pores and gills on the undersides of the caps of agarics. I always use a small hand-held unit, using grazed lighting to show the depth of the pores or gills. Using flash also frees the photographer from the vagaries of the weather, which in a damp year productive of fungi will be unsuitable for much available-light photography. Using flash, I have taken acceptable pictures of fungi in pouring rain, being careful not to select specimens with puddles on the caps, as this would cause too much reflection. The caps of some fungi change colour when wet, usually from lighter to darker brown; when possible photograph them in both conditions.

Fungi of grasslands

Grasslands are much poorer in species of fungi than woodlands, but a number of interesting and attractive kinds are to be found, especially in the genus *Hygrophorus* which contains some striking red or orange cap-fungi. Extensive gardening may be needed to show the underside of the cap in specimens which have pushed their way up through dense grass. Available light in grasslands lacks the green hue found in woodlands, so can be used without risk if you prefer it. A reflector or fill-in flash may be useful for showing detail on the stems of agarics. Luckily wind is not a problem as it frequently is when photographing flowering plants, so you do not need to carry windshields or stakes, and a tripod should seldom be necessary, as many pictures can be taken with the elbows pressed to the ground to provide firm support. A miniature tripod or ground-spike can be useful for most fungus photography, whatever the habitat.

Collecting and identifying fungi

Specimens should be carefully removed from the substrate, taking the whole of the stem, if there is one, including the base. Wrap each specimen in a polythene bag, and attach a tag showing the date, place of collection, type of woodland, how the fungus was growing, eg on a pine stump, high on a birch tree, in clusters in a beech wood etc, the name of the collector and your own reference number and film frame-numbers. All these details may be vital for naming the specimen, whether you attempt this yourself or send it to an expert. If you do it yourself, a spore print is often needed. This can be made by laying a fresh, open (ie mature) specimen, minus the stalk, cap upwards on a piece of paper overnight. As spores are released they fall on the paper, forming the print. This shows the pattern of the pores or gills, and the colour of the spores. Take care not to damage the print when removing the fungus. It is preferable to 'set' the print by spraying carefully with a clear matt spray before identification or photography is attempted.

Although there are many popular guides to the identification of the larger fungi, only serious works used by professional mycologists contain a comprehensive description of all the species. For the amateur it is often difficult to be certain about the identity of any but some of the commoner and more characteristic species. Many species of *Lactarius*, *Cortinarius*, *Agaricus* and *Russula* are, among others, very difficult to name, and even an expert may need a whole morning to name accurately a single specimen. Identification should proceed as soon as possible, as most fungi start to decay rapidly once they are picked. Keeping them in the refrigerator prolongs their life a little. It is usually almost impossible to name any fungi from colour slides alone, even to genus, so do not waste the time of

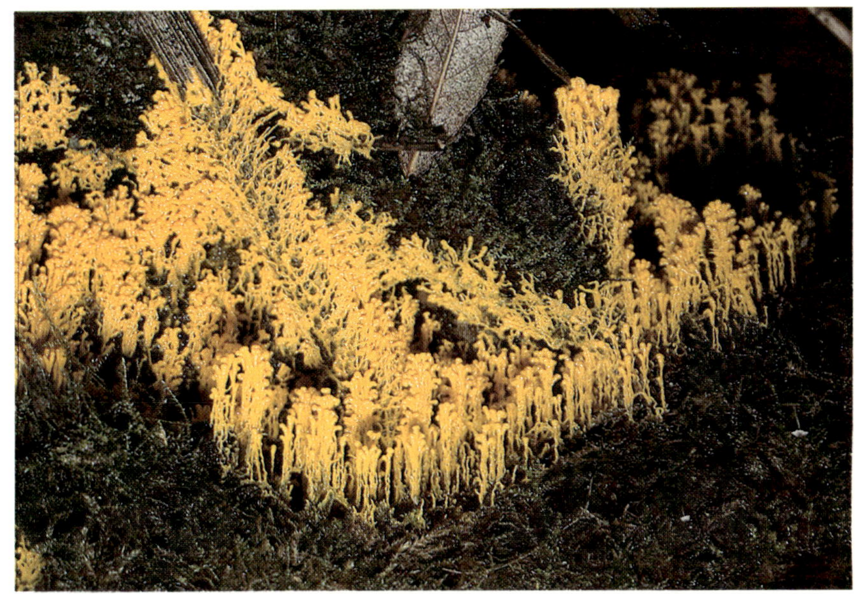

Physarum cinereum, a Myxomycete or slime-mould. The individual stalked fruit-bodies are beginning to differentiate from the mass. Taken in an extremely awkward position low down on a pile of logs next to a tree, so I had to lie and squeeze myself into a tiny gap, holding the camera and flash in a very awkward position.

experts by sending them batches of slides unless accompanied by good specimens with adequate provenance data.

Myxomycetes

Myxomycetes are peculiar organisms, with both plant and animal characteristics, which are usually called slime moulds. They are not really fungal moulds, but consist of a usually transparent mass of protoplasm which lives mostly in damp places, such as on rotting leaves on the forest floor, or old mouldering stumps. This simple organism would pass unnoticed were it not for the production at some stage of fruit bodies which release spores. As reproduction commences the protoplasm, frequently bright yellow, flows along set lines, some species forming a beautiful, intricate fan-shaped 'plasmodium'. I have seen large yellow splashes of plasmodium a foot long on stumps, very conspicuous and resembling a daub of yellow paint. Most species, however, are minute. They are worth searching for, however, as the fruit-bodies are often very beautiful, frequently clustering in masses of bright pink, deep red, burnt gold or brilliant orange. Many species go through several transformations of colour as they mature, and this makes an excellent close-up series.

I photograph these tiny organisms *in situ* using a single flash. I normally reverse the lens to achieve magnifications greater than life-size for these tiny subjects. Identification of myxomycetes is mainly for the expert with a microscope, but the amateur can quickly learn to recognise some of the commoner kinds in the field.

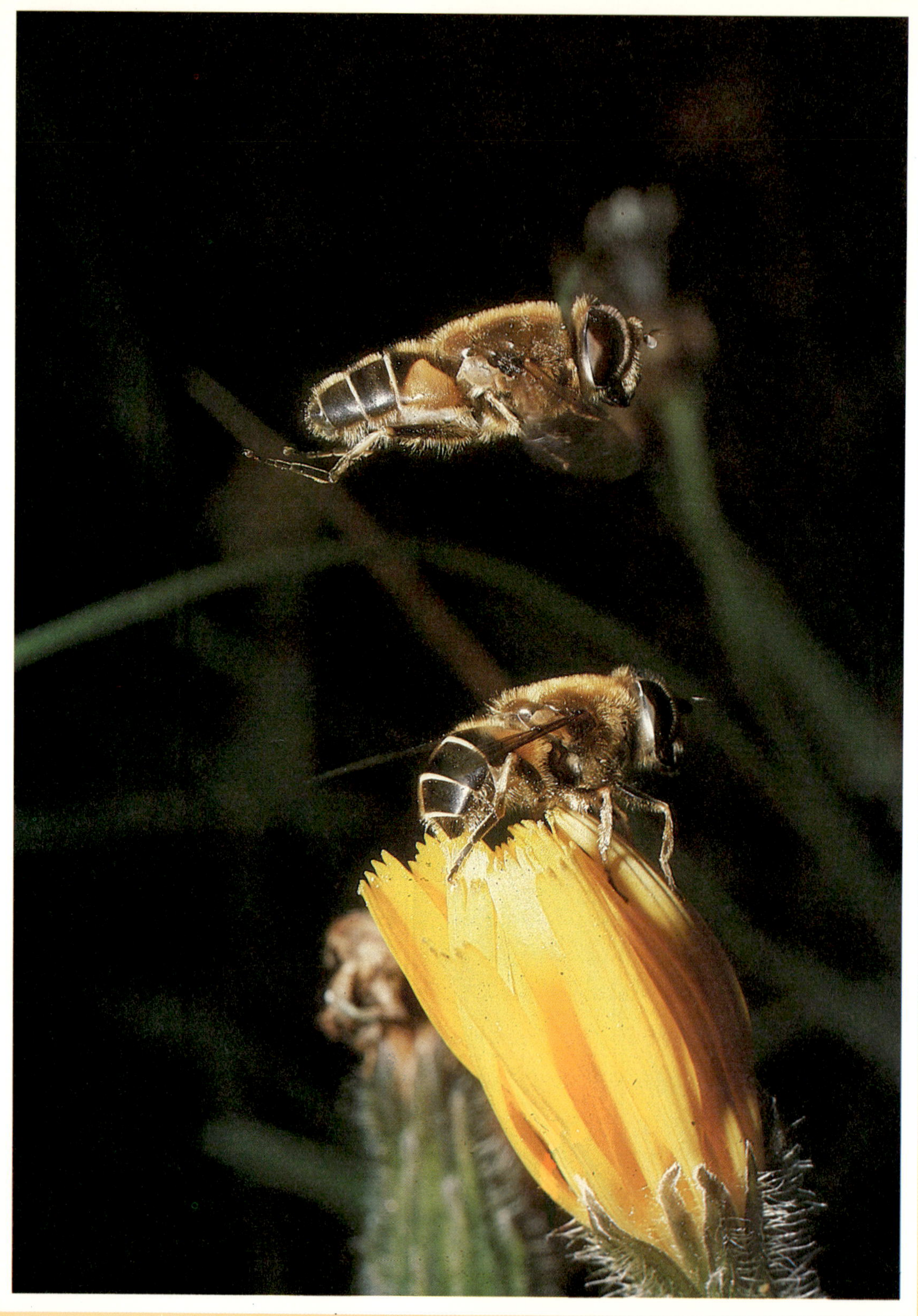

5 Invertebrates - Insects

If the chapters in this book concerning animal life had been written according to the relative abundance and importance of each type, this chapter would fill most of the rest of the book, with less than a page devoted to birds and mammals. Insects are the most numerous and successful animals ever known on earth and nearly one million species have been described and named. The 50,000 species of weevils (Curculionidae) outnumber all the species of reptiles, amphibians, birds, mammals and freshwater fish added together. And weevils are only *one* type of insect. Insects are a very ancient group and there are fossils of some primitive kinds that existed over 350 million years ago, 150 million years before the first dinosaurs.

This enormous time span has enabled insects to colonise successfully every terrestrial habitat, although they have never really conquered the sea. The ubiquity of insects is amazing. They have been found on mountains at over 20,000 ft, and also in deep caves hundreds of feet below ground. Some types of larvae live in water which is frozen in winter and others in hot springs at 60°C (140°F). Virtually every known vegetable substance is utilised by their larvae, including many considered to be poisonous. Animals, both alive and dead, and their dung are extensively used as food sources. Insects occur in the far north in areas where the ground is frozen in winter, reaching stupendous populations during the brief summers. In contrast they are equally successful in arid deserts where the temperature may climb to 49°C (120°F) in the shade. Although common in temperate areas, insects reach their peak in the tropics, especially in tropical rain forests. In these perpetual hothouses there is an amazing richness and diversity of insects. The tiny tropical island of Trinidad has over 620 species of butterfly, compared with approximately 60 in Britain and 380 in the whole of Europe. Nevertheless, even Britain has over 5,000 species of true flies (Diptera) and 3,500 beetles (Coleoptera), while Europe and North America both have rich and diverse insects faunas.

Insects probably provide the first living animal subjects for many wildlife photographers, for even a small garden in the

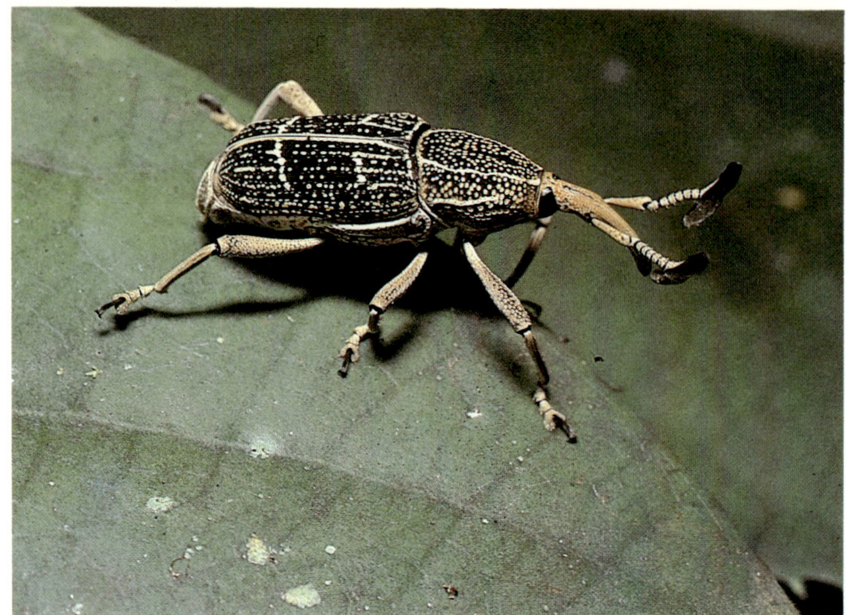

Cercidocerus indicator.
Taken in forest at 5000 ft
at Fraser's Hill in
Malaysia. This weevil was
walking around on a leaf
and made an awkward
subject as I wanted it
against another leaf rather
than a black background.
Taken from a standing
position with back bent;
single flash.

centre of a large city may support many different species. Their
accessibility, very interesting life styles, often bizarre shapes and
beautiful colours, combine to make insects among the most
rewarding and challenging of all wildlife subjects, particularly as
it is very easy to produce original work.

What are insects?

Insects are arthropods, that is they have an external (exo)
skeleton enclosing the softer parts of the body in a protective
shield. An insect's body is divided into three segments, the head,
the thorax and the abdomen. The head bears the mouthparts,
two compound eyes and a single pair of antennae, while the
thorax bears the wings and three pairs of walking legs. Any
small arthropod with more than this number of legs cannot be
an insect. Any arthropod with wings must be an insect,
although not all insects have wings.

It is unfortunately impossible to describe an 'average' insect.
Shape and colour vary greatly and also size, from tiny beetles
only 0.2mm long to tropical stick-insects which may have a
body length of 33cm. The general description given above
applies only to adult insects. Immature insects frequently show
no division into head, thorax and abdomen, and are always
wingless and often legless, sometimes with no obvious head or
indeed any external characteristics at all (think of a blow-fly
maggot). Fortunately few insect larvae other than moth and
butterfly caterpillars make good pictures, so this difficulty need
not concern us further.

Identifying insects Naming insects is often difficult. This is not surprising in view of their numbers and the fact that new species are constantly being discovered and named. It is easy to learn the names of your local butterflies, moths and dragonflies but it is difficult, unless you are an expert, to name more than a few of the more easily recognisable species of insects such as flies, wasps, bees or beetles. The best that can be expected is that you will quickly learn to recognise all the orders of insects in the field and then some of the more characteristic families, such as Hoverflies (Family Syrphidae), or Bush-crickets (Family Tettigoniidae). Expert entomologists are in short supply, but if you do know a professional or competent amateur who is willing to make determinations for you, then so much the better. Remember that *specimens* are required, as *reliable* identifications of most insects from slides is difficult and often impossible. Killed specimens of insects should be pinned through the thorax or wing cases after collection and labelled with the usual data of place and date of collection etc. Rare insects should never be collected.

I must stress, however, that for really successful insect photography knowing the names is not enough. It is absolutely vital to be at least reasonably familiar with your subjects' habits. Try to read some general entomological books or accompany a skilled entomologist on a walk in the country. This makes finding and identifying subjects far easier, helps you to search for and recognise what may be at first rather puzzling aspects of behaviour and generally makes photography more successful. Insect photography is highly specialised and there are no short cuts if really outstanding results are to be obtained.

Equipment for field photography
'Keep it simple' is my basic rule. Insect photography can be excessively frustrating, for most subjects constantly do their best to evade your attentions. Several hours spent chasing after elusive insects can be both irritating and very exhausting, especially in hot weather and in the tropics, so the less you are carrying the better.

Tripods I have never used a tripod for any of my 10,000 insect pictures. I always use a hand-held camera, even for close-ups using several inches of extension. Only a very small number of my slides are rejected because of focusing errors. Even small tripods are heavy, inflexible, difficult to set up quickly in the right spot, and are generally a liability in most insect work. If you cannot take hand-held close-ups with an acceptably high rate of success and are forced to use a tripod, you will be

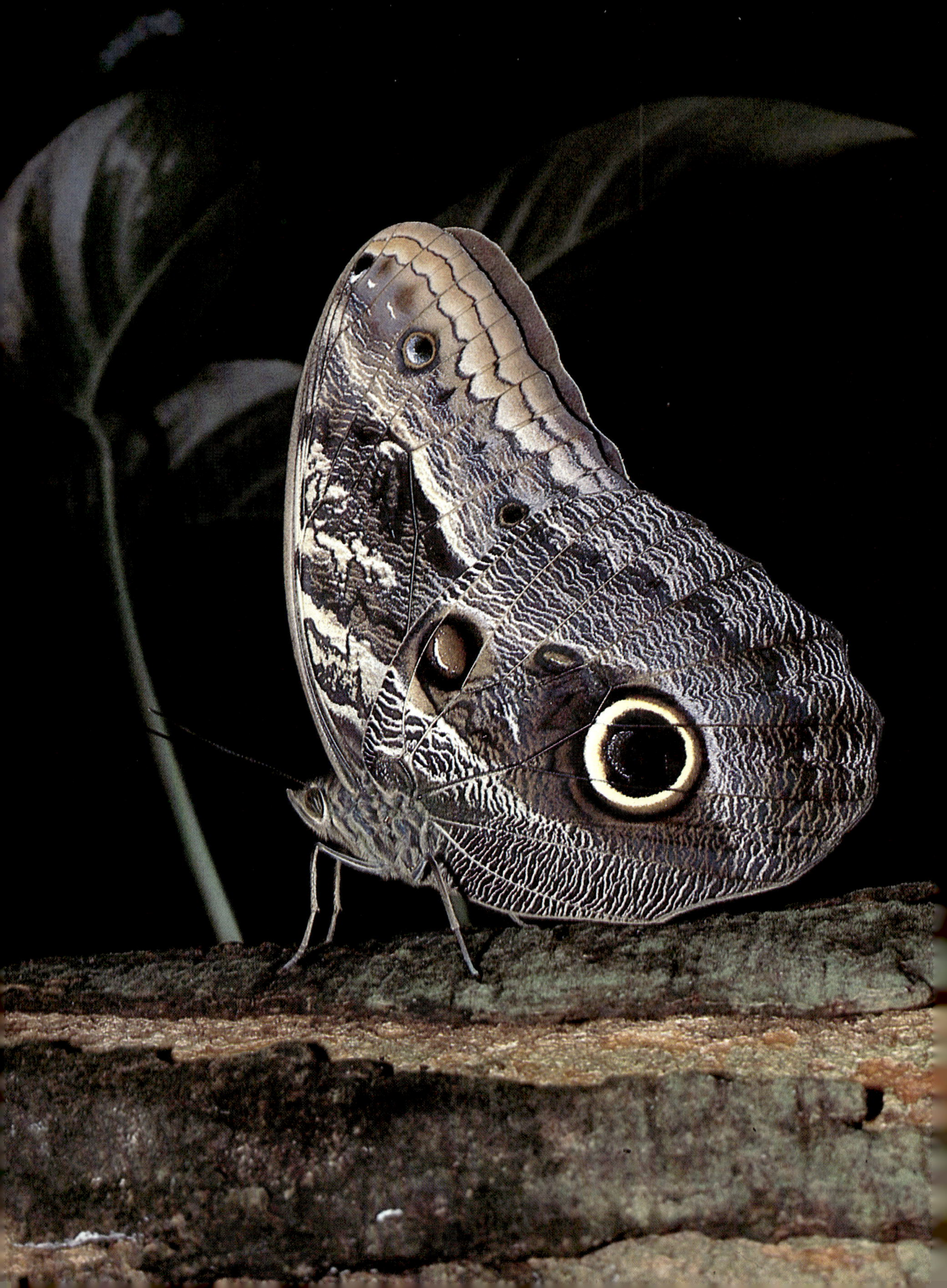

extremely restricted in the number and types of insect you can photograph. Moths resting on bark during the day, butterflies asleep in cool weather and in the evening, caterpillars on leaves and clusters of newly hatched nymphs can all be tackled using a tripod. It is also possible to set up a tripod near a flower head and wait for insects to arrive. This is, however, a very time-consuming and inflexible method of achieving very simple pictures. If you must use a tripod, choose a model which can be set up and levelled quickly. A focusing slide is essential for moving the camera nearer to the subject. It is better to practice hand-holding, as this will improve your performance and may enable you to dispense with a tripod. Some people can manage hand-holding from the very start, but others are never really successful.

Camera   An SLR is essential, preferably one with which you feel really at home. The type of focusing screen is very important in insect photography. If you have a central focusing 'aid', such as a split-image, you must completely ignore it and focus instead using the fresnel field on the rest of the screen. This is an acceptable method for 'standard' shots, at least with practice, but makes close-ups of the head very difficult, as this is normally in the middle of the picture and will be blacked-out by the central spot. The camera, therefore, has to be moved back to centre the subject after focusing has been carried out on the fresnel area. This introduces a high probability of mis-focus, so if possible choose a camera with interchangeable screens. A depth of field preview button is also useful, and a shutter with flash synchronisation at 1/125 sec for stopping insects in flight.

Lenses   Most of my insect pictures are taken using a 55mm Micro Nikkor. Even active insects such as dragonflies and butterflies can often be approached to within 2in for close-ups of the head. For close-ups of really small insects a lens of this focal length is better than a short telephoto, as it can be reversed on a fairly short extension to give good image magnification with excellent definition.

For full-wing shots of most dragonflies and butterflies I use a Vivitar 70–210mm Macro Zoom mounted on an automatic 25mm ring, which at *f*16 gives superb results. A short telephoto of 100mm or 135mm would do a similar job and be lighter, but framing is much easier with the zoom. With longer lenses the working distance is increased, so there is less chance of alarming the subject. However, I do not use the longer focal lengths on the zoom for smaller subjects as it requires a large and clumsy amount of extension. Close-up lenses are alright for larger insects as long as you use flash and stop down to at least *f*16,

when the definition will be acceptable. However, definition on
the more powerful close-up lenses most often needed for insects
is bad even at $f16$, so a set of tubes, macro lens or macro
convertor are a better solution.

Flash   I use flash for all my pictures of insects with the
exception of some butterflies and certain camouflaged insects,
and even then only if there is enough available light to stop
down to at least 1/60 sec at $f11$, a comparatively rare event in
close-up work. Even for larger insects maximum depth of field
is vital and flash gives spectacularly clear results for all insects.
With the 55mm lens I use a single low-power flash held in my
left hand, using my wrist to aim the light exactly where I need
it. With the zoom I use a larger flash mounted on a ball and
socket head on a bracket screwed to the camera. A little
practice is needed before you manage to get the flash in exactly
the right position. Some people mount a second flash, or white
reflector, on the other side of the camera to reduce the shadows
cast by a single flash and sometimes a third unit from overhead
to light the background. This is cumbersome to work with and
would have been impractical for the great majority of insect
pictures which I have taken. It is also largely unnecessary, as the
single flash seldom casts shadows more dense than those caused
by bright sunlight. With most subjects the main flash lights the
background quite adequately and it seems rather pointless to
burden yourself with three flashes for the very few occasions
when they may be needed. I never use ring flash for insects as
the light is too flat, but rings which are partially blocked off do
give really excellent results, although they are expensive.
Although you should avoid it whenever possible, a single flash
mounted on the camera can give acceptable results with most
insects when used with a telephoto lens. As with ring flash, the
lighting tends to be rather flat but the results are generally
acceptable, especially for flat-winged species such as butterflies.
When using flash for pale insects, or any insects on light-
coloured flowers, always use at least ¾ stop or a full stop less
exposure than normal. Insects on white flowers do not then
look underexposed, as the petals act as a natural reflector.

Stalking insects

I take all my photographs in the field and disagree most
emphatically with the advice that 'pin-sharp portraits of insects
can only be taken under controlled conditions in the studio'. I
hope that the pictures in this book show just how unjustified
this advice is. When I started to photograph insects, over 10
years ago, I faithfully followed this advice. I caught my subjects,

Right: *Acontista* species,
praying mantis,
photographed on a
roadside in Trinidad in the
Northern Range. This
female mantis, about an
inch long, is eating a fly
on a *Bidens* flower. Wind-
shake was a problem, but
flash stopped it; the dark
background thus produced
nicely emphasises the
mantis, which would
otherwise have tended to
merge into a cluttered,
out-of-focus background.

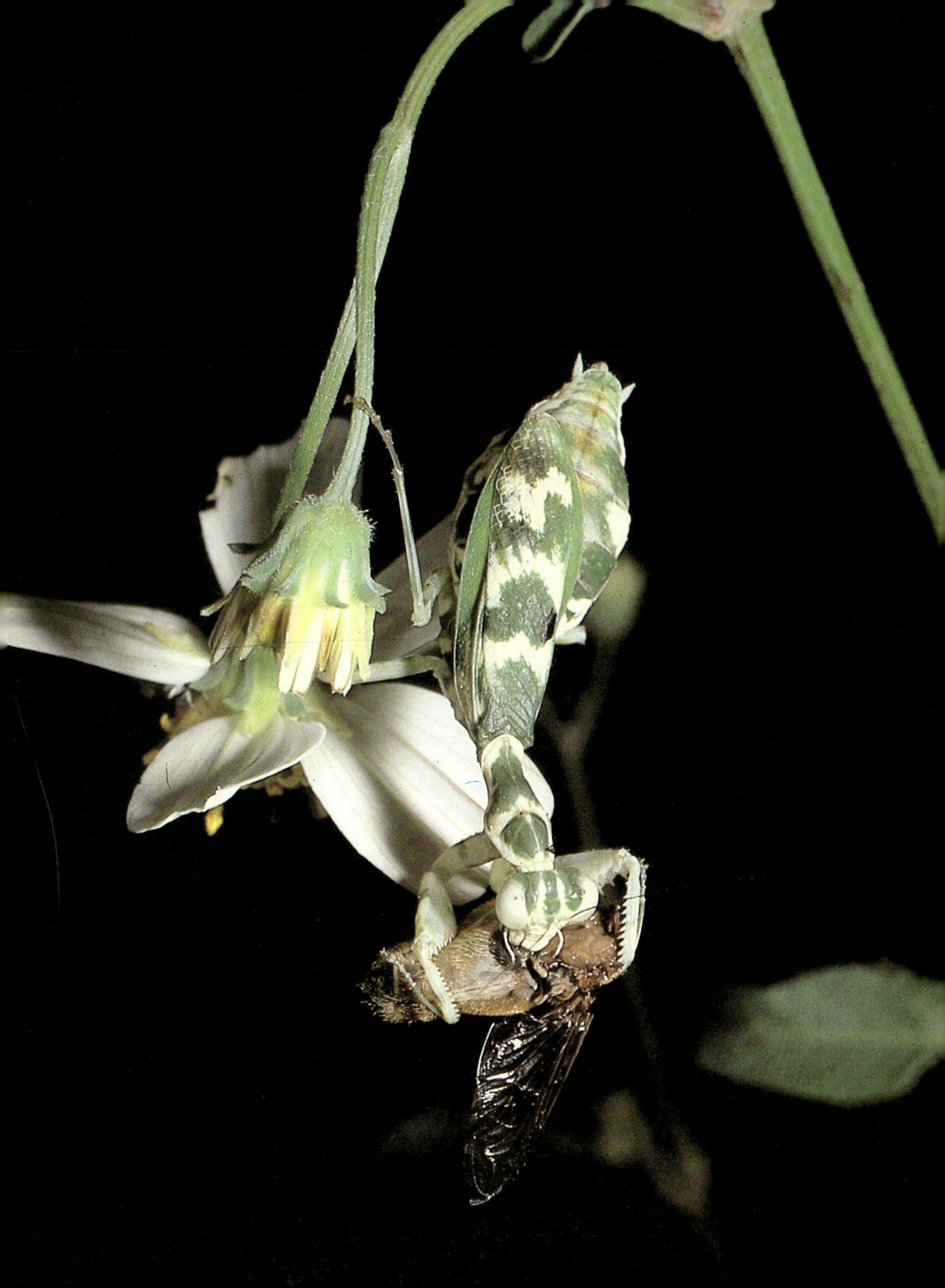

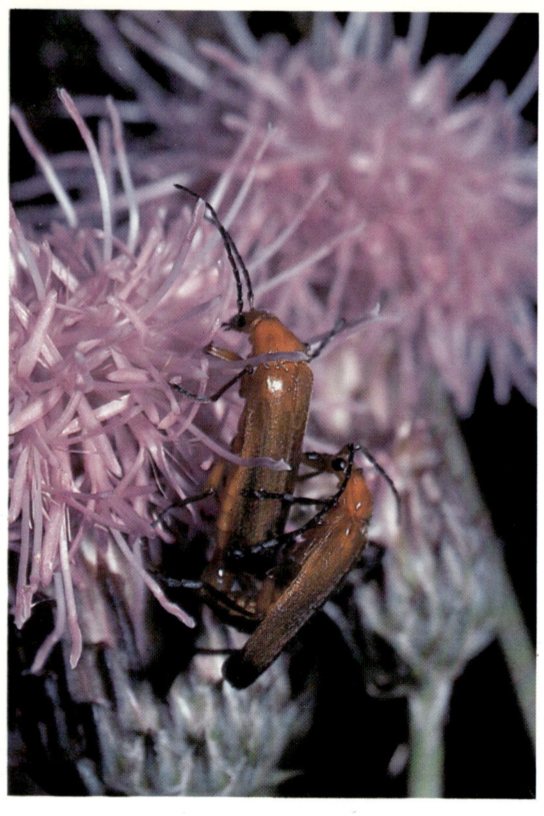

Rhagonycha fulva. Mating Soldier Beetles are one of the most numerous and easily-approached wildlife subjects in Britain and parts of Europe during July and August. Every thistle and umbel flower seems to be covered in masses of mating pairs, although beetles in the same family and equally attractive can in fact be found from early May onwards, and similar beetles are found all over the world. I used the thistle flower behind this pair as a background; 55mm lens with extension ring (actual length of the beetles is only 7–10mm).

transported them home, froze or gassed them and then put them on leaves in a box for photography. If they were still sufficiently comatose to be quiet enough to photograph, they looked exactly what they were — half dead insects. If they woke up and became active, they immediately jumped off my 'props' and ran around inside the cage. I spent frustrating hours getting a load of scientifically useless rubbish and then 'forgot' the advice of the 'experts' and went out into the field to start learning insect photography the real way. I have never looked back. Insects are *much* easier to photograph in the wild and pictures that may take hours to obtain in the studio, and may even then look artificial, can often be obtained literally in seconds in the field. The other advantage of photography under natural conditions is the ease with which complex behaviour can be photographed, resulting in pictures of much higher biological (and often aesthetic) value than the indoor fakes. Not least, there is also the thrill of accomplishment at photographing a completely wild creature going about its normal business.

Photography in the field will only be successful if your stalking techniques fit the subject. When using extension tubes select the required extension before you begin the stalk. This requires experience, and beginners often find that a bad decision has been made, and the subject appears either too small or too large. Up to life-size, a macro lens or macro convertor can solve these problems, but at greater magnifications even a macro lens needs reversing. Always carry spare extension rings or reversing rings in your pocket, as it is stupid to waste a careful stalk because you have left them in your case. Stalking technique comes with experience. Move slowly and stealthily, avoiding sudden movements. Constantly be aware of what you are doing, which requires concentration. You will need careful muscle control, especially when sinking very slowly to your knees from a standing position. If possible rest the camera on your knees when focusing, or press your elbows hard into your chest, taking up a comfortable and well-braced posture. This means being aware of what your legs and back are doing as well as your hands. The most difficult shots to hand-hold are those taken from a standing position leaning forwards with the back slightly bent. It is amazing what can be accomplished with practice and I have taken close-ups lying on my back with my head and shoulders raised 6 in or so.

Some insects are easier to approach than others, varying even within a single species, and luckily there are usually some phlegmatic individuals which are more approachable than their fellows. Insects such as butterflies, absorbed in feeding on flowers or dung, are often easier to photograph than when merely basking on leaves. A shadow falling on a basking insect normally leads to instant flight, so be careful with yours. Close-ups are easier in early morning and late evening as your subjects may be rather torpid, but if you want interesting action shots you will have to take pictures throughout the day.

Some insects seem hypersensitive, even to the most careful approach. On occasions I have sometimes resorted to a chamaeleon like stalk, keeping my body in a continuous swaying movement as if being blown by the wind. This makes you look intoxicated, so it is preferable not to do it with people watching, but it can be successful if everything else fails. Never give up, as subjects may suddenly become less nervous for no apparent reason. Luckily few insects notice the brief pulse of your flash, and those that do mostly 'start' violently but remain where they are. Drab, camouflaged clothes do not seem any better for insect photography than a coloured shirt, but do take care with your hands, which seem to be the most conspicuous objects. This is vitally important when winding on after taking the first picture. You are then very close, and all your actions should be very slow and deliberate.

Stalking any wild animal requires complete concentration

and however pleasant a companion may be, the best results usually come when working alone. You will have to learn to ignore the pain as you brush your hands against stinging nettles while bringing an insect into focus. Mosquitoes can also be a nuisance and I have many times felt them biting my hands just as a prized insect was coming into focus. Ignore such distractions and above all avoid sudden reactions. Swatting the mosquitoes can only give temporary respite and may cost you a valuable picture. If someone arrives at a vital moment, explain what you are doing in a low voice. Most people listen sympathetically and stand still until you have finished. Dogs never listen to such polite requests, so never take one with you and avoid areas which they frequent. This also applies to cattle which are inordinately nosy. Finally, after you have taken your first shot and are carefully winding-on for the next, remembering to move your hands with extreme care, do not spoil everything by breathing out a large pent-up sigh of relief. Your breath will frighten away most insects. I often perform close-focusing while taking only very shallow breaths at the maximum possible intervals.

Selecting the viewpoint   Angle of approach is decided both by the subject's position and how you wish to portray it. Butterflies and dragonflies with their wings spread, for example, need a top shot to show the colours. If you want to show the dragonfly's huge eyes meeting at the top of its head, you can still use this dorsal approach, but also take some head-on shots for more impact. If a butterfly is feeding rather than resting, a frontal angle shows the long proboscis probing the flower. Vary your approach as much as possible, assessing each subject on its merits. Try to show the anatomy and behaviour of insects to the maximum advantage and avoid the monotony of a series of shots from the same angle.

Selecting the background   The background is usually dictated by where the insect is sitting and from which angles you can approach it. There is often little choice. If you dislike dark backgrounds with flash avoid insects on isolated flowers on dull days. The same applies to dark-coloured insects which will be lost against a dark background and should if possible be taken against leaves or the sky. On sunny days this is less of a problem, as are flower heads with nearby vegetation. Colourful insects look striking against a dark background if you find this acceptable. Most insects look good against the sky but low viewpoints are often difficult. Avoid subjects on very shiny leaves, as these are distracting, as are really cluttered backgrounds with lots of criss-crossing plant stems.

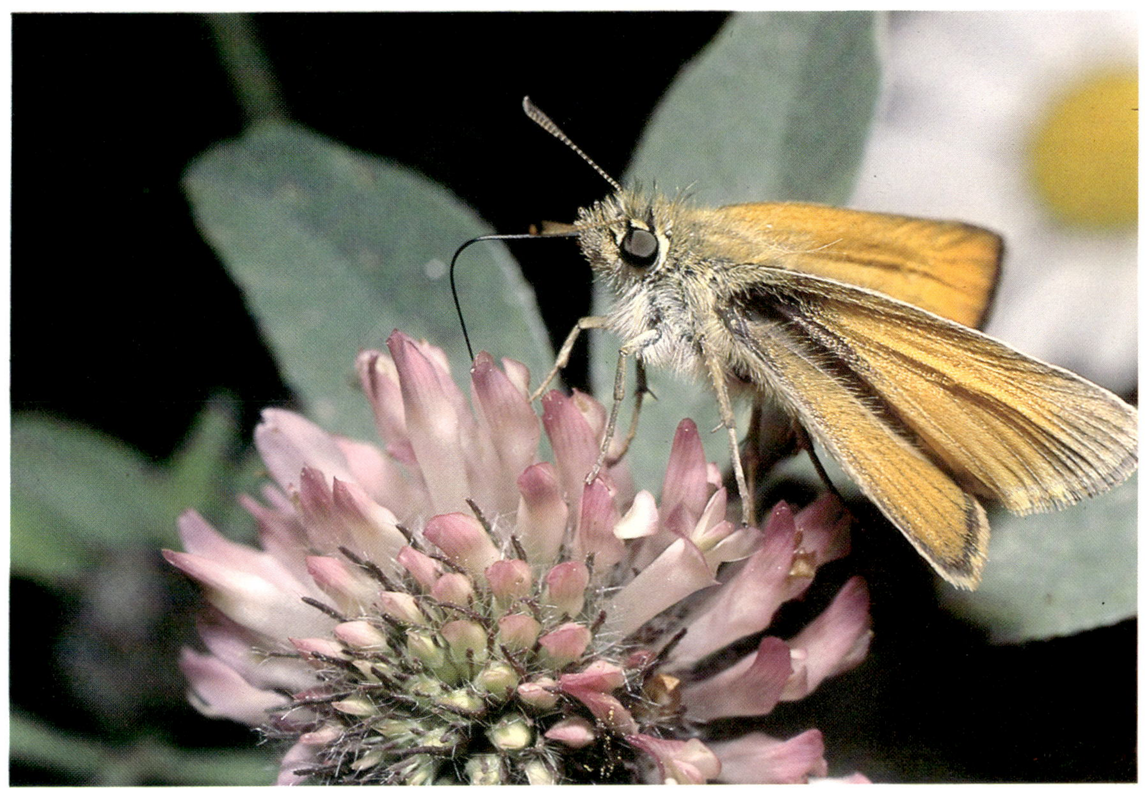

If your subject stays put, take a series of pictures, varying the angles and lighting and bracketing the exposures. Take advantage of a good 'sitter' by going for close-ups of the eyes or legs. Some people take 'insurance' shots as soon as they are within a reasonable distance. If only a bare scientific record is required this is alright. I always work on the assumption that the only picture worth having is exactly the one I want. If the insect flies off before I have approached as closely as I would like, then it does not matter, as I have only missed a second-rate picture. I never take 'insurance' shots now, remembering the boxes of wasted pictures of insects which usually then sat tight for perfect shots.

Stalking and focusing The picture of the leaf-cutting bee on page 92 has been chosen to illustrate a number of the above points, particularly the importance of working with a hand-held camera and flash.

Several of these bees were nesting in a greenhouse in temperatures of 40°C (100° F) in the shade. The female digs a burrow in which she builds cells composed of sections of leaf neatly fitted together. She fills them with pollen and nectar as food for her larvae. Several females were cutting sections from a rose bush growing in a shady spot in the greenhouse. This bee is

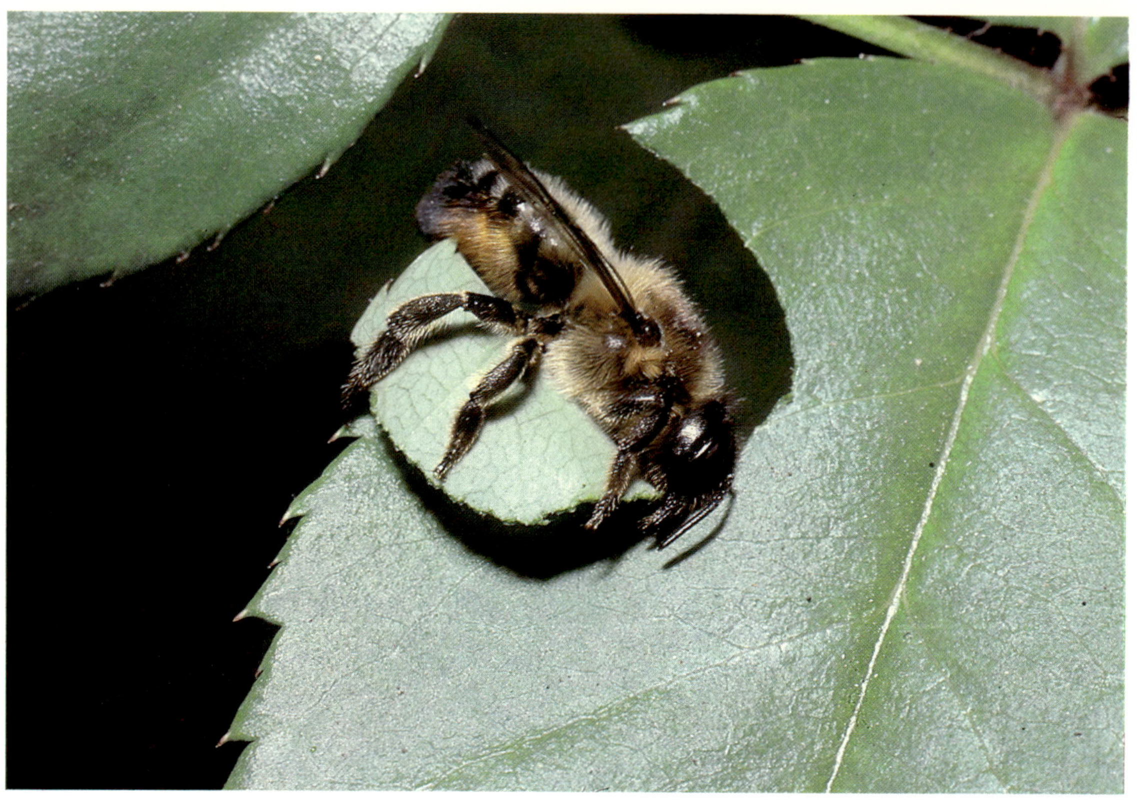

about 12–14mm long, so I had to use a macro lens focused right out at 1:1. Once they have landed on a leaf the bees cut the section and fly away in less than 10 seconds, so rapid focusing is necessary. The technique I used was to stand by the bush with the camera wound on and the flash charged. As soon as a bee started cutting I bent quickly, but not so fast that I would frighten her away – a difficult compromise to achieve. As I wanted only side-on shots, I had to twist my body at awkward unbraced angles for many of the pictures. By the time I had a bee in focus, she was usually more than half finished. At this stage most bees start to wobble from side to side as they become unbalanced, making focusing particularly difficult, but luckily the flash stops the movement. After quickly checking that the background would catch some light (they are dark bees) I pressed the shutter, usually having time for one shot only. The whole process from first seeing her alight to pressing the shutter must be accomplished in around seven seconds. I took over 20 shots, and they were all much the same as the one above. Not one had a focus error. Just imagine trying to shoot these using a tripod, or with available light (it was 2 sec at $f3.5$). Luckily this is not a typical example of insect photography, as most subjects give you far more time in which

to work, but it does show what is possible in difficult conditions, and what rubbish the 'only in a studio' advice is.

Where to find insects
The best place to start looking for insects is in your garden (if you have one), especially if there are a few nettles or other weeds in shady corners, and plenty of nectar-rich flowers such as michaelmas daisies or sedum. Bees, wasps, ants, butterflies, moths, flies, beetles, bugs and earwigs can be found in most gardens and provide excellent practice for perfecting hand-held close-up techniques. The hoverflies on p. 80 were photographed in my garden in Warwickshire. Woodland edges, hedgerows, scrub, downland, marshes, the sides of ponds and rivers and heathland all have large populations of insects, many of them characteristic of certain kinds of habitat. In the USA the deserts of the south west are very rich in different species of insect, many of them very colourful and interesting. The richest places on earth for insects, however, are the tropical rain forests. These support a huge number of species, but they are not teeming with specimens and can be very dull places to visit.

Probably the best places to see numerous kinds of insects in large numbers is in temperate areas in summer and in deserts after rain. A good time to go out is on the first warm sunny day after a period of cold wet weather. The insects are forced to telescope activities such as feeding, mating and egg-laying into a short space of time during the available sunshine. They are often easy to stalk as they are absorbed in these activities. In areas where there are weeks of perfect sunny weather they are able to spread their activities evenly over a long period, making photography that much more difficult.

Photographing immature insects
Immature insects usually make easier subjects than the more mobile adults. Insect eggs are very tiny, and are often deposited inside plant tissues or in soil. Those of butterflies, moths, alder flies, bugs and some beetles are the easiest to find. Eggs of Lepidoptera (moths and butterflies) are usually laid on the undersurface of a leaf, which may have to be picked for photography. Even if a whole egg-batch is photographed you still need a reversed lens and a lot of extension, while single eggs need specialised lenses with manual diaphragm control. Most female butterflies and moths lay their eggs on only one kind of food plant. This can be searched for eggs but they are never easy to find.

Larvae are usually more conspicuous than eggs and can

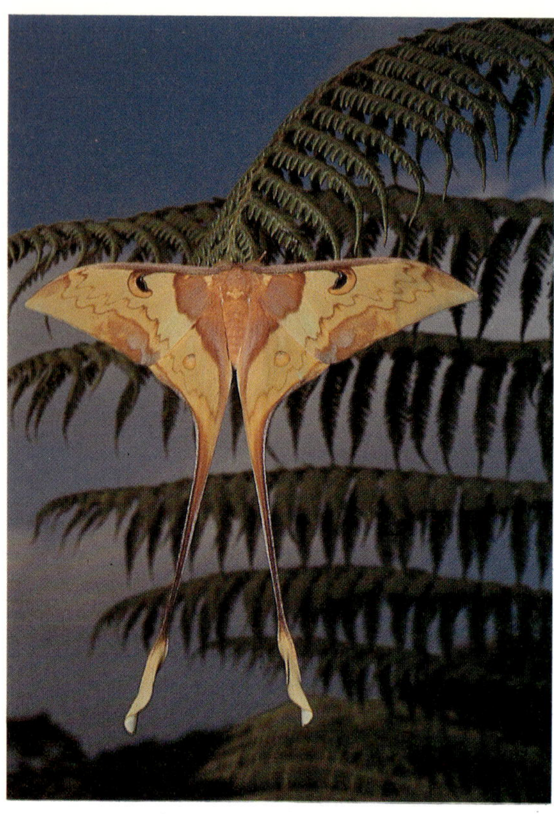

Argema maenas, a Moon Moth, photographed in highlands in Malaysia. This lovely moth was hanging from a tree fern on the edge of the road. It was blowing around in the wind, and was impossible to keep in the viewfinder most of the time. It was never completely still, but flash has frozen the movement to an acceptable level. After taking some pictures I carefully picked the tip of the frond so that a companion could paint the moth. After a while it suddenly flew away, and was instantly eaten by a large black bird, before our startled gaze!

sometimes be located more easily if you look for signs of damaged and eaten leaves. Some caterpillars feed in conspicuous aggregations and are easy to spot. Many caterpillars are extremely hairy. Never touch these, as they can sting violently, causing an irritating and long-lasting condition like nettle-rash. Some caterpillars have very long hairs sticking up vertically and out at the sides and it can be a problem to decide where to focus. I usually choose just above the base of the nearest hairs which ensures that most of the important hairs are in focus.

Insect larvae develop through several stages called instars, moulting the skin between each stage. At each moult there may be a change of colour which can be spectacular. For this reason different instars should be photographed and if possible the larvae should be reared through to the adult.

Most caterpillars feed by biting neat semicircular pieces from the edge of a leaf which they straddle. If you want shots of them feeding be careful with your approach, because when frightened they may stop feeding and curl into a semicircle, or else fall off the leaf. Close-ups from the front show the jaws and simple eyes (*ocelli*). In certain shield bugs (stink bugs in the USA) the eggs and young larvae are guarded by their mother, who sits over them shielding them with her body. In Europe the

94

Parent Bug (*Elasmucha grisea*) can be found in June by looking up into the foliage of birch trees, where the females may be spotted sitting over their babies on the undersides of the leaves.

Butterfly pupae are seldom found in the wild and many of them are very well camouflaged and therefore hard to spot. Moth pupae are usually buried, and can be dug up if you want to rear the adult. A complete egg to adult series is difficult to obtain in the wild unless you devote a lot of time to it. If a series is desired, particularly the adult hatching from the pupa, then a studio approach is probably the best, one of the few occasions when this is so.

Photographing behaviour in adult insects

The enormous variety of insects has led to many fascinating and diverse behaviour patterns.

Feeding   Feeding is the easiest of all insect activities to observe and photograph. The type of mouthparts often gives a clue to the type of food taken. The dagger-like proboscis of an assassin fly is plunged into the body of another insect, while the broad pad-like labellum of a house fly is used for mopping up liquid food. Butterflies and moths generally have a long proboscis which is probed into flowers for nectar and is coiled like a watch spring when not in use. Grasshoppers, cockroaches, dragonflies and beetles all have biting and chewing mouthparts, or mandibles for munching their food.

Plant-feeding insects   An enormous number of insects eat plants, usually when the insect is in an immature stage. Butterfly caterpillars chew and destroy a plant's leaves, while the adult may be feeding harmlessly on the nectar in its flowers, helping the plant by effecting pollination. The most destructive insects as adults are grasshoppers, especially the large swarming locusts, together with leaf beetles which chew the leaves and bugs which suck the juices. British grasshoppers are fairly small and feed mainly on grasses. The USA is home to some large and beautiful species such as *Chromacris colorata* which I have seen in desert areas where it feeds in groups on the leaves of various bushes. Take side shots of feeding grasshoppers and bush-crickets (katydid in USA) and also front shots to show the jaws. Photograph clusters of aphids on a plant stem, and look for larger bugs feeding on plants so that you can go for a close-up showing the mouthparts piercing the tissues. Groups of brightly coloured metallic leaf beetles can often be found feeding on leaves and whole plants are sometimes defoliated.

Insects on flowers   A hoverfly feeding on a flower is often the first insect photographed by many people. This is one of the most frequently seen and accessible of all subjects. The colours, shapes and scents of flowers (except wind-pollinated kinds) exist solely to attract animals (insects, birds or bats) so that pollen can be transferred from the stamens of one flower to the stigma of another. There are many devices to ensure cross-pollination, those of the orchids being the most interesting. Orchid pollen is cemented together into two masses called pollinia. These are attached to the visiting insect by adhesive pads, usually on the head or proboscis. Orchid pollination is a fascinating subject and if orchids grow in your area it is worth spending some time looking for insect visitors. Pollination in many orchid species has never been photographed and a series of pictures covering several species would be most valuable.

The best flowers on which to photograph pollinating insects are those with broad flat heads, such as those of the Umbelliferae. Umbels of white flowers are mainly visited by short-tongued insects such as beetles, ichneumon-wasps, wasps, sawflies and flies. A wide range of insects has been recorded on plants of this family, which thus present excellent opportunities for portraits of numerous different species of insect. Hoverflies (Family Syrphidae) seem especially attracted to umbelliferous plants, and also to Ragworts (*Senecio* ssp), and on a warm day in late summer these plants may be a mass of busily feeding flies. *Eupatorium* flowers seem to be especially attractive to butterflies, which often crowd the flowers in large numbers.

Top shots showing the whole insect are the easiest to obtain on umbels and other flat-headed flowers. Close-ups of the proboscis can be taken, but wind-shake is then more of a problem. Umbels are often so productive it is probably worthwhile rigidly staking a number of stems within a small area to eliminate problems with wind. Do not take too many shots of insects on white umbels, as the lack of colour and uniformity of flower shape leads to rather boring pictures.

Thistles are also very popular flowers, especially with bumble bees. Avoid dark backgrounds for bumble bees, as they have a lot of black on them and tend to blend into dark backgrounds, when flash is used. I usually adopt a slightly overhead angle so that a large thistle flower forms the background to the bee. Hive bees are difficult subjects because in warm weather they work at great speed and good pictures require quick reflexes.

Insects on dung, urine and sap   There are many kinds of lovely butterfly, especially in the tropics, which never visit flowers, but obtain all their nutritional requirements by feeding on animal dung, urine-soaked ground, the edges of ponds and fermenting

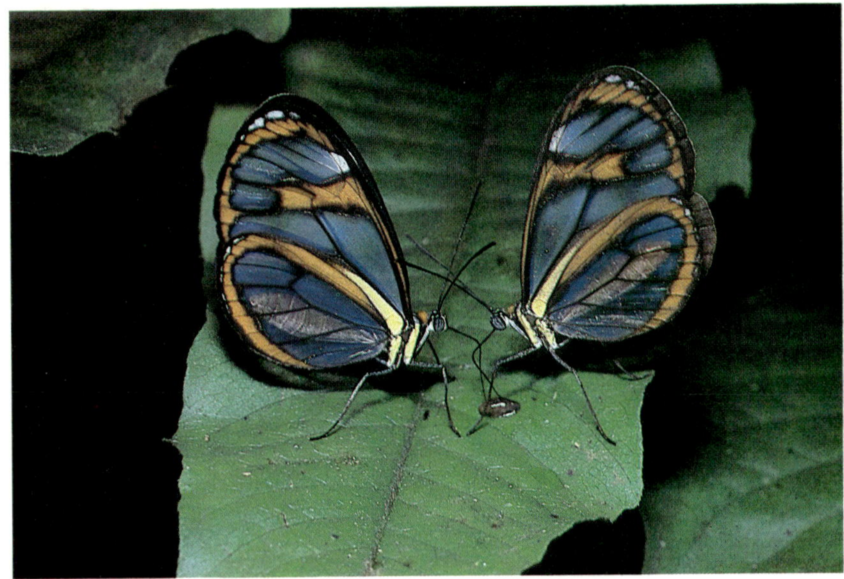

Ithomia pellucida butterflies, sitting opposite each other feeding on a small bird-dropping in gloomy forest in Trinidad. Note the transparent wings through which the abdomens can clearly be seen, and the long thin proboscis of each butterfly. To get the camera low enough to obtain a flat field so that they would be in focus from proboscis to wing-tip I knelt on the wet ground and held the camera out to my left, focusing with the left eye and holding my head parallel to the ground; single flash.

tree-sap. In a Kenyan forest I once discovered a small amount of predator dung which was completely buried under a mass of beautiful butterflies, all pushing and shoving to get a share of the feast. They were so absorbed in feeding that I could even get close-ups of the probosces from 2 in. Indeed, in the tropics one of the best ways to attract a large number of butterflies quickly is to urinate on the ground.

Injured trees ooze sap, which is very attractive to butterflies and beetles. Photographic techniques for butterflies on trees are the same as when they are on flowers, ie telephoto or zoom plus flash for full-wing shots. Groups of butterflies feeding on the ground, however, look very fine with sunlight providing backlighting through the wings.

Predators   Most insect predators catch other insects, although some, such as ground beetles, often attack other animals such as earthworms or snails. Praying mantids are probably the most familiar of all insect predators, with their pincer-like front legs, armed with a row of hooks for grasping the prey. They are quite capable of drawing blood if you handle a large specimen carelessly. The head can rotate so that the insect always seems to be watching you in an uncanny way.

Mantids found with prey often continue to feed quite happily while you photograph them. Take some shots from the side to show how the mantis grasps its prey and then close-up from the front to show the triangular eyes and the mouthparts tearing open the body of the prey. Near water damselflies can often be found feeding on mosquitoes or caddisflies and require a similar technique.

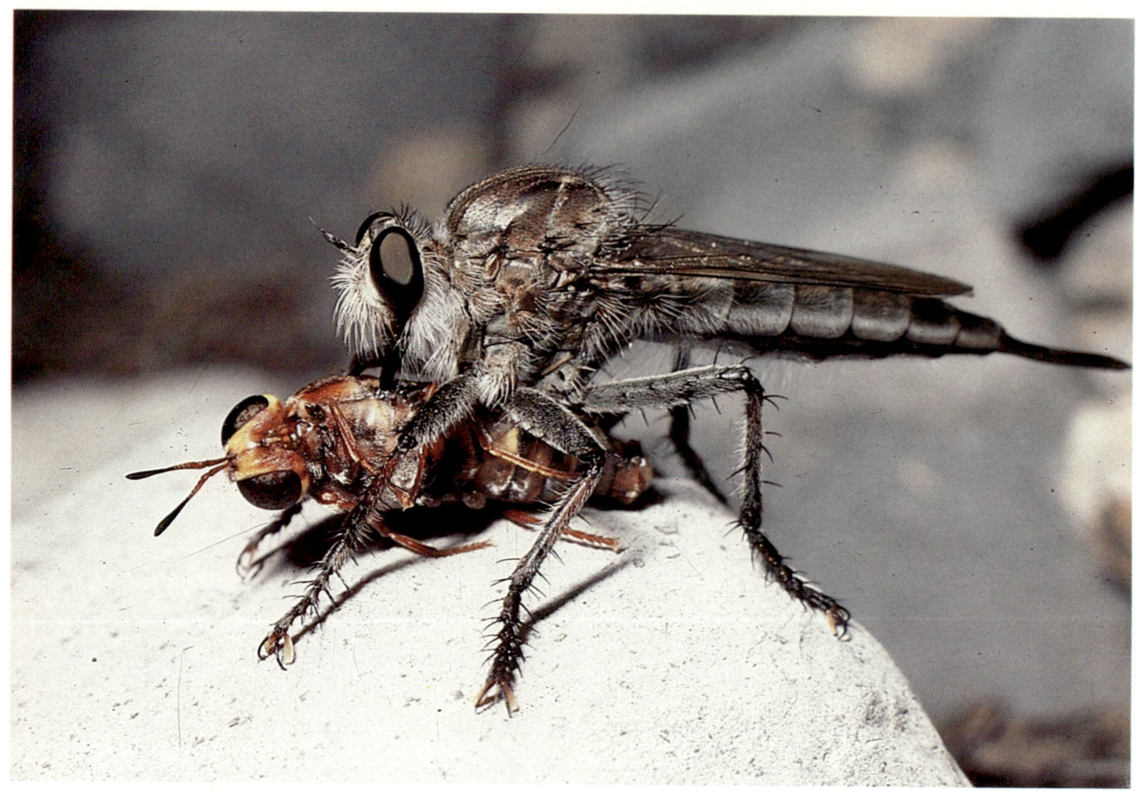

Most wasps are fierce predators, catching huge numbers of insects to feed to their brood. While photographing insects on umbellifers or other masses of attractive flowers, you may notice social wasps or yellow-jackets as they are known in the USA also taking a great interest in your subjects. If you wait awhile you may see a wasp pounce on the back of an unwary fly and kill it. Using its powerful jaws the wasp then cuts off the head, legs and wings and carries the body back to the nest. It is possible to wait for this to happen and photograph the whole sequence. But, as in the example of the leaf-cutting bee, speed is essential.

Assassin or robber flies (Asilidae) catch their prey on the wing and then suck the juices while at rest on a stone or leaf. Asilids have sharp eyes, so stalk carefully. There is no hurry, as feeding may take up to half an hour. Take close-ups from the front to show the moustache of bristles which protect the eyes from damage by struggling prey.

Ladybird beetles, both at the larval stage and as adults, feed on aphids. Being slow-moving they are good subjects. A reversed lens on at least 2in of tubes is needed for close-ups. Give less than normal exposure for these and all shiny beetles to reduce the highlights.

Efferia species robber fly eating another fly in the Chihuahuan Desert in Mexico. This shot required my sinking to my knees on hard, hot limestone rubble. The eyes of both insects should be in focus for this kind of shot. Flash. Note the robber fly's protective 'moustache'.

In the tropics, the most obvious predators are the dreaded army and driver ants. Columns made up of millions of individuals can be found scurrying across the forest floor. These aggressive subjects should be approached with caution, for they have a ferocious bite and photography can soon give way to retreat followed by a great deal of jumping up and down. Fast-moving ants can be 'stopped' using flash. Look for workers carrying prey back to the nest, and also go for close-ups of the huge jaws of the soldiers.

Courtship in insects   Finding insects actually courting is usually a matter of chance. Many flies have a fascinating courtship ritual, and if you know where the flies abound, then courtship pictures are more likely. In the Alps an Assassin Fly (*Cyrtopogon ruficornis*) lives in colonies and can be found on bits of wood. If you find a colony you may see the male wooing the females by waving his black-tipped abdomen from side to side and stroking her face with his legs. Male dolichopodid flies wave their wings at the females and can be found in swarms on almost any pond. Some male hoverflies hover an inch or so above the female on a flower and emit a piercing whine with their wings. Learn to recognize the whine and you can see this courtship every day over patches of flowers.

One of the most fascinating courtship displays can be found quite easily. Empid flies are common along hedgerows in early July. The males of some species catch an insect and present it to the female as a 'wedding gift'. The male hangs from a leaf by his front legs, supporting both his mate and her meal. Near my house there are several shady hedgerows where, after a careful search, mating 'trios' can be found low down in the vegetation. All courtship in insects tends to be rapid, so as usual flash is essential, both for overall clarity and for freezing motion. Fast focusing is also needed, but not too fast or you may scare your subjects.

Mating insects   Most insects are more approachable when mating than when alone. The most unusual subjects are dragonflies and damselflies. While mating, the male grasps the female behind the head, forming a wheel-like posture. They both face forwards and can fly extremely well, so take care with your stalking. Mating pairs of damselflies can be found without much trouble by water and should be photographed from the side to show the wheel-like shape. A short telephoto lens is best, although I have taken many pictures with a 55mm lens.

Soldier Beetles (*Rhagonycha fulva*) seem to be permanently mating, and several pairs can be photographed together on a single flower umbel. Grasshoppers attract their mate by sound,

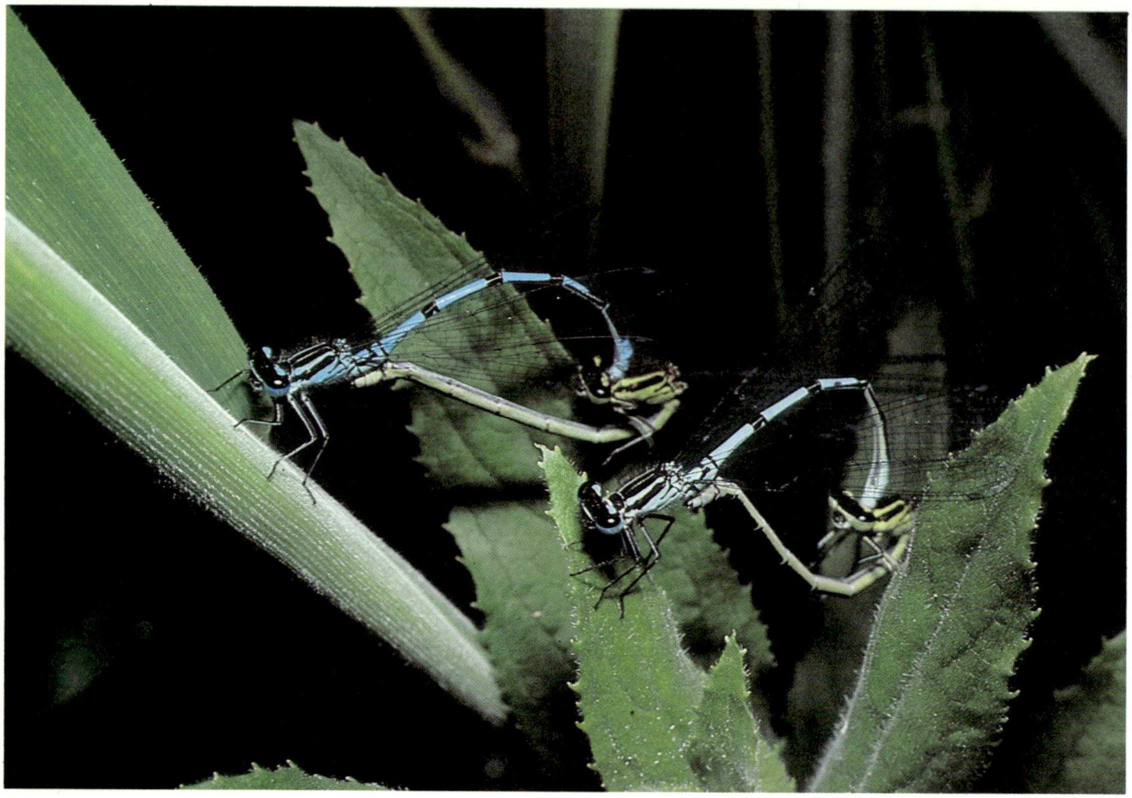

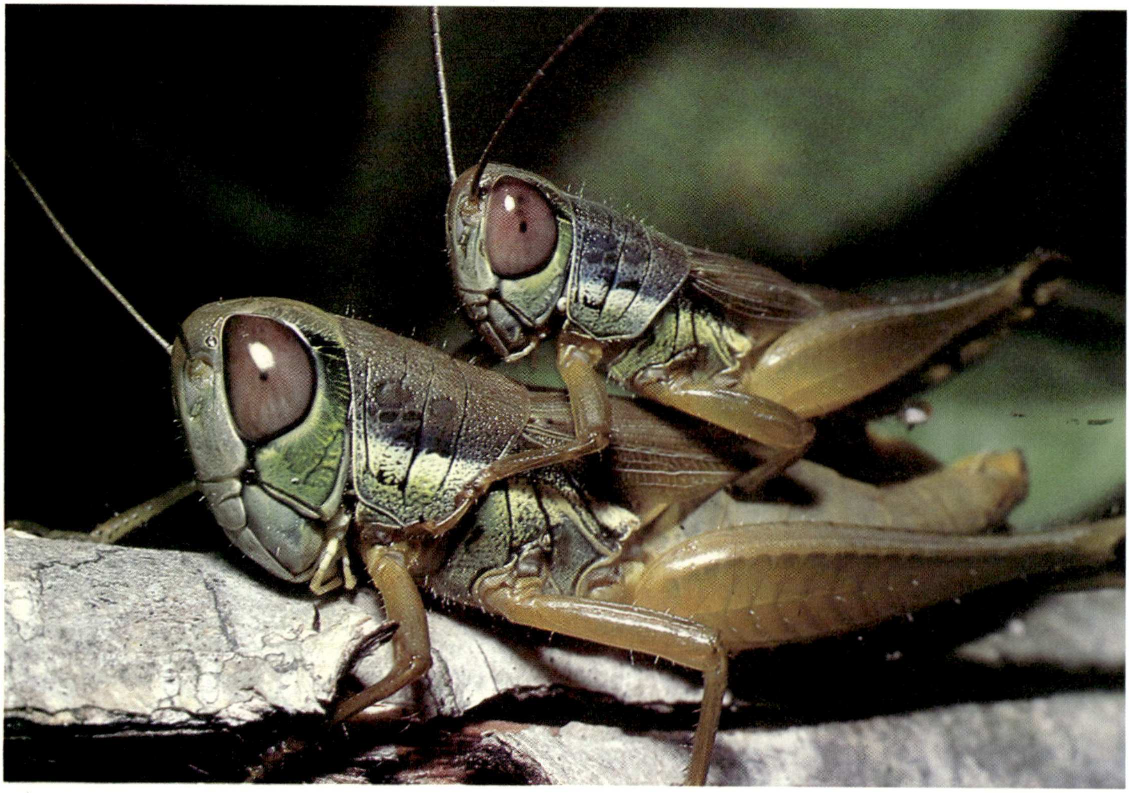

the male then sitting on the back of his mate. A picture taken from the side is best to capture this. Take care, for if frightened the male usually leaps off his mate. A female praying mantis sometimes eats her partner while still mating and may eat him all, except the very tip of his abdomen where it joins her own. This makes an excellent, if rather gruesome, series but it is not an invariable occurrence and many mantids mate normally. I have seen one pair mate for 32 hours, giving plenty of time for focusing!

On fresh cow pats there are usually numerous pairs of the Common Yellow Dungfly (*Scatophaga stercoraria*) mating, laying eggs and scuffling about on the wet surface. Photographing insects on fresh dung is not very pleasant and you have to take care not to get your camera messy. It also elicits curious looks from passers-by. It is, however, excellent for building up an interesting series of pictures of different visitors to the dung and for refining your close-up techniques.

Insects laying eggs Many insects only lay eggs at night or in concealed places, so you need to know the habits of those most likely to be abroad during the day. Dragonflies and damselflies are the best subjects, for they carry out all their activities near water, where they are easy to find. Female damselflies mostly lay their eggs inside waterplants, often accompanied by the male poised vertically above her as he holds her behind the head with his anal claspers. Large dragonflies, such as the splendid Emperor (*Anax* spp.) also oviposit in waterplants. Use a short telephoto or zoom with flash, although a 55mm can be used if you are extra careful. Be prepared to get wet, as you may have to enter the water to get close enough. Holding the camera vertically for ovipositing pairs of damselflies can mean submerging your arm, shoulder and the side of your head, while horizontal shots will probably leave you with a wet rear.

Some of the large *Aeshna* species of dragonflies lay their eggs in rotting wood or moss at the water's edge and make easier subjects. They usually return and resume their task even if they have been frightened away and are so absorbed in what they are doing that they provide excellent opportunities for taking close-ups of their eyes, as well as side shots of the curved abdomen when the female is laying eggs.

Dead and dying trees and logs should be searched for ovipositing beetles or horntails. Emergence holes left by previous generations are a sure sign that a tree is in use. You may even find ichneumon wasps. These wasps have very long ovipositors which they use for boring into the solid wood and laying eggs on the larvae breeding within.

Nesting insects   The nests of social insects such as ants, wasps and termites may be conspicuous objects, those of some termites being taller than a man. A series of pictures showing the outside of the nest is instructive but if you want to show the activity within, you have to cut the nest open. This is obviously very destructive and I myself have never done it. It is really only excusable if done for a specific scientific purpose.

Wasps' nests can be photographed with their occupants sitting on the outside, especially *Polistes* which is very common in North America. The nests of these wasps vary greatly in shape and can be spotted hanging from branches, in bushes and under overhanging rocks and the eaves of houses. Only the cells containing pupae are covered, so the eggs and developing larvae can easily be seen and photographed. *Polistes* adults sitting on their nest usually wave their abdomens threateningly as you focus. Resist the impulse to retreat and get an interesting behaviour shot. I have photographed many species of wasps and have managed to avoid being stung so far. Do take care, however, as even a single sting from some tropical wasps can be both painful and dangerous.

The majority of wasps are not social but solitary, and the females normally feed their larvae on very specific types of prey. Some species take only spiders, some take caterpillars, others grasshoppers. The prey is often stung and paralysed rather than killed, so that the wasp's larva has fresh food. Portraying the actual stinging is not easy unless you know the habits of the species. In Britain, *Mellinus arvensis* takes only flies, which are mostly hunted on cow pats. I spent two days crouched over a pat, photographing the females as they pounced cat-like on unfortunate flies and stung them. Once again quick reflexes were needed, as I only had a few seconds to shoot each picture.

Photographing the females returning to their nests with prey is much easier. Nests are often in colonies in sandy ground, or in bare woodland banks. Sand dunes are particularly good. Once you have found a colony, all you need to do is sit patiently and wait for females to return with prey. Sometimes they enter their nest so quickly that photography is impossible. The best species to photograph are those which close their burrows on leaving and have to dig them out on returning, giving you a few precious seconds for focusing. Many females cannot locate their nest while you are sitting near it, as you are an unexpected landmark. This means that you may have to move back from the nest, which gives less time for focusing when she finally finds it. Sand is very reflective, so use less exposure for species nesting on sandy ground.

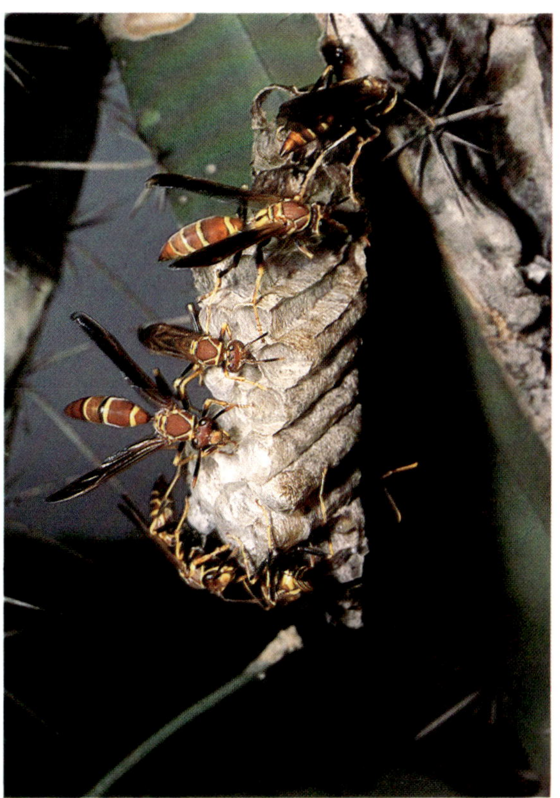

Left: *Polistes instabilis.* Social wasps photographed in Veracruz State, Mexico. The nest, low down in an awkward prickly spot in a 30ft tall candelabra cactus, was hung underneath a stem, and insinuating myself between the prickles while getting the flash onto the subject was very difficult. As I focused they waved their abdomens in a threat display at me.

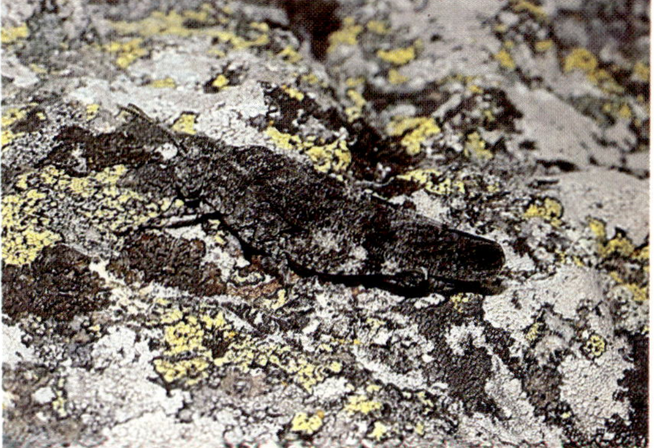

Below: *Oedipoda germanica,* red-winged desert grasshopper. As mentioned in the text, these are cryptic and flash red wings when they fly. Photographed on a rock in the Pyrenees, France. I could only approach from this side, which was in heavy shadow, so I used single flash.

Flight   Some insects are relatively easy to photograph in flight in the field. Hoverflies are the best subjects, as they often hover for a second or two next to a flower before they alight. While hovering they are fairly stationary and with rapid focusing you may be able to take a successful shot. Use flash to stop most movement.

Bees visit tubular flowers such as Foxgloves (*Digitalis purpurea*). When they are inside the flowers, only their rear-ends are visible, so try to picture them just as they fly backwards off the flower, or as they hover momentarily in front of another. This is not easy, but good results are possible without wasting much film. Ovipositing dragonflies can be photographed in flight as they dip up and down and wash their eggs off into the water. Beetles which are about to fly off often open their wingcases slightly just before. Be prepared and then shoot as they open them fully, showing the wings unfolding beneath.

The great value of this kind of photography is to record flight as a facet of behaviour in the lives of insects. It is not the primary purpose to freeze the wings, although this sometimes happens anyway. Wing-stopping photography requires the use of high-speed flash and complex electronic equipment, and is

normally undertaken in the studio. The results are of course
highly artificial, lacking the biological interest of the pictures
shot in the wild. An endless succession of highly stylised studio-
portraits of insects showing their wings stuck out at varying
angles soon becomes very boring. The scientific value of in-flight
analysis claimed for this technique is nonsense, as it has all been
done many years ago with high-speed cine. Not too much
importance should therefore be attached to these indoor flight
techniques.

Grooming   Grooming is an important part of an insect's
behaviour and so is worth some pictures. After feeding at
flowers, many hoverflies, for example, protrude their proboscis
to its greatest extent and clean it with their front legs. Be
prepared for this while photographing at flowers, so that you
are ready to take your chance. Some flies sit on a leaf and go
through a careful process of grooming their whole body. This
makes an interesting and unusual sequence.

Survival techniques
Camouflage   Camouflage is used by many insects as an aid to
survival. A green insect on a green leaf is obviously more
difficult to spot than a red insect on the same leaf. Many insects
are coloured to blend generally with their surroundings.
Grasshoppers are often striped or mottled in greens and browns,
matching grasses or sandy ground. Many day-flying moths rest
during the day with their wings held flat against tree trunks.
The wings are usually coloured to match the lichen-mottled
bark. Caterpillars rest on tree trunks or twigs, the dense row of
hairs fringing their bodies concealing their outline and
eliminating shadows. Weevils fall off a leaf onto the ground,
where they remain still and resemble small bits of debris. Some
tropical insects, such as bush crickets and mantids, have bizarre
outgrowths on their bodies to break-up their outline. Most
butterflies have camouflaged undersides when resting with the
wings closed. Many cryptically coloured grasshoppers have
brilliant red, blue or yellow wings. When disturbed, the insect
flies and reveals the wings startling and distracting the predator,
before landing and 'disappearing' into the background. These
grasshoppers are very common in Europe and the USA but are
not found in Britain.

Photographing camouflaged insects All camouflaged insects
must be photographed *in situ* on a natural background, for if
they are removed to a different background they immediately
become conspicuous. If there is enough available light for
adequate depth of field at 1/60 sec, take some pictures without

flash, showing how the natural interplay of light and shade effectively conceals the insect's outline. Take some flash shots as well, just to make sure, but try to choose an angle which does not cast heavy shadows, rendering your subject more conspicuous. Tree trunks in tropical rain forests often support many cryptic insects with flattened bodies. Available light here is always inadequate, so flash is essential.

Finding cryptic insects means 'getting your eye in', but is easy once this is achieved. Luckily many kinds rely on their camouflage for protection and will allow you to get really close if you do it carefully. Do not be tempted to fill the frame with the insect, as this makes the camouflage less obvious and may even conceal it completely. Take some shots of the insect on its chosen background, preferably not in the centre of the picture every time. Then take some medium close-ups which still show the camouflage but also show more detail of the insect. Finally shoot close-ups showing fine details such as outgrowths or concealing hairs.

Warning colouration   Whereas cryptic insects seek to conceal themselves from their predators by colouring which matches their background, some insects go to the opposite extreme and advertise their presence with bright combinations of colours which contrast strongly with their surroundings. Insects with warning colouration fly by day so that predators can see their bright colours and often aggregate for increased effect.

Such insects normally have protective stings or possess noxious secretions, which make them smell and taste nasty. Many feed on poisonous or unpleasant smelling food plants and these properties are absorbed by the larvae which then use them for their own defence. Many Lepidoptera have warning coloration both as larvae and adults, an example being the Monarch (*Danaus plexippus*) whose larvae feed on poisonous milkweed plants. The plant's poisonous glucosides are harmless to the larvae but fatal to any predator which ignores the warning colours and eats the larvae. Warningly coloured stink-bugs and grasshoppers may have a very pungent and obnoxious odour which is difficult to wash off the hands. The blue and red Painted Grasshoppers (*Dactylotum* spp) of Americas's western deserts are beautiful examples of warningly coloured insects, while the most familiar are the yellow and black, or red and black ladybird beetles which secrete an unpleasant liquid when molested.

Photographing these insects is very straightforward. Use flash to render the colours as brightly as possible and separate the insects effectively from their backgrounds. With aggregating

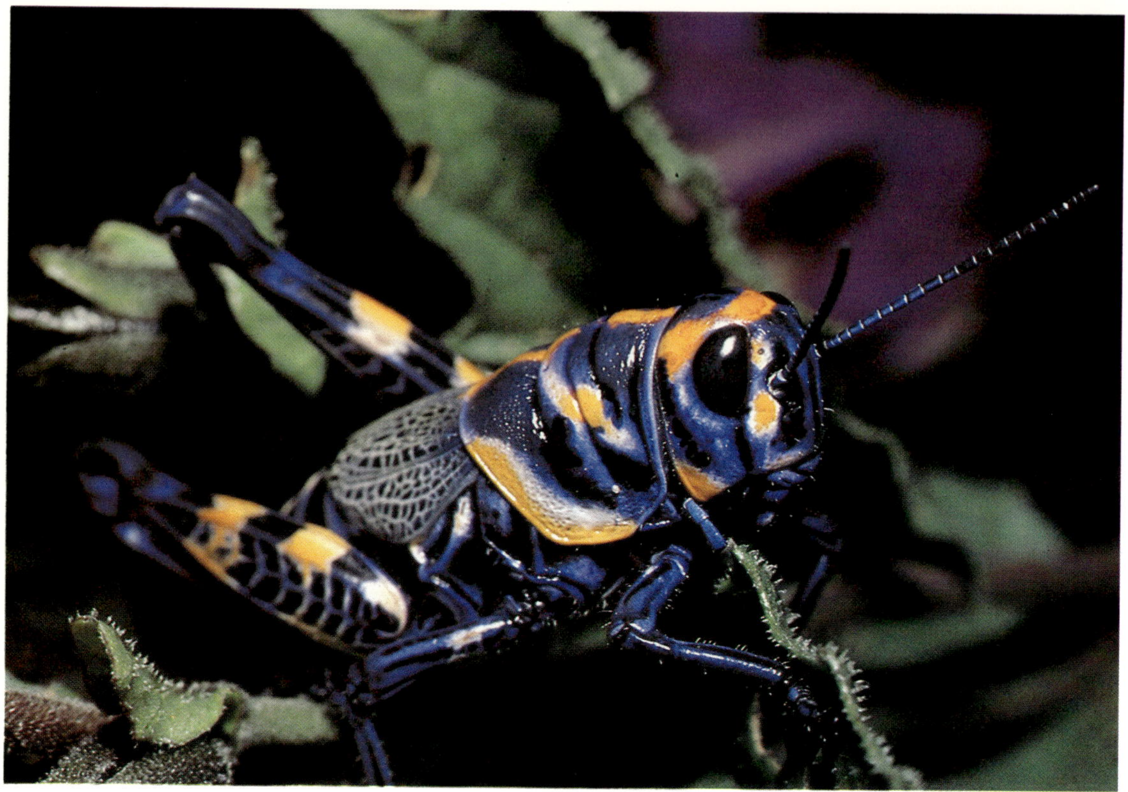

species, take shots of the whole group and then close-ups of individuals to show colour and pattern. One might have thought that being 'protected' warningly coloured insects would be easier to approach, but this is seldom the case.

Mimicry   One of the most fascinating adaptations of insects is the phenomenon of mimicry. This can be of inanimate objects such as leaves and twigs, or other insects which are themselves noxious. Mimetic insects do not try to conceal or confuse their outline but rely for protection on their close resemblance to an object regarded as inedible by potential predators.

The mimicry of inanimate objects is extremely varied, although living and dead leaves are probably the objects most often copied. Many moths resemble dead crinkled leaves, spending the day sitting in full view on green leaves where they are mistaken for a leaf which has just fallen. Some butterflies, such as the Comma (*Polygonia c-album*) in Europe and Question Mark (*P. interrogationis*) in America, have undersides resembling dead oak leaves. Numerous tropical bush crickets or katydids mimic green leaves with remarkable perfection of shape and colour, sometimes even including the blotches caused by mining insect larvae. Stick insects and stick caterpillars of geometrid moths mimic twigs and sticks. Elongated

Dactylotum species, Rainbow Grasshopper. Photographed during a stop of only a few minutes in semi-desert near Pachuca, Hidalgo State, Mexico, during a long drive towards Oaxaca. Numbers of these grasshoppers were found amongst grass and large Agaves on the roadside. Many shots were taken, including this close-up showing the coloured head and black eyes. I adopted an angle which ensured that the leaf made a background to the insect; single flash.

grasshoppers look like grass stems or seed heads. In the
American deserts, groundhoppers closely resemble the pebbles in
their arid habitat. Many insects mimic bird-droppings, for
example adult moths, bush-cricket nymphs and swallowtail
butterfly larvae. The only criterion seems to be that the object
mimicked is not the normal food of insect-eating predators.

The main problem with photographing these insects is
spotting them in the first place. This comes with practice. In the
tropics peer closely at every bird-dropping or dead leaf you see
lying on top of green leaves. Use the same techniques as for
photographing camouflaged insects. For example, take shots to
show how a leaf-like bush-cricket resembles the real leaves in its
habitat and then close-ups showing how the insect is like a leaf
in its own right. Luckily many insects of this type rely heavily
on their camouflage and sit still if approached carefully.

Some harmless insects mimic noxious warningly-coloured
species. For example, the harmless Viceroy butterfly (the mimic)
copies the distasteful Monarch (the model). Noxious insects also
mimic each other to gain a mutual benefit. Wasps are typical
models. Their familiar colouring of black and yellow bands is
copied by harmless insects such as the Wasp Beetle (*Clytus
arietis*), various sawflies, several clearwing moths and numerous
hoverflies. The mimetic colouring may also be accompanied by
modified behaviour, such as jerky wasp-like movements. Furry
bumblebees are mimicked by various flies, the commonest being
Volucella bombylans which has red-tailed and buff-tailed forms
which mimic the corresponding bees.

A good project is to build up a series of pictures showing
various models and as many mimics as possible, photographed
from the same angles to show the similarities in pattern and
colour. Many of the pictures in such a series can be obtained by
regular photography on umbellifers or ragwort flowers.
However, you will need some experience in entomology before
you can separate the models and mimics. I wonder how many
people watching the very common Drone Flies (*Eristalis* spp) on
flowers realise that what they are seeing are not hive bees but
flies which are close mimics.

Defence by surprise Some camouflaged insects, and also a
number which mimic leaves and twigs, resort to another device
if their camouflage is detected. If touched or approached too
closely they may suddenly open their wings, revealing large eye-
spots or bright combinations of colours. Such 'shock tactics' are
intended to deceive small predators into thinking that they
themselves are threatened by a larger one. The photographer
may elicit this response unintentionally while stalking, and it

can be an unexpected bonus. Try to obtain shots of the insect in its normal cryptic pose and then in full display. Unfortunately, some of the more spectacular tropical insects seem to sense the futility of displaying to a huge creature such as man, and only perform when threatened by genuine smaller predators such as birds. Trying to provoke a reaction in these reluctant performers is very frustrating and I have several times wished for a stuffed bird which might elicit a more vigorous response.

Insects in the studio
The case for studio photography of insects has been vastly overstated. Generally speaking, indoor shots cannot compare in quality and biological value with those taken in the wild, and a studio should only be used as a last resort when all else has failed. There are, however, a few occasions when a studio approach may be necessary. For example:
1. Underwater shots of aquatic insects (see Chapter 10).
2. An egg to adult series. These *can* be obtained in the wild, but if you want a series of a particular species and time is limited then a studio approach is unavoidable. The adult hatching from the pupa, in particular, would be a rare find in the wild but is simple indoors.
3. Showing oviposition. Many insects oviposit in soil where it is impossible to see what is happening. If you want, therefore, to show how an insect such as a locust extends its abdomen like a telescope into sand in order to lay its eggs, a studio set-up is needed. Similarly, nocturnal moths are seldom found laying eggs in habitat but often lay freely in captivity.
4. If it is absolutely imperative that you obtain a picture of a certain species of insect, which has proved impossible in the wild, then as a last resort try an indoor shot. This is especially applicable to scientists and research workers.

Catching insects for studio work   Insects can be swept from vegetation using a sweep-net, which is a strong net with a triangular frame and extendable handle. Insects on trees can be beaten onto a white cloth or tray. A glass pooter can be used to suck up smaller insects such as flies, and flying beetles can be netted on the wing in a butterfly net. A mercury vapour lamp can also be used for catching insects. *Never* imply on your resulting pictures that the backgrounds on which you have posed insects were naturally selected by your subjects in the wild. You are not an insect and are only making educated guesses as to a suitable background. Pictures all too often do not make this clear and I have seen some terrible mistakes in the selection of habitats.

Insects can be taken home in glass or perspex tubes, or in pill-boxes, preferably with a few leaves or some damp moss to maintain humidity. Never leave boxed insects in the sun, as this is the quickest way to kill them.

Keeping insects Caterpillars are best kept in a breeding cage. This is normally a wooden box with gauze side-panels and a gauze or glass front. Fresh pieces of the food plant should be inserted daily. Never crowd larvae, which succumb more easily to deadly virus diseases if they are in overcrowded conditions.

Setting up the studio If you are used to working with a hand-held camera in the field this is fine for studio work. Otherwise use a tripod which can be set up in advance. Photofloods are not recommended as they emit too much heat and light, making the subjects hyperactive. Use a desk lamp for focusing and flash for the exposure. Vegetation to be used as 'props' can be put in a container of water. An egg to adult series can be photographed quite simply by taking the caterpillars on their food plant out of their cage and photographing them on a table against a blue or green card. Butterflies hatching from pupae attached to twigs can be treated likewise.

You can use several different coloured cards as backgrounds or large photographic enlargements of out-of-focus vegetation. Whichever type you use try to vary the effect, as a whole series taken against, for example, a blue background can look boring and artificial. You may need special set-ups to photograph certain insects. For example, ovipositing locusts can be photographed by confining a female between two sheets of glass filled with sand. She is then forced to extrude her abdomen close to the glass where it can be photographed. This is similar to the technique for aquatic animals described in Chapter 10.

If you must obtain a portrait of an insect which has proved impossible to photograph in the field, perhaps because it lives high in trees, it can be posed on a leaf for studio photography. Unfortunately many subjects do not like sitting still in studios with lights shining on them and people moving around. Many workers first chill their subjects in a refrigerator or give them a whiff of ether. The trick is to photograph the insect just after it has ceased to look moribund but before it awakes sufficiently to spring across the leaf and disappear over the edge. This is normally far more time-wasting than photographing insects in the field can ever be and the results are usually vastly inferior.

If you do resort to indoor photography *always* caption your slide 'studio subject'. If you have used something to slow it down always label the slide 'temperature controlled' or 'etherised' so that no deliberate faking is involved.

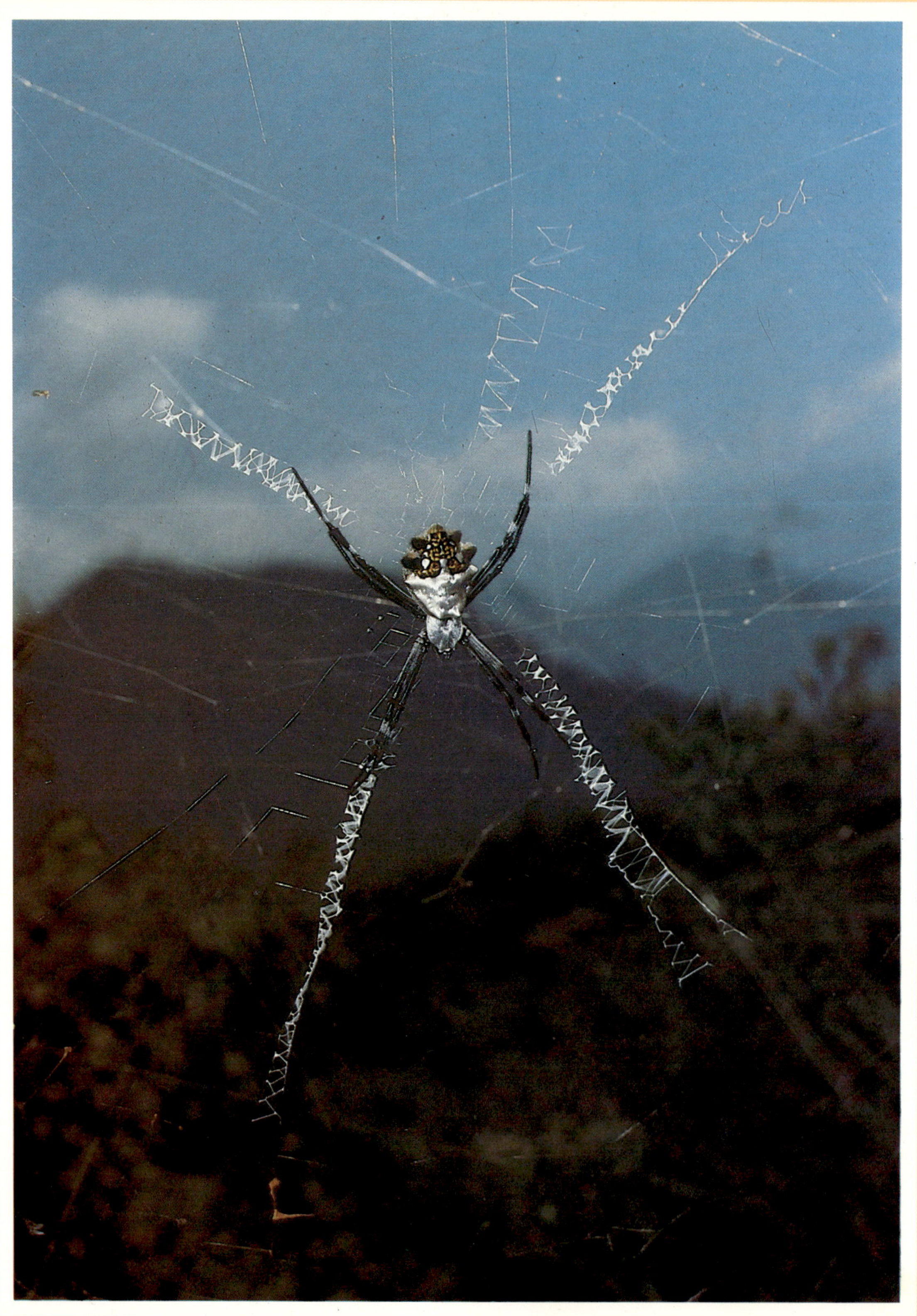

6 Other Invertebrates

ARACHNIDS

Like insects, arachnids are arthropods. Included in this group are spiders, scorpions, harvestmen, ticks and mites, plus some less obvious creatures. Arachnids have only two parts to their bodies and four pairs of walking legs. They do not go through a larval or pupal stage in their development and they lack the compound eyes of insects. The larger arachnids frequently arouse feelings of fear and revulsion in man, but they are interesting creatures and make excellent photographic subjects. Spiders are the most commonly seen arachnids, and offer the widest scope as subjects. Most of this section is, therefore, devoted to spiders, with only a brief mention of other arachnids.

Spiders

The most obvious creations of spiders are their webs. Not all spiders, however, construct webs for catching prey. Some, such as wolf spiders, are active hunters, while crab spiders lie in wait for prey on flowers or leaves. The most familiar web-builders are probably species of *Araneus* and *Argiope*. The female of the European Garden or Cross Spider (*Araneus diadematus*) is frequently to be seen sitting head-downwards in the centre of her beautiful orb-web. *A. cucurbitinus* is a common pretty green spider whose web may only span a single oak leaf. *Argiope* are also very attractive spiders, often boldly marked in yellow, black or silver. The web often has a zig-zag of silk in the form of a cross radiating from the centre where the female sits. *Argiope bruennichii* is a European species with striking transverse yellow and black stripes. The lovely American *A. argentata* has a strangely lumpy silvered abdomen. *Tetragnatha* species mostly build their rather scrappy webs near water, the long slim spiders sitting well-camouflaged on a nearby grass stem. The Linyphiidae, a huge family of mostly tiny spiders, would be missed individually were it not for the spectacle of their massed webs on dewy mornings.

Crab spiders are usually flat and walk sideways. *Misumena*

vatia is a very common species in Europe and the USA. The
white females usually sit on white flowers and wait to ambush
unwary insects. If they are transferred to a yellow flower, they
gradually change colour to match their new background.
Thomisus crab spiders often have rather humpy bodies, and are
frequently found on pink flowers, especially heather. *Peucetia*
are quite large green spiders, well-camouflaged on the leaves
among which they hunt.

Wolf spiders are mainly brownish, with long legs and
excellent eyesight. They generally make rather drab subjects,
except when the females are carrying their white or greenish
egg-sacs.

The jumping spiders of the Family Salticidae are easily the
most appealing of all spiders, mainly because of the 'intelligent'
way they turn their heads to watch what you are doing. The
European species are rather small and dull, but larger and
prettier species are found in the USA and the tropics. For
example, Arizona is rich in species of the genus *Phidippus*,
which are often strikingly marked with red and orange. Jumping
spiders have large eyes which are used for spotting prey. Despite
their sharp vision they are not generally difficult subjects,
especially if they are feeding or mating.

Many of the large Mygalomorphs, often called tarantulas,
spend the day in burrows, emerging at night to feed. They are
fearsome looking creatures, but their bite is generally not nearly
as serious as that from an american black widow or violin
spider.

Finding spiders   Many spiders are commonly found in the same
habitats as insects and so can be photographed at the same
time. Most woodland spiders live up in the trees, where
photography is impossible. Meadows, woodland-edge, marshes,
roadsides, gardens and semi-desert, however, yield an
abundance of species which live at lower levels. Certain kinds
only live near to or on water, while others must be sought
under peeling bark, logs or stones, where female *Trochosa* with
their white egg-sacs or glossy black *Zelotes* may lurk. Some
spiders live with man, such as the long-legged house spiders of
the genus *Tegenaria* and the charming little Zebra Spider
(*Salticus scenicus*) which lives on garden fences and in
greenhouses. Some spiders have an unusual and specialised
habitat. In the tropics there are crab spiders which only live
inside pitcher plants, feeding on the insects which fall into the
water contained in the plant's pitchers. Close scrutiny of
flowers, especially white, yellow or pink varieties, and also of
tree trunks should reveal a variety of cryptically coloured

spiders which frequent these habitats. Generally speaking a careful search of any kind of vegetation should reveal an interesting variety of spiders for photography.

What to photograph   Simple portraits are the most obvious first approach. Most of the spiders which you see are females, the males usually being very much smaller and more difficult to find. A low viewpoint is best for spiders sitting in their webs, if possible showing at least some of the background and preferably some sky. Take some pictures of the whole web and its occupant and then close-ups of both the upper and underside of the spider. Orb-web spiders have multiple eyes, usually eight, and a close-up of these makes a very effective picture. Side shots of web-builders show how the spider clings to the web. For female wolf spiders choose a side-on viewpoint to show how she carries her egg-sac beneath her. When the baby spiders hatch they crawl onto their mother's back and cling there in a little ball. Watch closely for this, as it makes an unusual shot. It is, however, much harder to obtain a picture of a mother with her babies than with her egg-sac, as she becomes far more retiring. With their large staring eyes, jumping spiders make the best subjects for face-shots, but take some pictures from the top as well to show the patterns on the body.

Always watch for signs of male spiders courting the females, for this is a fascinating procedure. A male *Araneus* enters the web of a female of the species and tweaks the web with his legs in a special code to signal to her that he is a mate rather than a meal. Male jumping spiders use their front legs to signal in semaphore fashion, the object as always to avoid being eaten by the fierce female.

As you walk through any kind of vegetation numerous frightened insects will leap and fly away in front of you. Some of these end up in webs and you may arrive just as the spider rushes from its lair and enshrouds the insect in silk. This always makes a good picture but requires rapid focusing and composition. Always examine webs for spiders feeding on interesting prey, such as colourful butterflies or large bees. Some people kill insects and then throw them into a web but this is not to be recommended, as the insect might have been capable of escaping from the web and therefore would not be the spider's normal food.

In spring, nests of baby spiders are common. Balls of several dozen golden yellow babies of *Araneus diadematus* can often be found in gardens. When focusing take care not to shadow or breathe upon these spiderlings, as they immediately scatter defensively in all directions. If this does happen, photograph the defensive behaviour and then wait for them to reassemble, taking more care this time. Female *Pisaura* wolf spiders construct a silken nest on plants and stand guard for a while over their newly hatched babies. *Therdion sisyphium* mothers catch food for the young, and even feed them with fluid from their own mouths. This is a difficult series to obtain, but is worth waiting for. The webs are often very common on gorse bushes.

Like insects, spiders have various means of survival. Many simply have cryptic colouring, such as the European *Drapetisca* and American *Tama*, which live on bark. Some small *Cyclosa* make spirals, decorated with the husks of their prey, in the centre of their web and then sit in the middle where they are virtually invisible. Many tropical spiders resemble dead crinkled leaves and some mimic bird-droppings. Ant-mimicking spiders are worldwide, but the best mimics are probably from the USA and the tropics. Some spiders are so ant-like that they are very difficult to spot when running with ants. Watch out for them, and if possible photograph both model and mimic together.

Taking the pictures The general techniques are the same as for insects and I always use a hand-held camera and single flash. A low viewpoint, suitable for orb-web spiders, entails lying on the ground to include the background and some sky, especially if close-ups of the spider's face are being taken. These may require several inches of extension, but it *is* possible to hand-hold this lying on your side and pulling your arms back to your chest. Wind-shake on webs is a general problem and the only solution is simply to wait for a still moment, although flash freezes some movement, especially on dull days. If you cannot hand-hold a camera very well, spiders in webs make good subjects for tripod work, as long as you do not touch the web or any trip-lines when setting it up. If you do, the spider may hurry into its lair and may prove slow to re-emerge. Approach crab spiders on flowers with great care as, if they spot you, they often sidle slowly over the edge and sit on the underside. Wolf and jumping spiders have very sharp eyes and can spot the slightest movement, so be especially careful when stalking them.

Collecting and identifying spiders Although some of the larger and more common spiders can be identified with ease in the field or from slides, most species must be collected for examination under a microscope. Even then identification may be lengthy and difficult and is best left to a specialist. Spiders should be preserved in spirit, as they cannot be dried and pinned like insects. Many tropical spiders may be impossible to

name, even with specimens, as they are often imperfectly known
and catalogued.

OTHER ARACHNIDS

Scorpions are among the larger and more interesting of the
remaining Arachnids. They are normally nocturnal, hiding by
day under stones or bark and emerging at night to hunt and
mate. Their sting can be fatal, so always take great care when
lifting stones or bark to search for them. All photography of
scorpions should be carried out with extreme caution. Strangely
enough, the smaller species are often the deadliest and some of
the hugh tropical species have stings of little consequence.
Courtship in scorpions is fascinating. The male seizes the
female's pincers in his own and performs a 'dance' which may
last for some time. Baby scorpions cluster on their mother's
back and quickly return when dislodged. Deserts or other stony
arid places at night are the best places to search, using a red
torch to locate the subjects and to allow focusing. Scorpions,
however, are one of the better subjects for studio work and
have recently become very popular as pets. Once they are used
to their owners they can be photographed very easily from the
top of the cage or through the glass sides using flash.

Mites (Order Acari) are distributed throughout the world
except in the polar regions and over 10,000 species are known.
They are mostly very small, the largest being the ticks which
carry many dangerous infectious diseases, both to man and
animals. Ticks can be photographed *in situ* on their host, using
extension tubes or bellows and flash. The main problem is to
keep the host still. Rolled-up hedgehogs sometimes carry large
ticks and keep still long enough to obtain pictures. Ticks can be
an irritating nuisance, especially in grasslands in warm areas. In
Kenya, for example, I frequently found 20 or 30 baby ticks
clinging around my ankles. After they were removed the
wounds continued to itch for several months.

Mites are normally tiny, the African Giant Red Mite being
an exception. This splendid velvety red species can be found on
the ground after rains. Small red cylindrical objects are often
seen clinging to the bodies of butterflies, moths and other
insects, usually on the thorax. These are small mites which are
simply using the insects as transport in a phenomenon called
phoresy. The whole insect, complete with mites, should be
photographed, although close-ups of the mites themselves
require several inches of extension. Butterflies sleeping during
cold weather or in the evening should be examined for phoretic

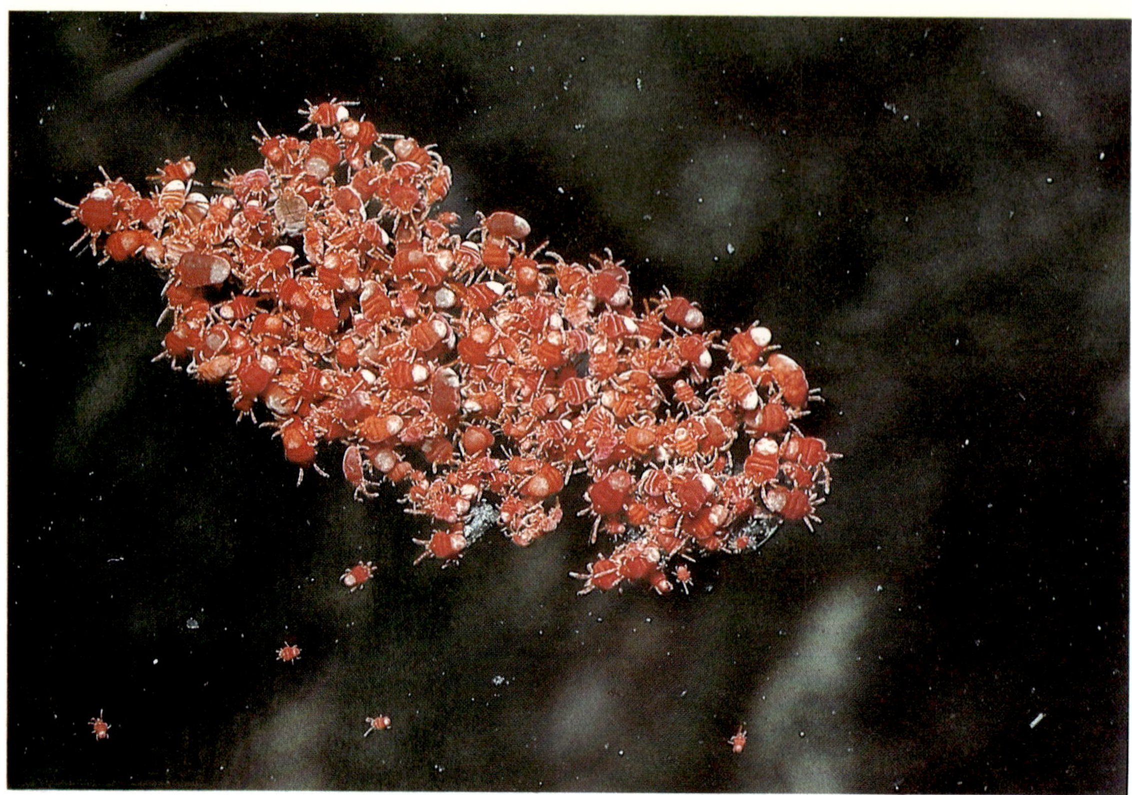

mites, as the insects will not fly away when you approach closely. Aggregations of thousands of tiny mites can be found in webs on bushes and some species congregate in floating 'rafts' on coastal rock pools.

In summer the long-legged harvestmen or Opilionids are common, wandering over the vegetation in an apparently aimless way. They often carry red phoretic mites, presenting an opportunity to photograph one order of arachnids riding upon another. Harvestmen have very ugly 'faces', with their eyes often raised on lumps and make good close-ups. They can sometimes be found stealing the prey out of spiders' webs, and several may sit together on tree trunks or walls. Most of the smaller arachnids are difficult to identify but this should not deter you from taking pictures of them.

CENTIPEDES

Centipedes belong to a separate class of Arthropods, the Chilopoda. The narrow extended body is composed of anything from 15 to 173 separate rings. Every ring bears a pair of legs. The head has a pair of long sensitive antennae and two pairs of small jaws for feeding. The front pair of legs is modified into a

Velvet-mites of the family *Trombidiidae*. This particular aggregation was found on the surface of a rock-pool on the Kenyan coast. Photography was the same as for other water-surface inhabitants, eg water-skater bugs, using 55mm lens reversed on 50mm extension (plus sunken lens), flash. Taken from a painful position kneeling on sharp coral and hanging out over the water, difficult as a slight breeze kept on blowing the raft of them all over the pool.

pair of strong claw-like organs, which close like tongs and are equipped with poison glands. Centipedes are always carnivorous, hunting at night for small arthropods, molluscs and worms. The tropical giant centipedes are fearsome creatures up to 25cm long, capable of attacking small vertebrates and of giving a painful and dangerous bite to man.

Centipedes found in temperate climates are smaller. The common European brown centipede *Lithobius forficatus* grows to a length of about 3cm. It lives in damp earth in gardens, forests and beside fresh water. Search for it under stones and pieces of loose bark. When exposed to bright light it can move extremely quickly but it may stay long enough for some pictures if unearthed carefully in dull conditions, especially in dark woodlands. Using flash creates numerous highlights on the shiny skin but is unavoidable as the subjects shun bright available light. Female centipedes guard their eggs and young by curling their bodies around them. This makes an exceptional shot if you can find one doing this.

MILLIPEDES

Millipedes (Diplopoda) generally make better subjects than centipedes as they are less strictly nocturnal and may be a conspicuous and common sight during the day, especially in the tropics. They move much more slowly than the swift aggressive centipedes and are vegetarian. The body segments each carry two pairs of legs and are usually cylindrical, although the common polydesmids have flattened bodies. Millipedes up to 30cm long are found in the tropics.

In temperate areas look for millipedes under stones and bark, where they may be found with centipedes, woodlice and spiders. Pill millipedes roll themselves into a closely fitting armoured ball, while the larger and lengthier kinds coil into a spiral like a watch-spring.

In the deserts of the south west USA and Mexico, as the sun sets and the ground cools, many animals which have been sheltering from the heat of the day venture forth in search of food and a mate. Among these nocturnal wanderers are many big *Spirobolus* millipedes, which appear like magic in large numbers at dusk and climb the vegetation to feed on the leaves. In Kenya lovely glossy black millipedes with orange legs are a usual sight along the coast. Mating pairs are common, the male caressing the female's head with his mouthparts and legs. **Photographing millipedes**   As with most smallish subjects, I use a hand-held camera and flash. However, most millipedes are

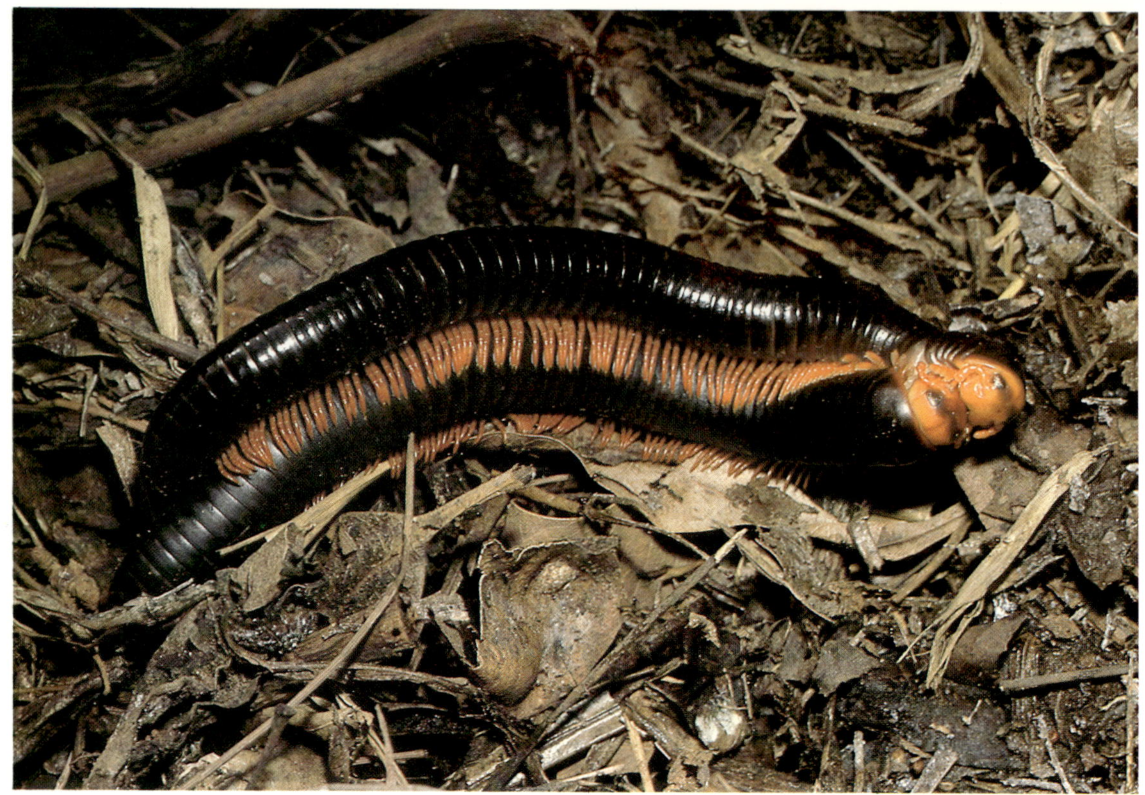

good subjects for photography if you use a tripod, or ground spike, especially when they are sitting still while feeding or mating, or when coiled into a spiral. The large tropical kinds often walk around in bright sunlight, so available light can be used if preferred. I always take a series of pictures, showing the animal at full length while walking, coiled defensively, feeding and turning round on itself to groom its legs. Mating pairs are the best subjects and close-ups of the faces are most attractive. When using flash do not worry about the highlights on the body as this is natural, even in sunlight. Identifying millipedes is difficult and it is probably best not to bother unless for specific scientific reasons.

Giant Millipedes. These are the black and orange ones mentioned in the text, but nobody seems able to give me a generic name for them. Large numbers were in the garden of the house in which I stayed on the Kenyan coast. This pair are mating, photographed as I knelt; single flash. Note how the male is much shinier than the female.

MOLLUSCS

The phylum Mollusca is one of the major divisions of the animal kingdom, containing over 112,000 species. Marine molluscs include squids, whelks, limpets, clams and oysters, while non-marine forms include slugs, snails and freshwater mussels. Molluscs of the seashore are mentioned in Chapter 10. In this section I shall deal only with slugs and snails of the order Gastropoda which are to be found on land.

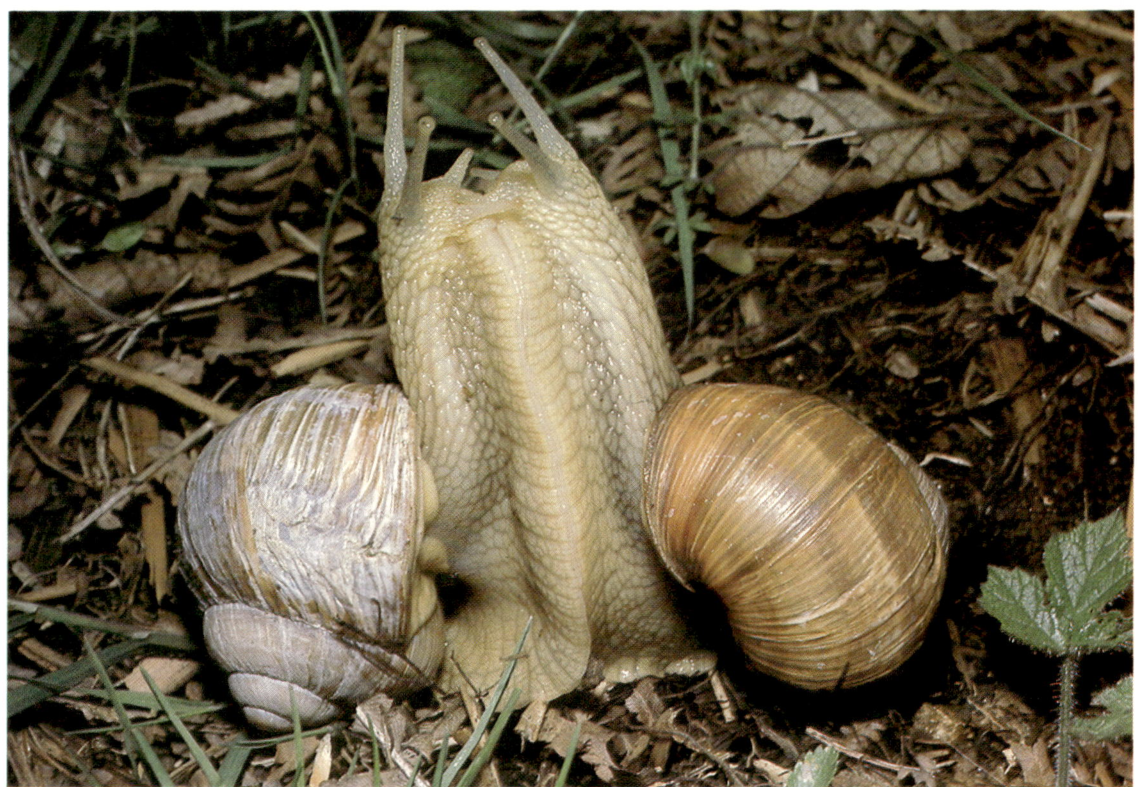

Slugs and snails

Slugs are rather unpopular creatures, usually arousing feelings
of revulsion rather than interest. Nevertheless, they are
fascinating animals well worth the attention of the wildlife
photographer. Snails are more popular, mostly because some of
them have attractively patterned shells, which conceal the more
unpleasant aspects of the slimy body. Most land molluscs feed
on plants, both living and dead, but some are predators and
feed on earthworms and other soft-bodied prey.

Snails and slugs are hermaphrodite, each animal fertilising
another and at the same time being fertilised itself. There is
often an elaborate and lengthy courtship which is worth
photographing. In wet weather it is easy to find large Roman
Snails (*Helix pomatia*) courting in grassland on the Cotswold
hills in England. The two animals face each other and rear up
off their creeping soles so that their bodies are vertical. In this
position they weave from side to side, caressing each other with
their tentacles, which become enlarged. Finally they shoot a
'love dart', a sharp, pointed chalky concretion up to ½in long,
deep into each other's body. After mating, roman snails lay
their eggs in soft ground, extruding the whole body downwards
beneath the shell as the large pearly eggs are produced.

Finding molluscs   Grassland, scrub and ancient woodlands on chalk and limestone soils are the best places to search. Heathlands and areas with generally acidic soils are less productive, as snails need lime to manufacture their shells. On a warm summer evening after rain you should find numerous species crawling around, feeding and mating. During periods of drier weather, search for them under stones and bark and among moss and vegetation in damp places. Specimens discovered under stones can be placed on a suitable background and sprayed with water to encourage them to emerge from the shell.

Photographing molluscs   Larger molluscs can sometimes be found crawling around in the open on quite sunny days. Available light gives an excellent three-dimensional effect and beautifully emphasises the texture of the shell. For the bulk of your photography, however, flash is obligatory, as the conditions and habitat preferred by molluscs are always very dull. Molluscs are slow-moving so they can be photographed using a tripod or ground spike, although I always hand-hold the camera. I use the normal hand-held flash but it is important to position this correctly, otherwise the large shell may create an extensive shadow behind the animal. Avoid snails with wet or shiny shells, as the inevitable highlights may conceal details of the pattern. I usually take most of my pictures from the side to show the creeping animal with its tentacles and, in snails, the shape of the shell. Some snails have spire-like shells, others are flattened and some are even densely covered in 'hairs', for example the very common European Hairy Snail (*Hygromia hispida*). Unfortunately these soon rub off and a careful search may be needed before a really hairy-shelled specimen is found.

In damp weather many slugs and snails feed on fungi and leaves. Take some side shots of the whole animal and then go in close for a frontal shot of the 'face' with its tentacles and wrinkled 'mouth'. The courtship of slugs and snails makes a wonderful series, especially if you can spot the 'love dart' and go in for close-ups. If you want to show the eggs being laid, carefully dig away the earth from around the animal so that the eggs are visible and use flash.

Collection and identification   Identification can be tricky, requiring careful measurements of the shell, examination of small details and occasionally internal dissection. This is best left to an expert if *reliable* names are needed. Molluscs can be kept alive for some time in a container of damp moss. Never collect rare snails, as some species are threatened by overcollecting.

120

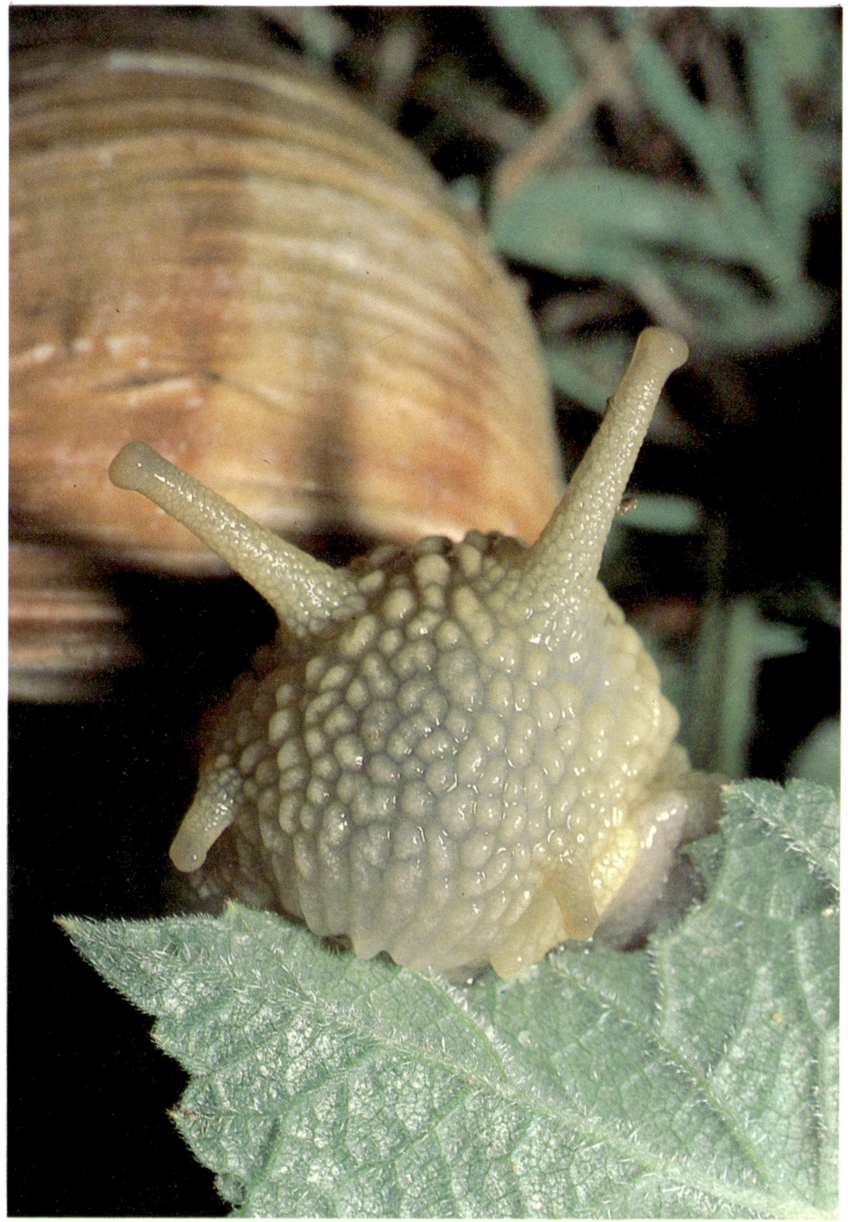

EARTHWORMS

Earthworms belong to the class Oligochaeta of the phylum
Annelida. Search for them at night using a torch, as they are
then out of their burrows. Do not tread too heavily or shine a
bright torch onto them too suddenly, as they instantly retreat
into their burrows. Mating earthworms lie beside each other
facing in opposite directions and joined at the clitellum (the
bulge near the front end). In this position they are simple to
photograph using flash and, if necessary, a tripod.

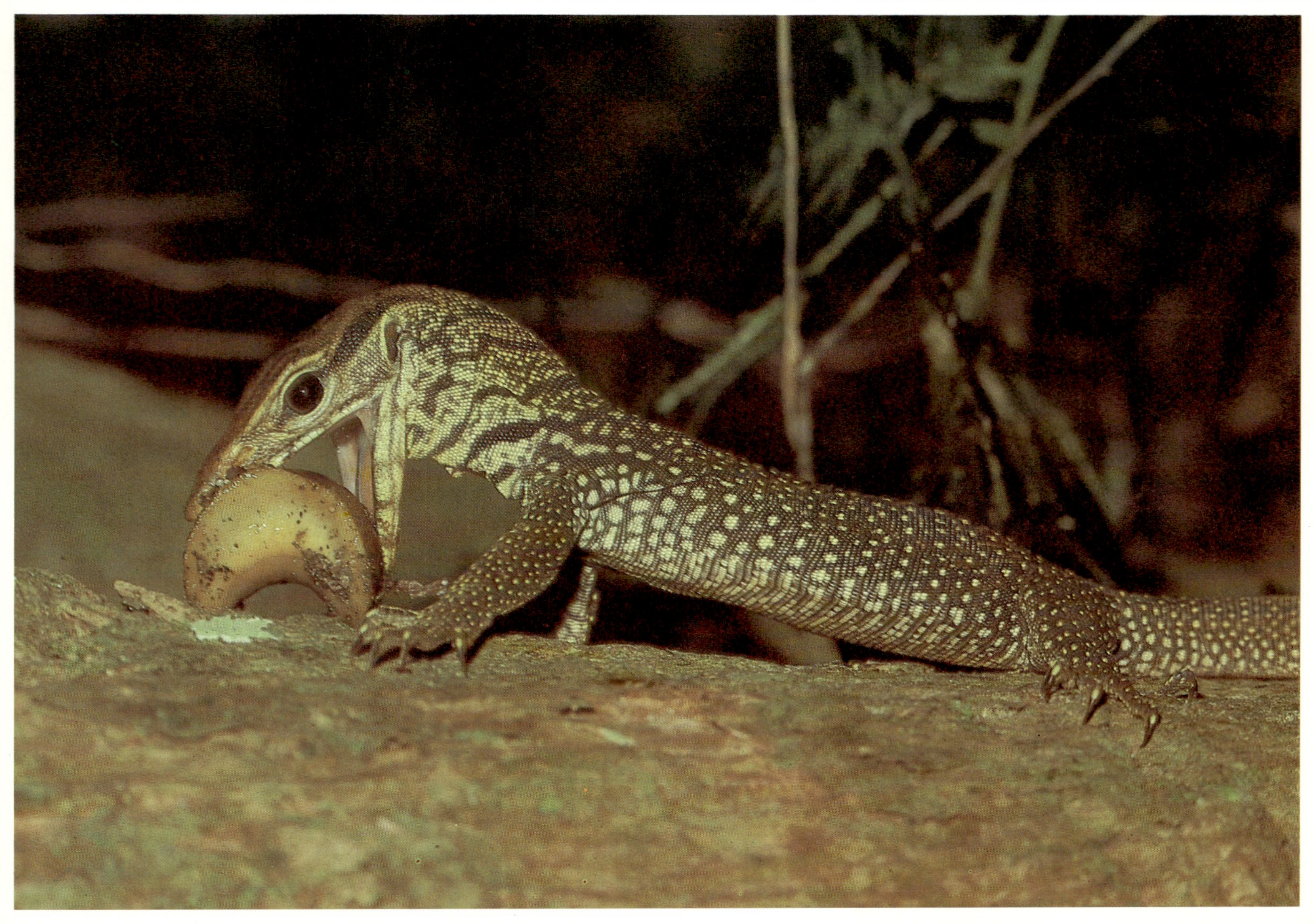

7 Amphibians and Reptiles

Amphibians and reptiles are vertebrate animals, like mammals, having an internal skeleton. Unlike mammals, however, they are cold-blooded and dependant for activity on the temperature of their external environment. For this reason they are far more abundant in the warmer tropical countries. The tiny Central American country of Costa Rica boasts over 130 species of amphibians, whereas the whole of Europe only has about 45 species. Britain has only six native species of amphibians, two toads, one frog and three newts. The situation with reptiles is similar. Britain has five native species, two lizards and three snakes. Europe has around 85 species, including terrapins and tortoises, in addition to many more kinds of snakes and lizards. North America is richer in reptiles than Europe, especially in the deserts of the south west, which are inhabited by many kinds of snakes and lizards, including the poisonous Gila Monster.

Although quite distinct biologically, amphibians and reptiles are often treated together, so I have considered them in the same chapter.

AMPHIBIANS

Amphibians generally have a soft moist skin. Their jelly-like eggs are fertilised externally in water. For this reason, most amphibians are still basically dependant on water, although certain tropical kinds are less so.

Frogs and toads

The most familiar amphibians are frogs and toads. Toads spend a great deal of time away from water and often turn up in gardens and greenhouses. At breeding times the croaking and bellowing of male frogs and toads makes it hard to ignore them and great intensity of sound can be generated even by a tiny male. British amphibians are quieter in comparison with those of most other countries, so few British people realise that frogs and toads can be among the noisiest of all wild animals.

At breeding times frogs and toads make for a particular

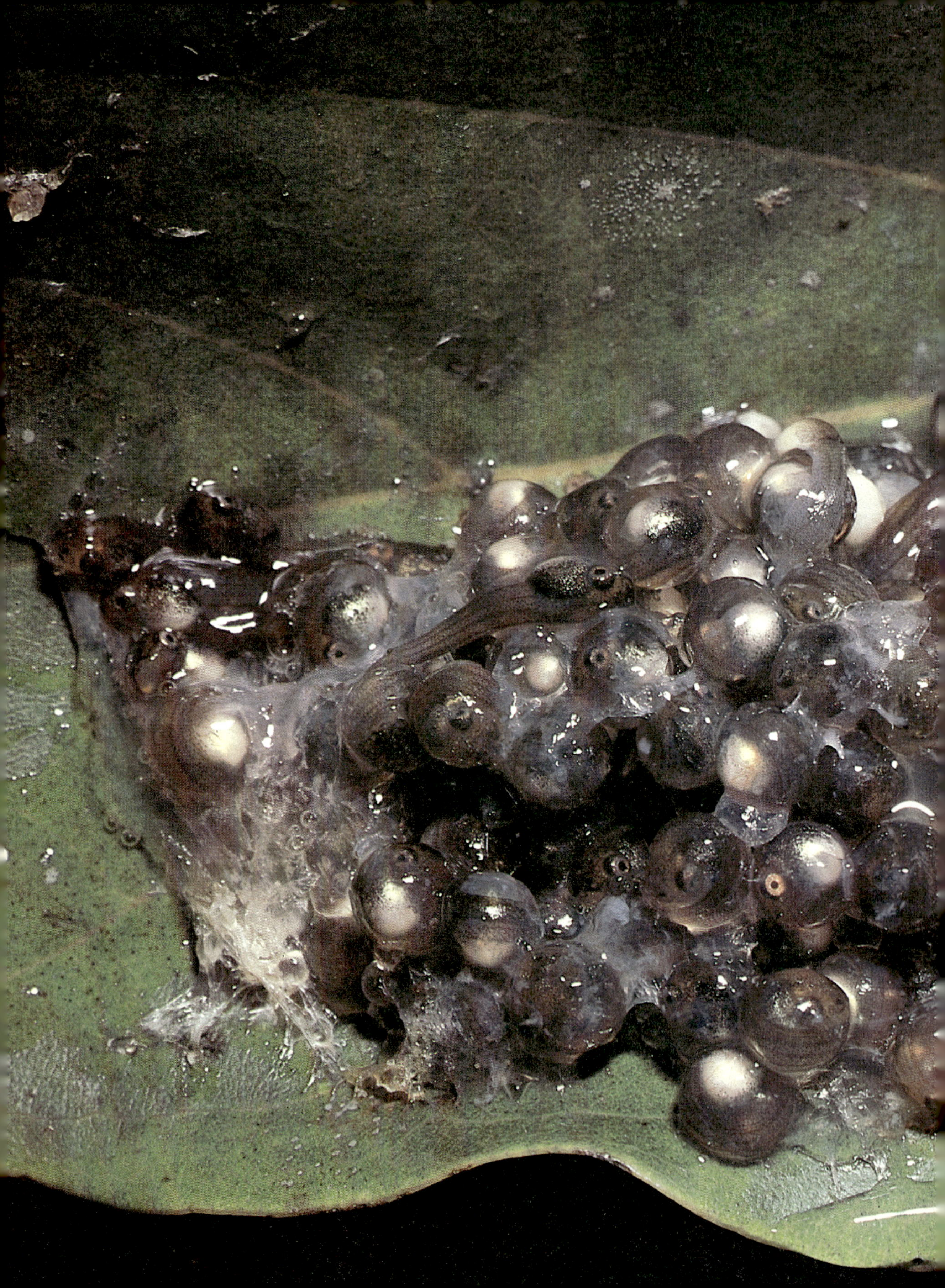

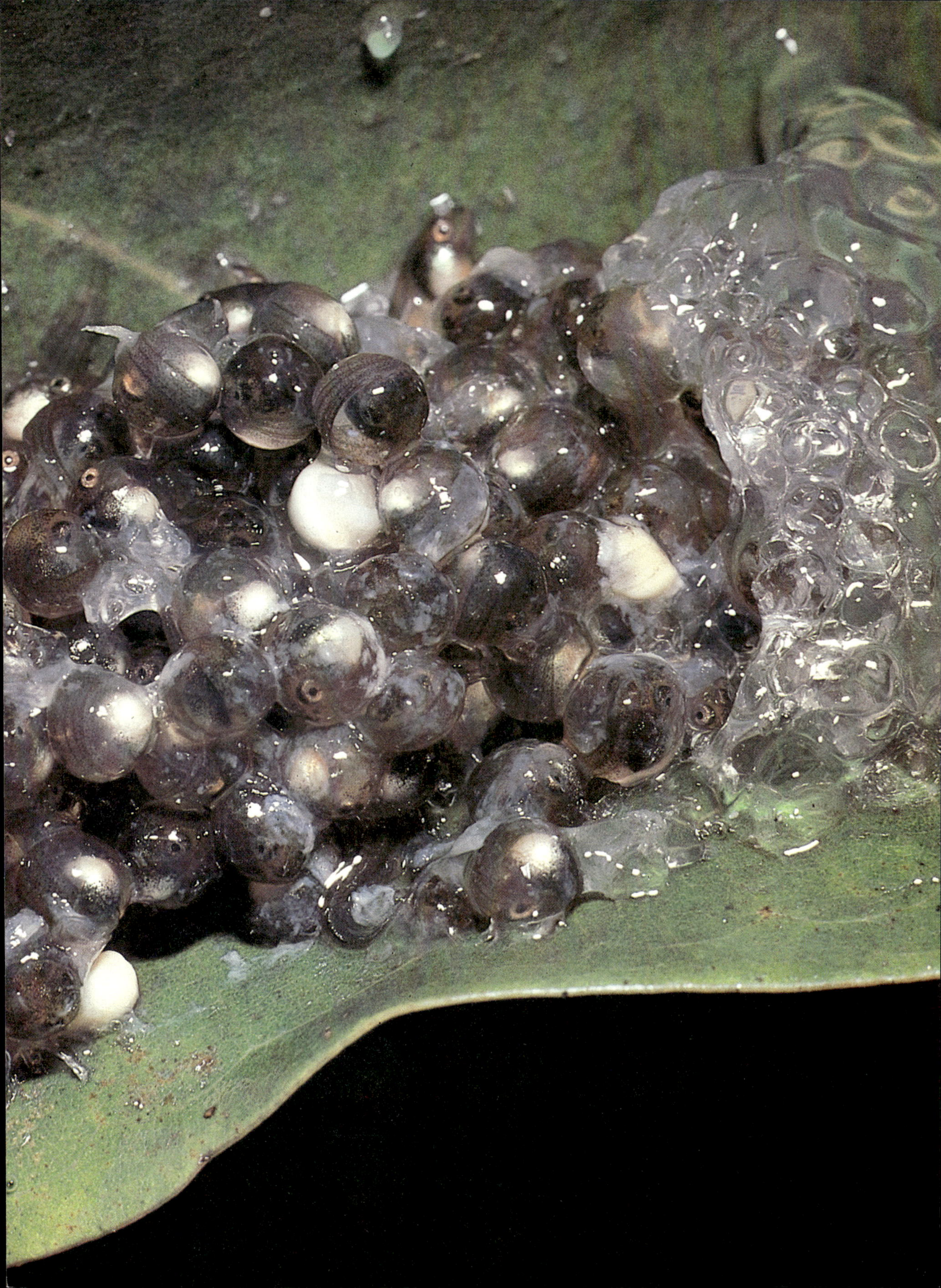

pond, often travelling several miles and bypassing other seemingly suitable areas of water until a favoured spot is reached.

Before breeding begins male Common Frogs (*Rana temporaria*) and Common Toads (*Bufo bufo*) develop both a nuptial pad on the first digit of each front foot and a strong instinct to grip anything they come across very tightly. The male climbs onto the back of a receptive female and grips her firmly underneath with his forelimbs. This is often accomplished before water is reached, so that pairs of frogs or toads can be seen hopping along through the vegetation and across roads and gardens. The eggs are laid in masses or strings in water, the male fertilising them as they are released.

Many non-British species of frogs and toads exhibit variations on this simple theme. In Europe the male midwife toad carries the eggs wrapped around his legs, regularly returning to water to moisten them. In the tropics, some tree frogs lay their eggs in masses of foam on leaves overhanging water. When the tadpoles hatch, they drop into the water. Some frogs lay their eggs on land, usually on the overhanging bank of a stream. When the tadpoles hatch, the male manoeuvres them onto his back and carries them around, often dipping them into the water. The female pipa toad carries her eggs in pockets on her back and the tadpoles stay there and develop right through to young toadlets before emerging.

Tree frogs are quite common in the warmer parts of Europe and America and most numerous in the tropics. They are not native to Britain. Many species spend the day sitting inconspicuously on leaves and tree trunks, with their legs drawn closely in to their sides. Some of the tree frogs of Central and South America are warningly-coloured and extremely beautiful. Their skins secrete toxins which are among the most poisonous of all known animal substances. Most tree frogs are nocturnal and their calls are varied and frequently very penetrating, sometimes resembling the calls of insects, birds or mammals. Many of the larger frogs and toads are very cryptic, blending in with their surroundings. Even the commoner European frogs and toads can be difficult to spot if they keep still.

Photographing frogs and toads Available light is adequate for more open sites, although I use fill-in flash whenever possible. Flash is also necessary for amphibians discovered in dull weather and in darker areas, such as forests. Night-time photography obviously requires flash, plus a torch for searching and focusing.

Stalking Frogs and toads on land are often surprisingly easy to approach in daytime. Most of my pictures have been taken using a 55mm lens rather than a telephoto. Tree frogs at rest during the day are usually very tame and often remain quite still, even when gently touched. Frogs and toads mating in water often rest with their heads above the surface and quickly submerge when they detect movement. Toads usually re-emerge quickly but with frogs you may have a lengthy wait.

Night is often the best time to search for amphibians, for then most species are active and can be located by their calls. If working alone, you will have to use some kind of head-mounted light instead of a hand-held torch. If accompanied, use a torch and request your companion to direct the light exactly where you need it. Tracking amphibians at night by their calls is not easy. The calls of many tree frogs have an amazing ventriloquial quality, which can leave you seething with frustration. In Trinidad one night I tried to locate a tree frog calling loudly with a single croak at intervals of a few seconds. After 20 minutes of flashing my torch in the apparent direction of the sound I had found nothing and had searched an area about 10m square, including the branches of a tree, low bushes and the sides of a pond. Finally, I found a single male *Hyla crepitans* sitting low down on a leaf, right in the centre of the area which I had searched several times. I am sure that he had never moved from that spot and yet at times I was convinced that his call was coming from several feet up in a tree several yards away! Once located at night, most amphibians will sit in the light of the torch for photography, as long as there are no sudden movements. They may be reluctant to call and show their inflated throat-sacks, however, while the light is on them.

In temperate countries, early spring is the best time to search ponds and lakes for signs of breeding activity. Sometimes the presence of frogs or toads is betrayed by freshly-laid spawn, or the soft 'plop' as an animal submerges. On occasion a pond may be filled with a seething mass of frogs or toads, several males frantically grabbing at every female who arrives at the water. At other times of the year you may spot frogs or toads when you are looking for flowers or insects, especially on damp days. They can then be photographed *in situ* among the vegetation. Toads may often be found under large stones, logs or pieces of corrugated iron, particularly if there is a pond or lake nearby. Some tree frogs spend the day resting on waterside plants, where they can be easily spotted. Others live in forest trees away from water, and it is often pure chance whether or not you come across them.

What to photograph Mating common frogs or toads can be

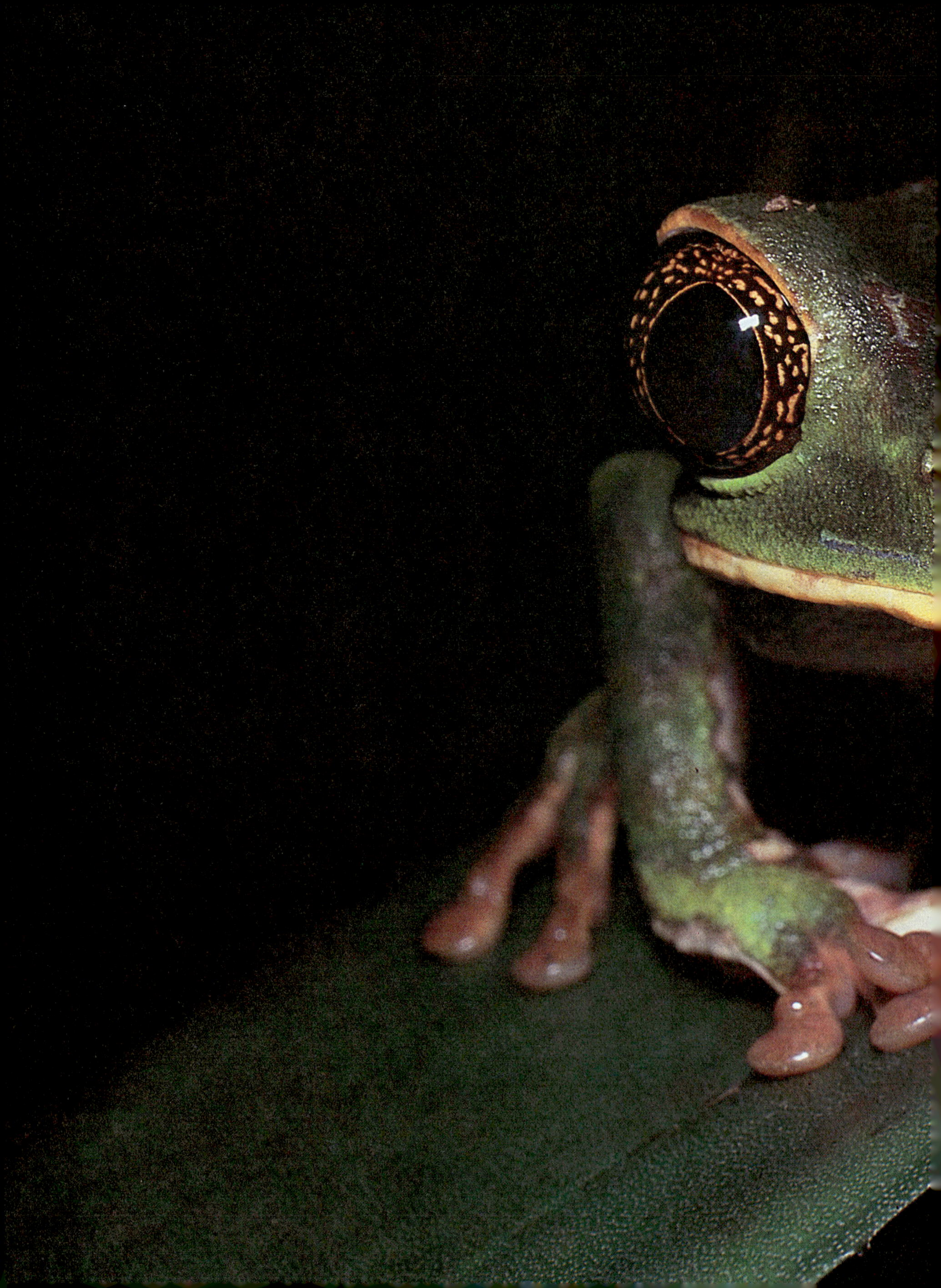

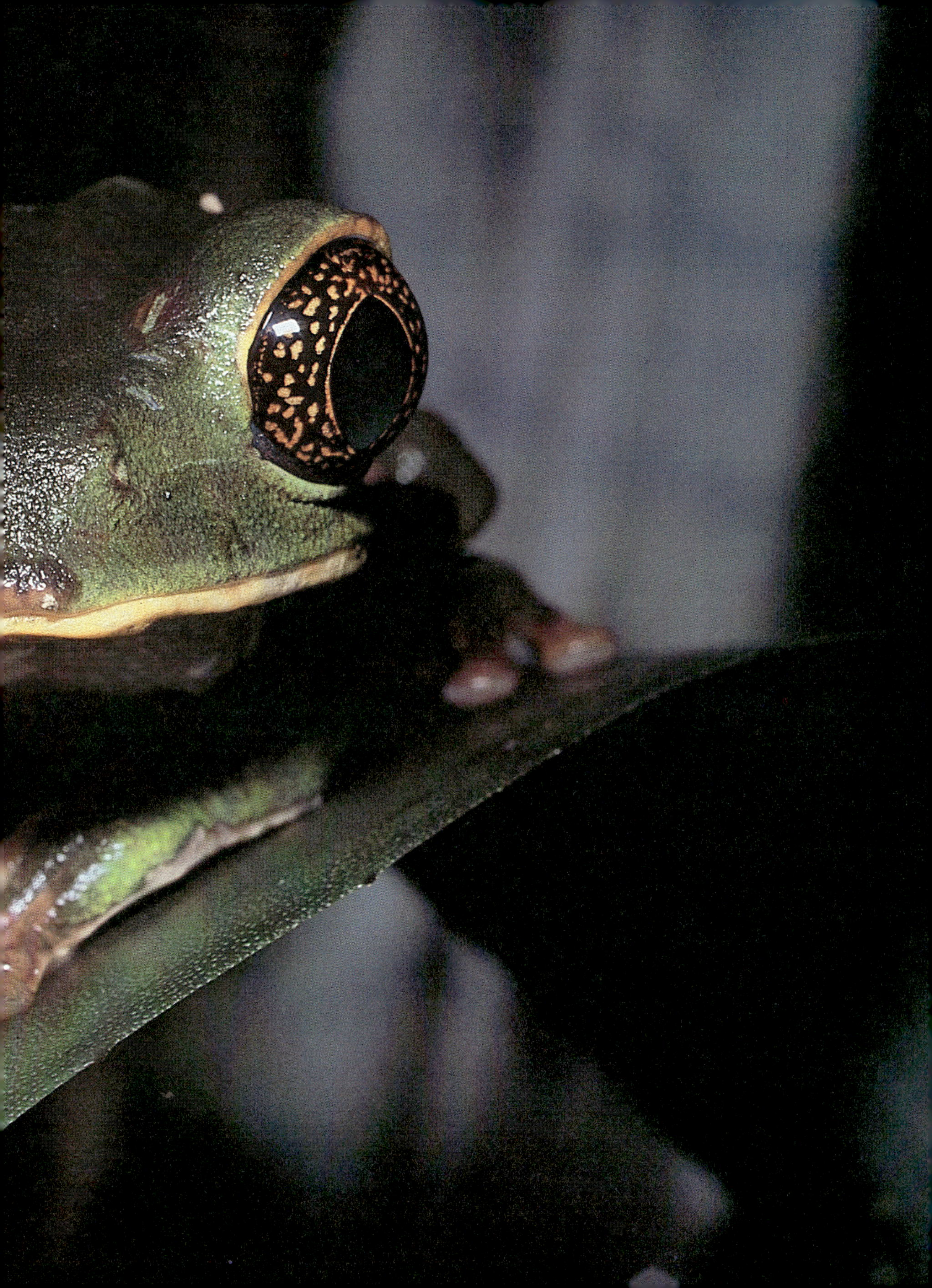

photographed partially submerged in the water, or as they make their way to the pond. Close-ups from a frontal viewpoint are very effective, showing the two heads with their large eyes, one above the other. Some toads, such as the American Giant Toad (*Bufo marinus*) inflate their bodies with air or else appear to attempt to stand on their heads in a defensive reaction. Your attempts to photograph their normal appearance may elicit this response, so take advantage of it and get some pictures. Close-ups of calling males with inflated vocal-sacs are very effective from the side or front. Low-angle frontal shots of the head are always dramatic but may entail lying full-length on the ground, unless a waist-level or angle-finder can be used. Cryptic frogs and toads should be photographed against a suitable background, preferably *in situ*.

Close-ups of the eyes, which may be very beautiful, make some of the most impressive pictures. The Trinidadian Tree Frog (*Phyllomedusa trinitatis*) has large black eyes densely patterned with gold filigree. The giant toad has gold-speckled eyes with a horizontal pupil. If you are taking pictures at night, the pupils will be fully opened when the toad is first discovered, and the eye will appear mainly black. Quickly take some close-ups and then keep the torch shining directly, but not too closely, into the eye. This causes the pupil to close-down, and the slit-like shape can then be photographed.

Tadpoles can be photographed *in situ*, particularly when they are swarming *en masse* at the edge of a pond. Sometimes hundreds of frog- or toadlets can be found hopping around the damp margin of a pond in late summer.

Newts and salamanders
Newts spend far more time in the water than most other amphibians and so are not really suitable subjects for photography in the wild. Salamanders are found mostly in mountainous areas, especially in eastern North America. Many species are warningly coloured and produce toxins on the skin. They are best photographed with flash *in situ* and may be found by searching under stones and logs in damp places.

Amphibians in the studio
I have never captured wild amphibians for studio photography, having obtained all my pictures in the field, even close-ups of the eyes from a distance of a few centimetres. However, some species are difficult or impossible to portray satisfactorily in the wild. It is also difficult to photograph behaviour such as eggs and sperm being released in a natural habitat, and on these

occasions you may have to resort to studio work.

Spawning pairs of frogs or toads should be taken home in a container of damp moss. Their tank should be large enough to hold them comfortably and be provided with emergent vegetation. Keep a close watch for the actual moment of spawning which can be easily missed. Tadpoles can be kept in smaller containers and photographed periodically as they grow. Young tadpoles are vegetarians, feeding on algae and weed. They later become carnivorous, when they can be fed on pieces of meat or chopped-up earthworms. Ensure that there is something for the emerging frog- or toadlets to cling to, such as a piece of wood or stone.

Newts have an elaborate courtship and the males develop a breeding dress. They can be photographed underwater using the methods given in Chapter 10. For studio photography in a vivarium out of water they can be photographed very simply from above using a flash, or else through the glass sides of the container.

Reptiles have thoroughly conquered the land and are so adapted to a life out of water that deserts are often particularly rich in species. Reptile skin is tough and scaly and the eggs, which are fertilised internally, have a protective outer shell. Most lizards, snakes and tortoises live on land, while turtles, terrapins and crocodilians spend most of their lives in water.

Lizards

Lizards vary in size from giant monitor lizards over 6ft long to tiny geckos only 2½in when fully grown. Many of them are agile creatures, capable of avoiding their predators by speed. Some larger kinds can rise up onto their hind legs and run like a man, often at a pace faster than many dogs. Even smaller lizards can disappear into the vegetation like magic when frightened. Some lizards have lost their legs completely, such as the European slow worm, which is often mistaken for a snake. Chameleons and some other lizards are slow-moving, relying on camouflage and stealth to catch their prey and foil their enemies. Many lizards lay eggs, sometimes in masses in one particular spot. Others, such as the European Common Lizard (*Lacerta vivipara*) give birth to live young. For the amateur, juvenile lizards can be difficult to recognise as they are frequently of a different colour from the adults and may be confused as separate species. The easiest way to tell a juvenile is that the large broad head looks much more conspicuous against the narrower body. An adult looks sleeker and better proportioned.

Lizards are not generally poisonous, the American gila monster being an exception. Some adult lizards are vegetarians, but most feed on insects, slugs, worms and other small prey. Geckos have suction-pads on their feet enabling them to run with confidence on the walls and ceilings of houses, where they reap a rich harvest of nocturnal insects attracted to the lights. Chameleons are famed for the length of their long sticky tongues, which are suddenly extended several inches to snap up insects. On the whole, lizards are seldom seen feeding in the wild, although in Borneo I saw huge monitor lizards raiding dustbins for food and I was able to approach to within 15ft of one which was feeding on dead fish washed up on the shore.

Many lizards are very colourful, with patches of green, orange or blue. The majority, however, are more cryptic, especially those inhabiting tree trunks in forests. The common house geckos of warm countries are usually of a pallid pinkish colour when in houses, but when living on trees in forests they are mottled in browns and olives and are very difficult to spot on the bark. Ground-running lizards such as the American Race-runners (*Cnemidophorus* spp) are often striped lengthways to break-up their outline, or else are speckled like sand. Certain lizards can change their colour to match their background, the most famous being the chameleons, which can do so quite rapidly, providing an excellent subject for a series of pictures.

The Australian spiny devil and the regal horned lizard of North America are examples of lizards with spiny projections, while some have frills. In Mexico I saw a small horned lizard *Phrynosoma modestum* which mimicked the limestone rubble in its desert habitat. This rubble was also mimicked by several grasshoppers and a cactus (see Chapter 2).

Finding lizards   Lizards seem to spend a lot of time sunning themselves, often choosing the same spot day after day. Bare patches of soil, rocks, stone walls and tree trunks, both upright and fallen, are good places to search. Some lizards live in colonies and may be locally abundant. While on holiday in Corfu my brother found a colony of the very pretty little Balkan Wall Lizard (*Podarcis taurica*) living in the grounds of his hotel. In France the Common Wall Lizard (*Podarcis muralis*) is often found on stone walls beside roads. Its mottled pattern allows it to blend in very well with the lichen-spattered stones.

It is always worth turning over any large flat object, as amphibians or reptiles may be underneath. Always replace

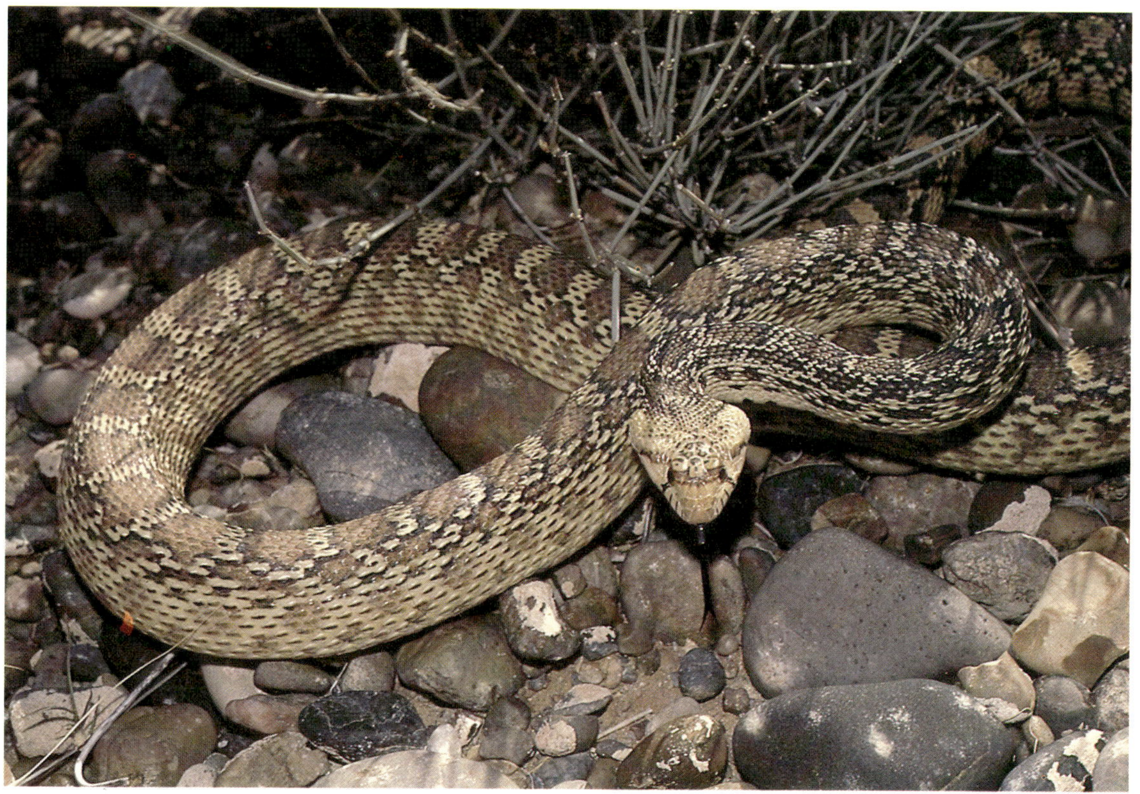

Pituophis melanoleucus, Gopher (bull-blow) snake, hissing loudly and ready to strike, although not poisonous. Taken in Arizona, USA.

anything you move, so that the creatures beneath do not lose their home. Early spring is the best time to photograph reptiles in temperate countries, as they are lethargic after emerging from hibernation. In the tropics or in desert areas early morning is the best time, before the sun has warmed them too much.

Photographing lizards   Before 1979 I took all my pictures of lizards using a 55mm lens. Surprisingly perhaps, I still managed to photograph quite a few species and in Mexico I took seven different species from as close as 3in. I now use a 70–210mm zoom lens, which has made things much easier, as it has greatly increased my working distances. Nevertheless, some lizards seem almost impossible to frighten, and individuals vary greatly in their degree of wariness. Some may even appear to be curious about what you are doing and put their heads on one side to get a better look. Even on warm days I have many times approached to within 2–3in of a wild lizard for close-ups of the head, sometimes taking several pictures without trouble.

As with insects, the key to successful stalking is to use extreme stealth. Any sudden movement, especially of the hands, is fatal, and a chameleon-like approach is often very effective. Take particular care when winding-on the film, as after obtaining one successful shot it is easy to relax and move the hands too quickly. Even now I still lose pictures in this way, which is inexcusable. Lizards which are being stalked usually show every sign of closely watching your approach, yet still look completely relaxed as long as no sudden movements alert them to a possible threat. Most of their enemies probably hunt with a quick rush, so a stealthy approach may arouse curiosity rather than fear. In Mexico I stalked a beautiful green lizard *Ctenosauras similis* to within a few inches, yet the slides show its muscles to be completely relaxed.

I currently use a 70–210mm zoom, usually mounted on a short automatic extension tube. On a bright but overcast day available light gives excellent results, and emphasises the scaly nature of the skin. On bright contrasty days, or in a situation where surrounding vegetation causes blotchy illumination, I use a fill-in flash mounted on an angle-bracket and ball and socket head as for the larger insects. I also use this set-up for photographing reptiles in forests on dull days and at night. For close-ups of exceptionally tame subjects I still use a 55mm lens and small hand-held flash unit. A tripod is generally useless for photographing lizards, unless you find very slow moving species or a spot to which a lizard returns regularly to bask.

Most photography of wild lizards is simply portraiture, as behaviour is unfortunately seldom observed. If you come across behaviour such as feeding, mating or laying eggs take plenty of pictures and count yourself very lucky. In most cases I simply take shots from the side and the top showing the whole animal, and then if it is sufficiently tame, close-ups of the head from the side and front.

Snakes

Snakes are far more strictly nocturnal than most lizards, and are seen less often during the day. During three months spent in Africa, with nearly every day spent in the field, I saw only 14 snakes, mostly very fleetingly, and hundreds of lizards. During nine weeks in the rich forests of Malaysia I saw only a single snake. This seems to be typical of rain forests in general, despite their being the richest areas on earth for snakes.

On several occasions, however, I have seen up to eight snakes all lying together in a tangled heap, and have been surrounded by poisonous snakes. This was not in the tropics but in Britain, with its three species of snake. However, of these three the Adder (*Vipera berus*) is fond of basking in groups in springtime and I was fortunate to discover a favourite spot on a pile of stones in the Cotswolds. Standing in full view against the skyline I was able to approach to within a foot, and I was able to photograph courtship and mating as well as basking. Large aggregations of snakes may also be found in North America, especially garter snakes emerging from hibernation.

European Grass Snakes (*Natrix natrix*) are most often found near water, where they chiefly prey on frogs. Basking grass snakes and some others often resemble a coil of rope which someone has left on the grass. I have missed pictures several times because I have failed to realise in time the true nature of the 'rope'. Like many snakes, grass snakes will bask day after day outside the same hole, so once such a spot is discovered, it is the most reliable way of obtaining pictures. Grass snakes exude an evil-smelling fluid when handled, which is extremely difficult to wash off. Unless you are experienced you should never handle poisonous snakes without adequate supervision or effective protective clothing. The bite of some snakes can kill a man, and at the very least you may lose a limb or be severely disfigured, a high price to pay for a few extra photographs.

A short telephoto or zoom lens is best for snakes, especially for poisonous kinds when a close approach with a 55mm lens would be courting disaster. Luckily most snakes have one main line of defence – retreat. This makes getting bitten unlikely, but it also reduces your chance of taking pictures. If you are lucky you may come across a snake which has just fed, making it reluctant to move very far. Newly fed snakes usually contain a fairly obvious bulge and often allow a close careful approach. But do not hurry, as otherwise they may regurgitate their prey and, thus lightened, make off at a rapid pace.

Terrapins, tortoises and crocodilians
Tortoises are common in certain areas, especially in semi-desert. They are easy to approach, but normally retract their heads into their shells and may be very reluctant to re-emerge. A long wait may be rewarded, but sometimes it is better to give up. Terrapins spend most of their time in water, but a really stealthy approach may be successful for photographing them basking on the bank. Crocodiles and alligators should always be approached with extreme caution. In Africa, man is still a regular item on the crocodile's menu, so ensure that you are not on it. Large crocodilians can move at an incredible speed, so do not be deceived by their lethargic manner. A telephoto lens is definitely required and is much safer. Approaching closely with a shorter lens would be extremely foolhardy.

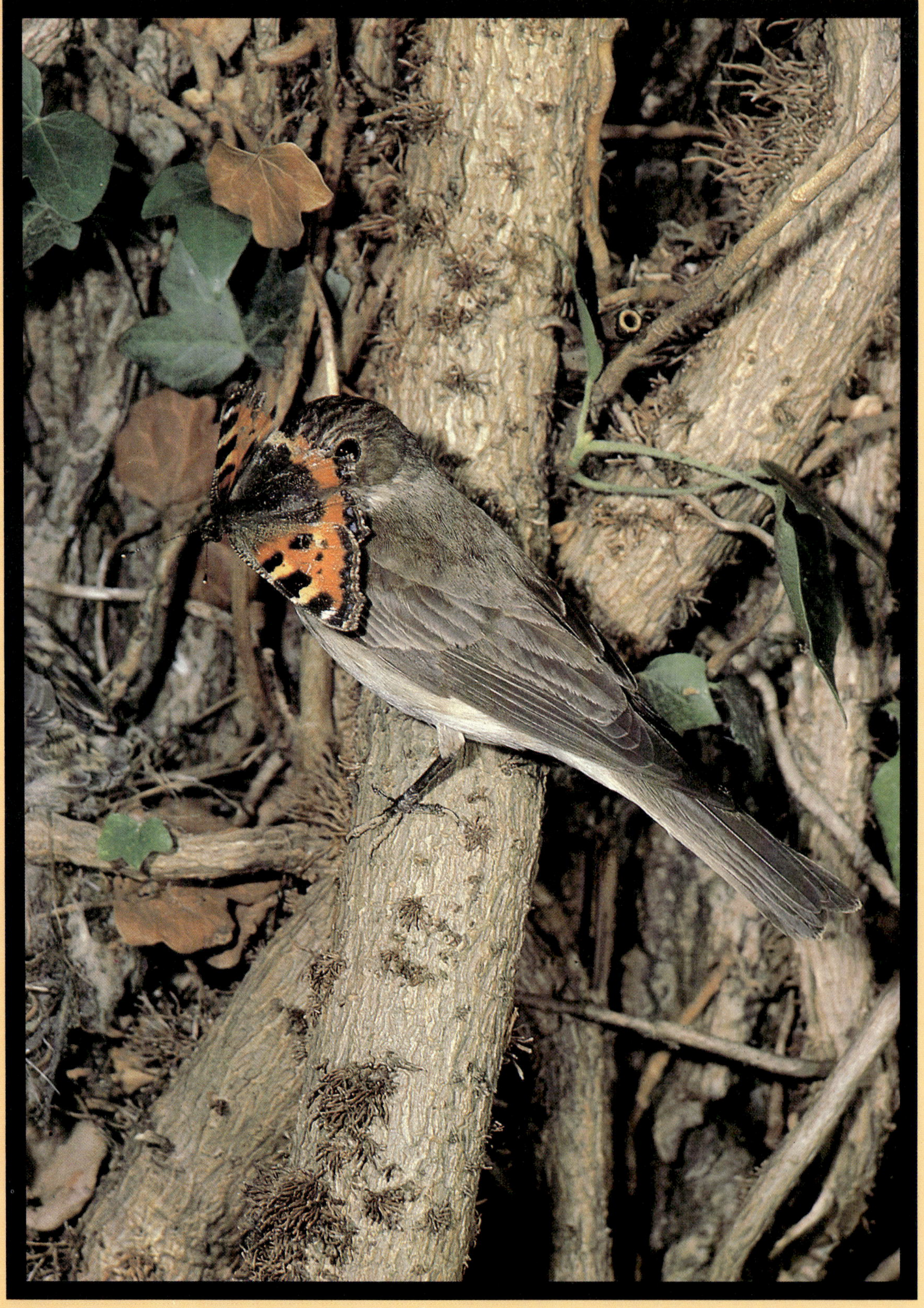

8 Birds

I must stress that I am not really a bird photographer, although I have photographed birds. The reasons for my lack of experience are mainly due to the nature of bird photography and the type of person who makes a success of it. Perhaps more than in any other branch of wildlife work, obtaining high quality pictures of wild birds requires a great deal of careful preparation, allied to a knowledge of the habits and likely whereabouts of the birds themselves. Once everything is ready and photography can begin, lengthy periods must often be spent in one spot before anything worthwhile can be achieved. A series of photographs of birds at the nest, from laying the eggs to the moment when the young birds leave, may take several weeks of careful and constant work. Several hours each day for many days will probably have to be spent in the confines of a hide, with the only view of the outside world through the lens of a camera or small peepholes.

This requires a great deal of dedication, which I lack, and this is why I have never really become involved in photographing birds. Above all, for real success it is vital to love birds. I do like birds and enjoy watching and listening to them, but I could never spend long hours confined in a hide, thereby sacrificing my freedom to observe and photograph all the other interesting types of wildlife outside. Insect photographers can photograph plants and other organisms in addition to their main interest, and so can plant photographers. Bird photographers are often forced to concentrate entirely on birds and are able to devote only relatively small amounts of time to other subjects. Therefore, although I have myself used most of the techniques described, this chapter is mainly a resumé of advice given by more dedicated bird photographers.

Birds figure constantly in the lives of most of us, but we become so used to seeing and hearing them that we take them for granted. Although they so frequently live close to man few wild birds, except those in isolated areas such as islands, are tame enough to allow a close approach for photography. To capture birds on film, therefore, usually requires the use of telephoto lenses or some form of concealment. The most frequently photographed aspect of avian behaviour has always been the brooding and feeding of young at the nest, for at this time the parent birds return repeatedly to the same spot. This makes it fairly simple to know with certainty where the birds will be. Photographing birds away from the nest is now becoming more popular and has been simplified by the advent of high quality but lightweight 35mm SLRs and telephoto lenses. These permit the photography of other activities such as feeding, singing, displaying, mating and preening, so that it becomes possible to build up a collection of pictures depicting the complete way of life of an individual species.

In Europe and North America, most birds have long ago been photographed comprehensively at the nest, so bird photographers are now attempting to record other aspects of behaviour. The situation in most of the tropics is quite different and relatively few good quality colour pictures are available, even of nesting birds in Africa, Asia and South America.

Although birds are strongly attached to their eggs and young, they are basically timid animals with an inborn fear of man. It is always possible that certain birds may be driven to desert their nests if the attentions of a photographer are too aggressively persistent. Causing a pair of birds to desert their nest is an unforgivable act, and helps to bring bird photography into disrepute. Many birds in various countries are stringently protected by law and it may be illegal even to attempt to photograph them while nesting, at least without a permit. Before starting out to photograph nesting birds, always ensure that you are acting within the legal as well as the moral code. Beginners should always serve an apprenticeship on the commoner birds, such as sparrows and pigeons, before moving on to the less common subjects. There are often, in fact, far more high-quality pictures of rare and therefore highly-prized birds than of common garden birds, which are ignored just because they *are* common.

Equipment for bird photography

When choosing a camera for bird photography remember that the shape of most birds is more suited to a rectangular than to a square format. For action photography the light weight and flexibility of a 35mm SLR is more attractive than a larger format. Photography from a hide entails the use of a tripod, so a heavier camera of larger format can be used. For general bird photography these days most people seem to use 35mm, which has the advantage of light weight, great flexibility, a vast choice of accessories and bargain prices. If possible choose a model

which offers interchangeable focusing screens, as split-image
rangefinders will not function with longer telephoto lenses. A
plain ground-glass screen is the best. A shutter speed of at least
1/000 sec should be available for action shots. Telephoto lenses
with an automatic diaphragm are preferable to preset types
which are slower to use. The extra cost is well worthwhile.
Modern 500mm and 1000mm mirror lenses are very short,
compact and lightweight. Their disadvantage is that they have a
fixed aperture, so carefully weigh up the pros and cons of
mirror versus ordinary telephotos before making a choice.
Modern zoom lenses are of very high quality. Many of them are
better than the best 'standard' lenses of only a few years ago.
Zooms permit framing of a whole nest and its occupants as well
as close-ups of the parents without changing lenses and risking
disturbance to the birds. A friend of mine, a well-known bird-
photographer, uses a 70–210mm zoom for most of his
hidework. The quality is superb, even on large monochrome
enlargements.

A tripod is vital, and should be equipped with a pan and tilt
head rather than a ball and socket. It is false economy to save
money and weight by purchasing a cheap lightweight model, as
a camera with only a modest telephoto or zoom needs a sturdy
support if camera shake is to be avoided.

Most photographers working from hides seem to use
electronic flash, either as the main or as fill-in lighting. While a
single small unit is sufficient for close-ups of plants or insects,
bird photography demands a higher-powered unit with its flash-
heads separate from the charging unit. You can then keep the
charger in the hide with you while the flash-heads (usually two)
are mounted outside closer to the subject. This is essential, as
the birds will be disturbed if your hand appears from the hide
every time you want to switch on the flash unit.

For photographing smaller birds with longer telephotos, a
bellows unit or extension tubes are necessary, otherwise the bird
will appear very small in the picture, even with the lens set on
its minimum focus. Despite the extra cost, a bellows unit is
probably preferable, as it permits constant and rapid adjustment
in magnification as your subject moves around. If you manage
to approach more closely than you had thought possible, it is
infuriating to find that you have to risk losing the subject while
changing the length of an extension ring.

Photography from a hide
The first requirement is obviously the construction of a suitable
hide. I constructed my hide from strong hessian cloth and four

broom handles, but metal uprights are lighter and more popular. Nurses' sleeves were sewn into three sides to take the lens, and some small peepholes cut. The entry flap is at the rear and can be tied down, whether or not the hide is occupied. I dyed the material dark green so that it blended in with the woodland surroundings. This is to make it more difficult for inquisitive humans to spot, the birds themselves not being especially fussy about colours. Ensure that the material is opaque, so that your movements inside are not revealed in silhouette. The material should not be of a kind which rustles in the wind, as this disturbs the more nervous kinds of bird. Have four strong guy ropes handy to attach to the corners in case of strong winds and sew some polythene into the roof so that you do not get soaked when it rains.

Setting up the hide   The most tricky part is probably finding the nest in the first place. People who are really familiar with the varied aspects of bird behaviour and who know their subjects intimately are in a better position to spot the clues to a nesting-site. Even then, some people are better than others at finding nests and a great deal of searching may be necessary before success is achieved. If a bird cannot be spotted singing near a nest or returning with food, the only way to locate the spot may be to walk up and down over a suitable area until a sitting bird is flushed. Needless to say, this should not be attempted in areas where damage to the habitat may result.

Once a nest is located, erect the hide at some distance and then gradually move it closer each day until within shooting distance. The final distance depends on the size of bird to be photographed, the length of lens in use and the power of the flash units (if any). The length of time needed to move the hide up to the nest also varies, depending on the tameness or otherwise of your subjects, but it should never be hurried, even if time is short, especially if the birds seem liable to desert their nest. Most birds completely ignore hides. Their shape may look angular, ugly and unnatural to us, but apparently not to the birds. An important point when selecting a suitable nest for photography is whether or not the hide, and therefore the nest, may be subject to human interference. Lack of disturbance is obviously impossible to guarantee, but conspicuous spots near roads or footpaths are best avoided. Nature reserves and enclosed private land (with the owner's consent) are good places for bird photography. When in doubt, it may be worth camouflaging the hide throughly with suitable local vegetation.

Using the hide   Some nests are totally unsuitable for photography, being buried deep inside vegetation which would

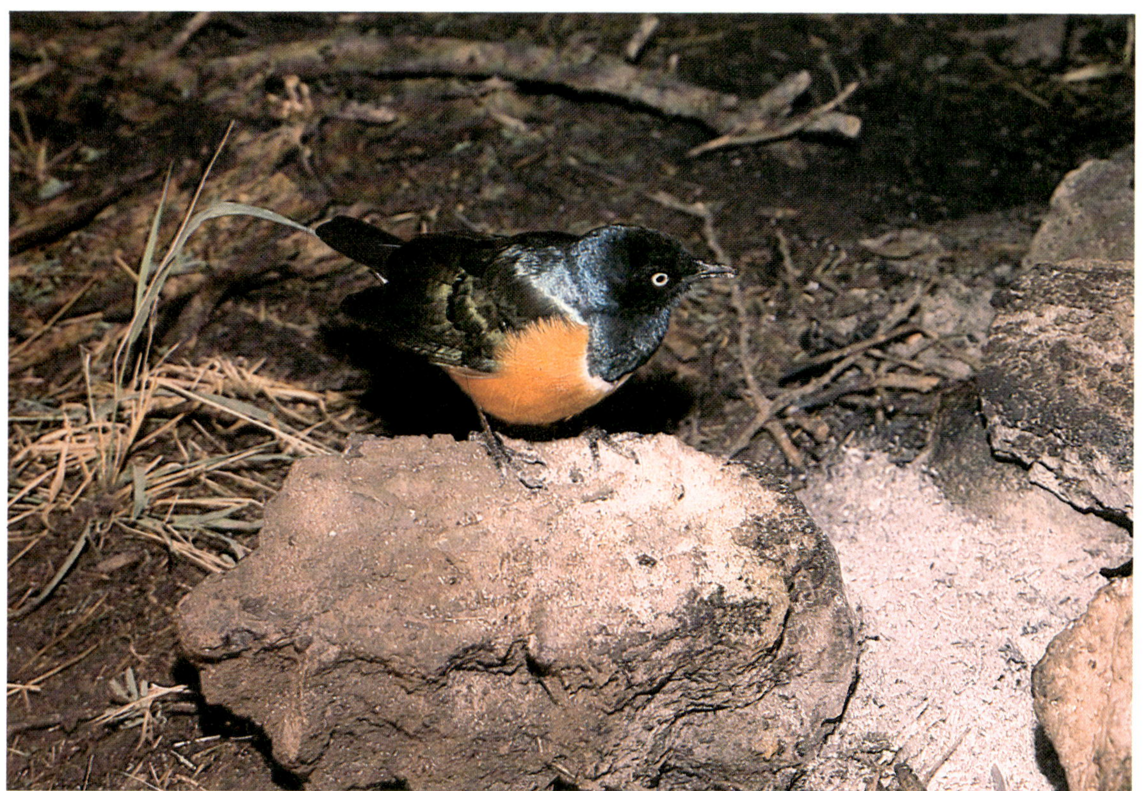

need wholesale removal to open the nest sufficiently for photography. Try to choose a site requiring little gardening. If possible nothing at all should be cut, but should be tied carefully back with green or brown string. Some vegetation in front of the nest may have to be cut, but this should be kept to a minimum, as otherwise the sun may roast the fledglings, as well as rendering the nest more obvious to predators. Whenever possible you should have a companion when you enter or leave the hide, as birds cannot count, and will think that the danger has passed when one person leaves. Working alone is possible but may place more stress on the birds and gives you less time to work as it takes them longer to resume their normal behaviour. Remember that anything which keeps the birds away from the nest places the young at risk from heat-stroke, cold or lack of food, depending on circumstances, and should be avoided at all costs.

Once inside the hide settle down on a comfortable stool, as it is not usually worth spending short periods in the hide, and a cramped and uncomfortable photographer is likely to lack the keenness necessary for the best results. Bird photography normally involves taking an excess of pictures. Hundreds of shots at a nest over a period of weeks may be required for the selection of a few really good ones. Never try to economise on film which always works out far less expensive than your time and effort in getting the pictures. Ensure that you always have plenty of spare film with you in the hide.

Before starting to shoot let the parents make several visits to the nest, to ensure that they have completely recovered from the disturbance caused when you entered the hide and that they are behaving naturally. A nervous animal always shows its tension by the way it moves and holds its body, so too much haste will only gain you a set of unrepresentative pictures of overstressed birds. Certain cameras have incredibly noisy shutters and mirrors. Some birds almost shoot off the nest when they first hear this and may never get used to it, in which case you will have to blimp the camera with a sound-absorbent cushion or else choose a different subject.

Most people try to shoot a series at the nest, including brooding the eggs, feeding the young, the male feeding the female, removing faecal pellets and the young birds fledging and leaving the nest. Many photographers place a convenient natural perch nearby on which the food-laden parents will often alight on their way to the nest. This enables variation to be included in a sequence of the parents actually at the nest.

In most situations flash is necessary, as it gives even lighting, an adequate depth of field and freezes the rapid motion of the birds so that shooting can take place at any time. Flash is obviously essential where the light is poor, such as in dark woodlands, and at night. Two flash-heads can be mounted on separate stands on either side of the nest, one slightly closer than the other to provide modelling and eliminate harsh shadows.

For birds which nest high in trees a pylon hide has to be constructed near the nest. This is a lengthy and complicated task, and should not be attempted until considerable experience has been gained with nests at lower levels.

Bird colonies

Seabirds frequently nest in densely packed colonies, often on offshore islands, where they may be extremely tame, allowing photography without a hide. Many of the better-known islands have hides overlooking the colonies, so that photographers can operate in comfort and without taking risks. When taking pictures of large colonies use a tripod and wide-angle lens with a slow speed and small aperture, so that nesting birds from just in front of the camera to the far distance are all in focus. A seabird colony presents unrivalled opportunities for photographing avian behaviour, such as greeting displays between pairs, quarrelling, fishing and flying.

Using bait

With the growing popularity of photographing birds away from the nest, bait is often useful to attract them within camera range. Food is the most obvious bait, but nesting materials may be useful and artificial drinking places are also effective. One favoured method of providing food is to bore holes in sticks and fill them with fat or sunflower seeds. Birds such as tits are attracted by such methods and it should be possible to obtain pictures without the bait being visible. Water can be provided by sinking a shallow container into the ground, concealing its edges with soil and vegetation. The British bird photographer, Mike Wilkes, did this to obtain his award-winning picture of a nightingale bathing, a picture which took many weeks of patient hide-work to achieve. Scavengers and raptors can be attracted by pegging-down a dead rabbit or sheep. Most published pictures of such birds feeding are obtained in this way. It is also possible to attract male birds to within camera-range by playing a tape-recording of their song. This method should be especially worthwhile in tropical rain forests, where many brilliantly plumaged birds are heard but seldom seen.

As well as using artificial baits, photographers can also use the wait and see method at various natural assembly points. Natural water attracts many birds, so a small pond is always worth watching. Waders can be photographed from a hide at low tide, and then again as they assemble at roosts at high tide.

Watching the feeding habits of smaller birds may also be worthwhile. In autumn many birds, especially thrushes and blackbirds, are attracted to berried trees. In Britain elder, hawthorn and rowan are very popular and are sometimes full of greedily feeding birds. In the Americas, hummingbirds visit tubular flowers in gardens. A hide can be erected near a favoured plant, and the birds can be encouraged to spend longer on your chosen flower if you fill it with a small amount of honeyed water. In Africa and Asia, sunbirds visit flowers in gardens, and a similar approach should be tried.

Perhaps the best place to gain experience in wait-and-see photography is in your garden, where birds can be attracted within camera range by a bird-table or bath. The food or water will attract the birds to a suitably placed perch where they can be photographed against a natural-looking background. If the table or bath are near a window the house itself can be used as a hide and the camera operated from inside the house. For subjects out of range, the camera can be operated by a remote release, or else a hide can be erected in the garden.

Stalking birds

In their attempt to record behaviour away from the nest many photographers stalk birds as they feed or roost. Even with a long telephoto or bellows, you may have to approach small birds to within 15 or 20ft, otherwise they will appear as a dot on the screen. Surprisingly, it is quite possible to approach birds this closely. When stalking with a long lens it is obviously impossible to use a tripod, so if a reasonably fast shutter speed is to be used, a fast colour film is necessary. As with hand-held close-ups, some people are better than others at holding long lenses without camera shake; frequent practice improves results.

Birds in flight

Learning to photograph birds in flight is difficult and will probably result in much waste of expensive colour film. It may be wise to use black and white film for the first few rolls. There are a number of common faults which the beginner makes. With long telephotos the birds usually seem to fill the focusing screen adequately and to be well-centred. However, the results are often quite different and the birds appear as barely discernible dots in various areas of the picture, resembling specks of dust rather than birds. So you have to learn when the bird is close enough to appear at a reasonable size on a slide.

The second problem concerns shutter speeds. Many people feel that speeds of 1/250 sec should be sufficient to freeze any but the fastest flying birds. Unfortunately this is often not the case, and speeds of 1/500 or 1/1000 sec are often required, even for slower fliers, while the faster movers require high-speed flash to stop all signs of movement. Lastly, focusing on flying birds can be a problem, especially as the depth of field when using a fast action-freezing shutter speed is severely limited. Be prepared for disappointing results at first but persevere, for there are few more graceful shots than those of gulls or terns in flight.

Attempt a series of angles, although panning shots as the bird flies by should result in the highest rate of success. Some of the larger waterbirds cannot take off directly from the water, but must first gain flying-speed by running along the surface. This kind of action is easier than pure in-flight photography, and makes a good picture, as do such stately birds as swans as they sweep in a flock low over the surface of a lake or river.

Photography of small birds using action-freezing high-speed flash is a specialised technique outside the scope of this book.

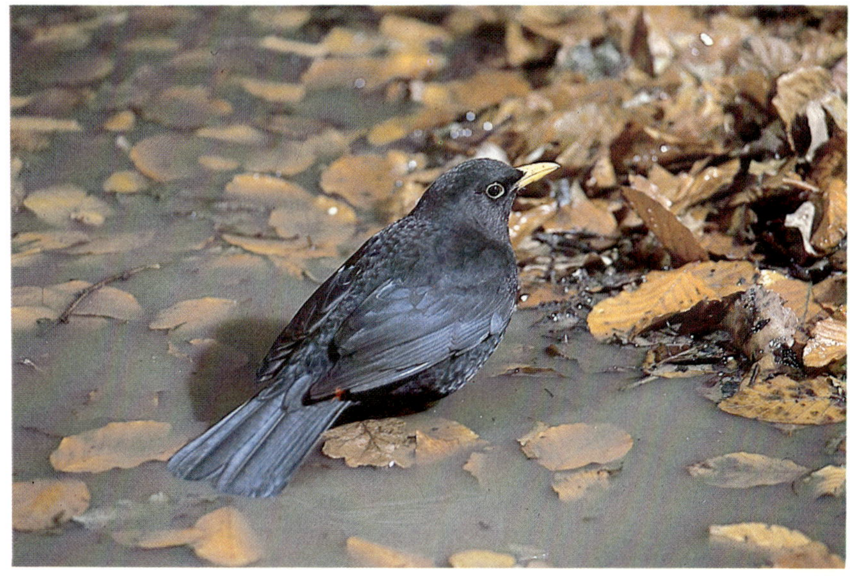

Blackbird bathing. Olympus OM2 with 70–210mm Vivitar zoom from a hide in a wood set up next to an artificial pool. Flash at 6 ft. Mike Wilkes.

Photographing captive birds

As most of the birds of Europe and North America have been photographed extensively in the wild over many years, there is little need to photograph them in captivity. However, the situation in the tropics is very different, particularly in those countries with large areas of rain forest. Here it may be difficult or impossible to locate nests for photography, and there may be inadequate time and limited opportunities for wait-and-see or baiting techniques. As the purpose may be simply to obtain high quality pictures of the plumage and attitude of the living bird, perhaps for the first time, it is often better to take the pictures under controlled conditions. This can be done either in a permanent studio or in a portable tent which can be carried to locations where the birds are found.

In Borneo I spent several days in a reserve where mist-netting of birds was in progress. Each day around 20 birds were caught, and most of these would be of different species. Only rarely were birds of the same species caught on the same day, or even on the following day. This is typical of the tropics, especially south east Asia, where the diversity of species is high but numbers of any one are low. Most of the birds which we saw netted in Borneo were seldom seen in the nearby forest and the warden had not seen some of them during his year's stay.

Captive birds often exhibit behaviour or stance untypical of the species. When kept for any length of time in captivity they may show differences in plumage due to climatic and feeding inadequacies. Any pictures of captive birds should be clearly captioned as such, so that no-one is misled.

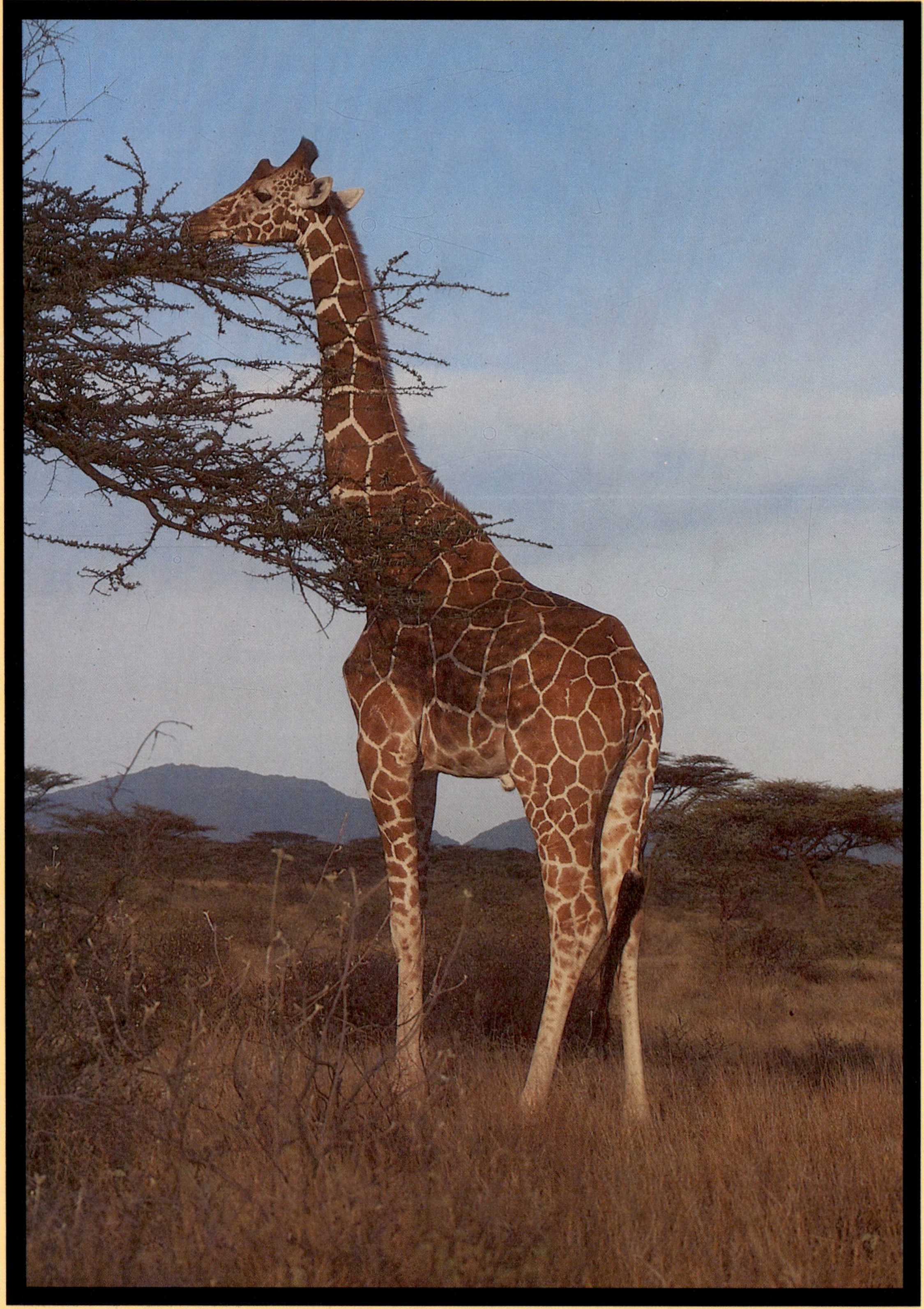

9 Mammals

In the wild, mammals are seen far less often than birds, and most kinds are seldom seen abroad during the day. Herds of large diurnal mammals are rare outside the savannahs of eastern and southern Africa, and the majority of mammals are small, very secretive and often nocturnal. Whereas the lives of birds are dominated by vision, resulting in bright plumage to aid in recognition and courtship, mammals spend most of their lives with their noses to the ground in a world where scent is the most important sense. As scent is normally the major sexual attractant, mammals have never evolved the bright colours of birds, and cryptic greys and brown predominate.

Mammals are highly evolved, warm-blooded, fur-bearing animals and the young are suckled on milk from the female's body. There is often some confusion as to the correct usage of the word mammal. The word 'animal' is often used incorrectly to describe mammals as distinct from birds and insects. Both the latter groups are, of course, also animals.

The 'big game' animals of Africa are perhaps the most rewarding and exciting of all natural history subjects. However, taking pictures of the great herds of antelope or zebra on the plains of east Africa is such a different experience from photographing any other kinds of mammal that I have given them a section of their own: 'Safari photography'.

Most smaller mammals are extremely difficult to photograph adequately in the wild. Many of them are small and nocturnal, often live high up in forest trees, seldom return to the same place twice (not having to return constantly to a nest), are highly agile and extremely wary, their sense of smell and hearing both being acutely developed. Mammals, therefore, generally require a quite different approach from birds, and are one subject which is often best covered in the studio under controlled conditions.

Finding wild mammals

Britain has an impoverished mammal fauna, with only about 40 native terrestrial species. Europe is much richer, with exciting species such as bear, lynx, ibex, chamois, bison, wolf and

"

beaver. North America may have lost its vast herds of bison
roaming across the prairies but there are remnant herds as well
as moose, elk, pronghorn, various deer, cougar, bobcat, several
kinds of bear, bighorn sheep, skunks, porcupine and many
more.

Generally speaking, relatively few mammals in temperate
conditions can be photographed in a chance encounter, for their
senses are far superior to our own. A fleeting glimpse of a tail
or a rustle of vegetation is normally the only evidence of their
presence. Knowing your subject's habits is the best way to
increase the chances of obtaining successful pictures. Get to
know where and when the animals habitually feed. Many
mammals are creatures of habit, rabbits for example, come out
to feed at approximately the same time every day. Some forest
monkeys have a regular 'beat' through the tree tops and can be
photographed crossing roads or feeding in certain trees at the
same time each day. Time spent observing wild mammals
through binoculars and taking careful notes will be worth the
effort when it comes to taking pictures. In the mating season
some male animals, such as stags, gather together a harem of
females, staying within a well-defined territory. The fruit of
certain tropical trees is eagerly sought by monkeys and the
location of feeding groups can be ascertained by listening for
their noisy chatter and crashing sounds as they move around.
Many of the most outstanding and biologically unusual pictures
of diurnal wild mammals have been taken by research workers
who spend almost every day for perhaps one or two years
following and recording the activities of their study-species. The
group being followed often learns to recognise this constant
companion and eventually becomes used to close human
presence. In this way superb pictures have been obtained of
unusual and seldom-photographed activities in, amongst others,
mountain gorillas, baboons and bighorn sheep.

In desert areas water is a powerful lure for many birds and
mammals, enabling you to set up a camera and hide at a
predetermined spot which you know will be visited regularly by
certain species. While some animals may drink in the early
morning or late evening, others only come at night, posing the
usual problems involved in night-time photography (see below).
Some of the small desert rodents obtain all the water they need
from their food and so cannot be photographed at water, in
which case they may be attracted to suitable bait such as
sunflower seeds. Bait can be used for various mammals, but be
careful when handling it as the human scent may deter your
quarry. Many small mammals such as pikas and hyraxes can be

carefully stalked in the open using a long telephoto as they sit among rocks. An open stalk can even be successful for rabbits and hares, especially in the mating season. At this time I have had a pair of hares run by within a few feet of me, both totally ignoring my presence. This is indicative of the way in which on occasion certain mammals may be unusually tame. Several years ago I stood in full view as a family of seven stoats played and gambolled in the grass only a metre or two away. Now and again one would sit up on its hind legs to study me, but generally I was completely ignored. Needless to say I had no suitable camera equipment with me, which shows that you should *always* be prepared.

Some mammals, such as rabbits and prairie dogs, can be photographed from a hide. Remember to position the hide downwind so that your scent does not betray your presence. Squirrels make excellent subjects and can be attracted to nuts put out for them on a suitable stump or log and photographed against a neutral background, using a hide or from a concealed position in the house.

Equipment for photographing diurnal mammals
If you are going to do much stalking a proper military style camouflage outfit would be useful. At the very least wear a green jacket of a non-rustling material. If you are stalking from downwind an animal cannot detect your scent. However, it can immediately identify you as human, and therefore dangerous, by your characteristic upright stance. As the only two-legged animal man is instantly recognisable. Stalking on all fours enables a slightly closer approach to certain mammals and draping yourself in an 'animal' costume to disguise your most obvious characteristics may also help. This will not fool your subjects, but it may make them curious about the nature of the unfamiliar creature approaching them, so that they stay a few vital moments longer before fleeing.

A 35mm camera is best when stalking because of its light weight and range of accessories. A good lightweight automatic telephoto lens is essential. A zoom is especially useful as it enables you to take groups of animals as well as close-ups of individuals without changing lenses. As with birds, many of your first pictures will prove to have been taken from too far away. It takes time to learn when the frame is correctly filled when using long telephotos. It is sometimes possible to shoot from behind suitable natural objects such as tree trunks, fences and bales of hay. In these cases it helps to cover your face with a camouflaged mask, with the outline of the head broken up by tying on pieces of vegetation. This may make you look silly, but anything which helps to conceal the typical aspects of the feared human form is worth trying. A good lightweight pair of binoculars is invaluable for spotting the animals and discerning what they are doing. Successful photography of mammals requires a great deal of dedication allied to an intimate knowledge of the subjects. Like bird photographers, mammal photographers do tend of necessity to be specialists.

Nocturnal mammals
Most small and some larger mammals are exclusively nocturnal, although they may occasionally be seen in daylight towards sundown and in the early morning. In Britain the most popular nocturnal mammals for photography are undoubtedly badgers. The advantage for the photographer is that badgers live in a precise spot in a burrow or 'set' where they may be found throughout the year. Even so, watching and photographing badgers can be a cold, cramped and very frustrating occupation, often requiring endless patience and dedication. All too often the animals do not put in an appearance on the night you are there, or else they spend the whole time playing and feeding temptingly out of camera range. The best shots of wild badgers have been obtained when regular visits over a long period have accustomed a particular group to the presence of the photographer, usually assisted by the regular provision of food. This ploy also works with foxes.

At night focusing has to be done by the light of a very dim torch or one with a red transparent covering, badgers' eyes being insensitive to red light. Flash is obviously essential and if working at a fair distance with a short telephoto lens you may require a large bulb to give you adequate light or a powerful and therefore expensive electronic unit. Shooting really first class pictures of badgers requires great patience and many visits, although as in all wildlife work, the beginner may be lucky and come up with some excellent material the first time.

In forested areas in the tropics and in Australia, mammal-spotting is often carried out at night using a head-lamp. The large eyes of nocturnal mammals will reflect its light from quite a distance. Some creatures are 'mesmerised' by the bright light and can be photographed as they sit on a branch, although their attitude will be rather unnatural as they stare fixedly at the torch. This method is probably more useful for collecting arboreal nocturnal mammals for later photography in the studio.

At night some mammals become extremely vocal, and I have

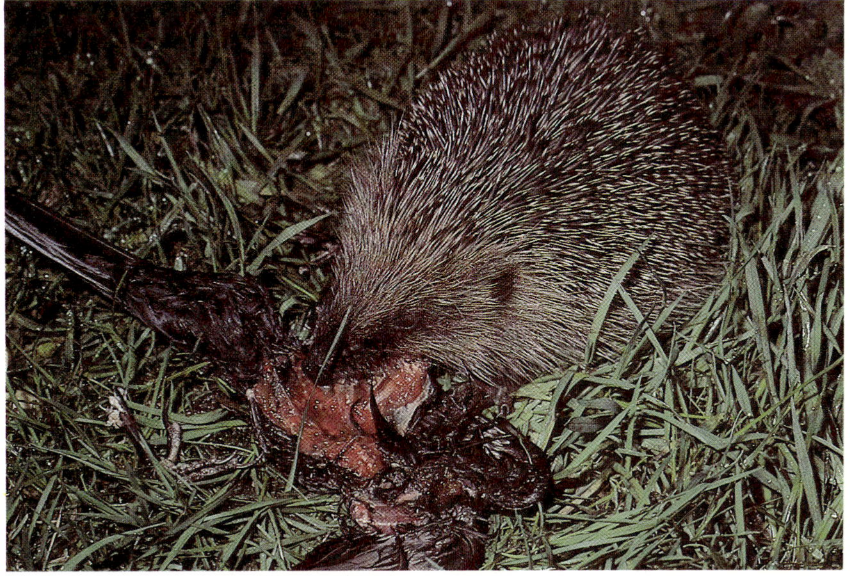

been awakened when sleeping under canvas in Africa by the unearthly screaming of bushbabies in the trees above my tent. Needless to say, as soon as I carefully ventured outside with a camera and a torch everything became deathly quiet. Voles and mice feed mainly at night and can be attracted to regularly placed bait. They are not easy to photograph to a high standard in this way, however, and the best results are usually attained in the studio. In the forest at night do not be too hasty in identifying the animals you spot in the light of a torch. A research worker in Malaysia one night spent some time carefully following and recording the movements of a jungle cat which he had spotted some distance away in the beam of his torch. After some time the cat suddenly switched on a torch and began walking towards the researcher! The 'jungle cat' was a fellow scientist who was also conducting nocturnal studies!

Safari photography
Fortunately these days 'shooting' usually means with a camera rather than a high-powered rifle. A visit to the national parks of East Africa is probably the most vivid and exciting experience for any naturalist. Although the big game animals do not occur in anything like the numbers of a century ago, it is still awesome to see herds of thousands of wild animals. On many occasions it is even possible to approach to within a few yards without frightening them away. Insects were my chief quarry on my first trip to Kenya, and I had intended to spend little time on the larger game, which has already been so well covered by more experienced mammal photographers. In addition I have

never been much inspired by mammals, which is perhaps
understandable when you live in Britain. I was therefore totally
unprepared for my reaction to the sheer beauty and grace of
most of the larger African game. Animals such as the
Thomson's Gazelle proved to be so beautiful that I simply sat
and gazed for ages, totally enthralled by their wonderful
daintiness and elegance. It is virtually impossible to avoid
becoming 'hooked' on these animals and I am sure that on my
next visit to Africa I shall devote more time than I should to
photographing and watching them. It is worth remembering,
however, that East African big game is not really the ideal
subject if your primary intention is to sell your pictures. It has
been photographed almost to saturation over many years, and
there are several extremely talented photographers permanently
resident there. These people have many advantages over the
casual visitor, having had far more time to devote to mammal
photography. They consequently have an intimate knowledge of
their subjects, making it easier for them to be in the right place
at the right time for that exceptional picture. But regardless of
commercial considerations, the parks of East and South Africa,
such as the Kruger, are worth a visit purely for the pleasure of
seeing the large numbers of lovely animals roaming the wide-
open savannahs of their natural home. No English safari park
could ever be quite the same.

What to do and how to do it on safari   Whether you go on an
organised safari or plan the trip yourself you will need a vehicle,
as without one you will not be allowed into most parks. A
vehicle also acts as a mobile hide and as long as you stay inside
(leaving the vehicle within a park, except at certain places, is
strictly illegal) most animals completely ignore your presence,
however enthusiastically you may be brandishing a large
telephoto lens in their direction. In some of the less visited parks
the animals are not so used to visitors and they may stop
feeding and amble away as soon as you stop the engine, which
is absolutely essential to avoid vibration with long lenses. In the
more popular parks most game continue feeding quite
unconcernedly within a few feet of the car while you snap
away.

   At first, most people find it impossible to resist shooting
masses of film every time any kind of animal appears on the
horizon. Many of these first pictures are taken from too great a
distance, and this soon ceases when experience teaches you just
how closely you can approach your quarry when you are in a
car. You then become more selective, taking time to choose the
best groupings and backgrounds. By force of habit most

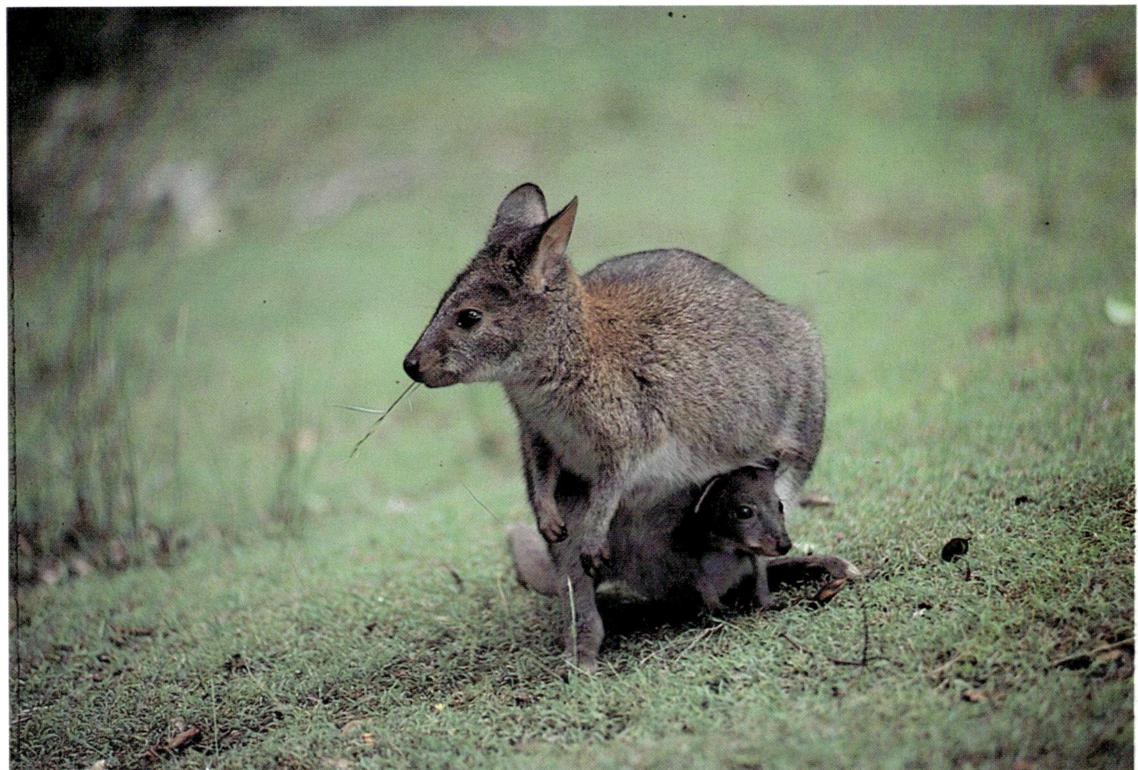

photographers wait for an animal to become still before pressing the shutter, so it is quite easy to forget that pictures of gazelles jumping gracefully or giraffes pounding along may be far more spectacular than animals simply standing around. It is worth wasting some extra film in pursuit of a single really outstanding action shot.

When shooting single animals ensure that there are no others standing behind with just their legs showing, as your subject will appear to have sprouted several extra pairs of legs. In the excitement and novelty of being so close to so many wonderful animals it is also easy to forget the importance of picture composition, particularly the horizon, and many otherwise excellent safari pictures (including too many of mine) are ruined because the animals and trees are all apparently leaning precariously on steeply-sloping ground. When using a telephoto in the dry season, the dark animals on the bleached grasses give very difficult lighting conditions. A TTL meter cannot compensate for such lighting and the grass usually appears very burnt out. Bear this in mind when using TTL or automatic cameras, or try using an incident light meter which is excellent for the cloudless skies of Africa.

As more time is spent with the animals you will increasingly want to record aspects of their behaviour, such as feeding, courtship, mating and fighting. Even the way a topi stretches when it stands up is worth a picture, or buffaloes wallowing in a muddy pool. Always be on the lookout for any less obvious aspects of behaviour which you may have missed. Really think hard about why you are taking a particular photograph before pressing the shutter.

Even though you will undoubtedly want some close-ups of each new species as it is encountered, do not constantly keep a long telephoto on the camera. Pictures showing the animals in their natural habitat are often far more attractive and instructive than an unbroken series of close-ups which could have been taken in a zoo. I found my 70–210mm zoom lens especially useful when working from the car, as it permitted both close-ups of single animals and pictures of the whole herd without changing lenses or having to start the engine and move the car. Remember that zooms are very prone to flare in difficult lighting conditions, so always use the largest lens hood possible and keep an eye on the direction of the lighting.

In a car it is so easy to approach large wild animals to within a few feet that there is a danger of forgetting that they *are* wild and therefore potentially dangerous. The laws against leaving your vehicle are made for the benefit of both animals and humans and should never be broken in an attempt to stalk game on foot. Leaving the car usually results in a mass exodus of any game, so there is little to gain and everything to lose. Outside the parks, or under expert guidance within them, it is possible to stalk game on foot or on horseback, but this is certainly not for the inexperienced working alone. Even the smaller antelopes can effortlessly outrun a man and you then realise just how far you have strayed from your vehicle in pursuit of yet closer pictures. Even when photographing insects outside the parks I always kept a careful eye on groups of trees or dense scrub which might harbour elephants or buffalo. Many people in Africa are still killed and maimed every year by animals which are surprised at close quarters, resulting in a murderous charge rather than panic flight.

During the middle of the day most animals avoid the heat by retreating to the shade of bushes and trees. Groups of impala or waterbuck can be photographed resting in the dappled shade, but for action shots of a variety of animals early morning and late evening are the best times. Unfortunately this means less light for photography and this is just one of the annoying little problems with which you will have to learn to cope. During the rainy season many animals are active in the open throughout the day but are far more difficult to spot in the long lush grass. In the wet season most of the game leave the parks and spread out over a huge area feeding on the plentiful grass, so if you intend to visit East Africa specifically for game, go in the dry season. There will then be more tourists and vehicles around to get in your way and spoil your sense of getting away from it all in the 'wilds', but at least the animals will be more concentrated and easier to see among the shorter dead grasses. Even in the busiest season the larger parks have plenty of backroads where few vehicles go and you can spend the day in peace. From July to around early January is usually a good time to visit East Africa for game, as it is usually fairly dry for most of this period, and parks such as Masai Mara in Kenya will have massive concentrations of game.

Mammals in captivity

Most of the published pictures of many smaller and some larger mammals such as rodents are taken in captivity in studio conditions. Some of the studio set-ups of mammals which I have seen are sentimentalised or stylised and, as explained in the appendix on ethics, I feel very strongly that all pictures of captive animals should be appropriately captioned to avoid mis-information. This is not to say that studio photography of mammals has no place in recording their appearance and behaviour, which for many species would be impossible in the wild.

Catching them   How you catch your subject obviously depends on how large it is and where you intend to catch it. Anyone interested in reading hilarious but instructive accounts of the complications involved in capturing wild animals for zoos should read Gerald Durrell's various books. To catch certain small animals it may be necessary to smoke them out of tall hollow trees, or else crawl down narrow rock crevices after them. This is obviously not the kind of thing which should be attempted by a novice and apart from possibly harming the animals it is also illegal in many countries. As already stated, in some countries it is illegal to collect *any* wild plant or animal without a permit.

If the intention is to photograph mice or voles these can be caught in a live trap baited with grain. In Britain the Longworth trap is much used for sampling the small mammal fauna of certain areas and is excellent for catching them for photographic purposes. When setting traps always ensure that you can visit them again within a reasonable time, otherwise the unfortunate occupants may starve to death. Small rodents are much more delicate to handle than birds of equivalent size and may have a tendency to expire in your hands if roughly handled, so take care. Traps baited with meat for shrews must be revisited every two or three hours, as shrews have to feed constantly to maintain their very high metabolic rate.

Keeping and photographing them Most small mammals are quite happy kept in a glass-sided vivarium as used for amphibians and reptiles. It is normal to provide a set of natural-looking 'props' in the form of patches of moss, small stumps and branches with fungi on them. If possible, natural food should be left in the same spot each day so that the animal becomes used to sitting there to feed. You should obviously choose a spot which is suitable for the pictures you want. Try to get the animal used to feeding during the day, to avoid the complications of working at night. Once the subject has been introduced to its new home it should soon settle down after thoroughly exploring its strange new territory. Most animals which are kept for long periods become very tame and photographing them will be as simple as taking pictures of your pet hamster or guinea-pig. If the set is only temporary and the subject is to be released quickly, you must at least give it time to settle down and lose the attitude of fear and uncertainty which it will inevitably have after being caught and handled. With timid animals you will need to mount the camera on a tripod with the lens poking through a black mask so that the subject cannot see your movements. The clunk of the shutter and sudden flash as you take the first picture will probably send it scurrying into hiding, but as long as you remain invisible this will soon be ignored.

Electronic flash is generally used to obtain adequate depth of field and overall sharpness for these small subjects. Photofloods are impractical as they give off too much heat and light which are not conducive to natural activity in small nocturnal animals. Use two flash units, one from the front and one from overhead and to one side, to give reasonably natural lighting without dense shadows. This set-up does cause a very unnatural double highlight in the eyes. However, a single flash usually casts unacceptable shadows onto the background, so two flashes are probably the lesser evil.

Studio photography of small active mammals which are not being kept long enough to become tame is certainly no easy option. To obtain really outstanding pictures requires careful and imaginative preparation of the studio and lighting, as well as skill in looking after the living subjects and keeping them in a healthy state.

156

Right: *Aepyceros melampus*, Impala antelope, part of a large herd of females, the harem of one male. Taken in the Masai-Mara Game Reserve, Kenya, during the rainy season.

Right: *Rhynchotragus kirki*, Kirk's Long-snouted Dik-dik. I was able to approach these in the car for shots showing the whole animal, but sometimes a picture is more natural if it shows the more typical pose of this basically shy little animal peeping out from behind long grasses. In Buffalo Springs Game Reserve, Kenya, from a car, 70–210mm Vivitar zoom.

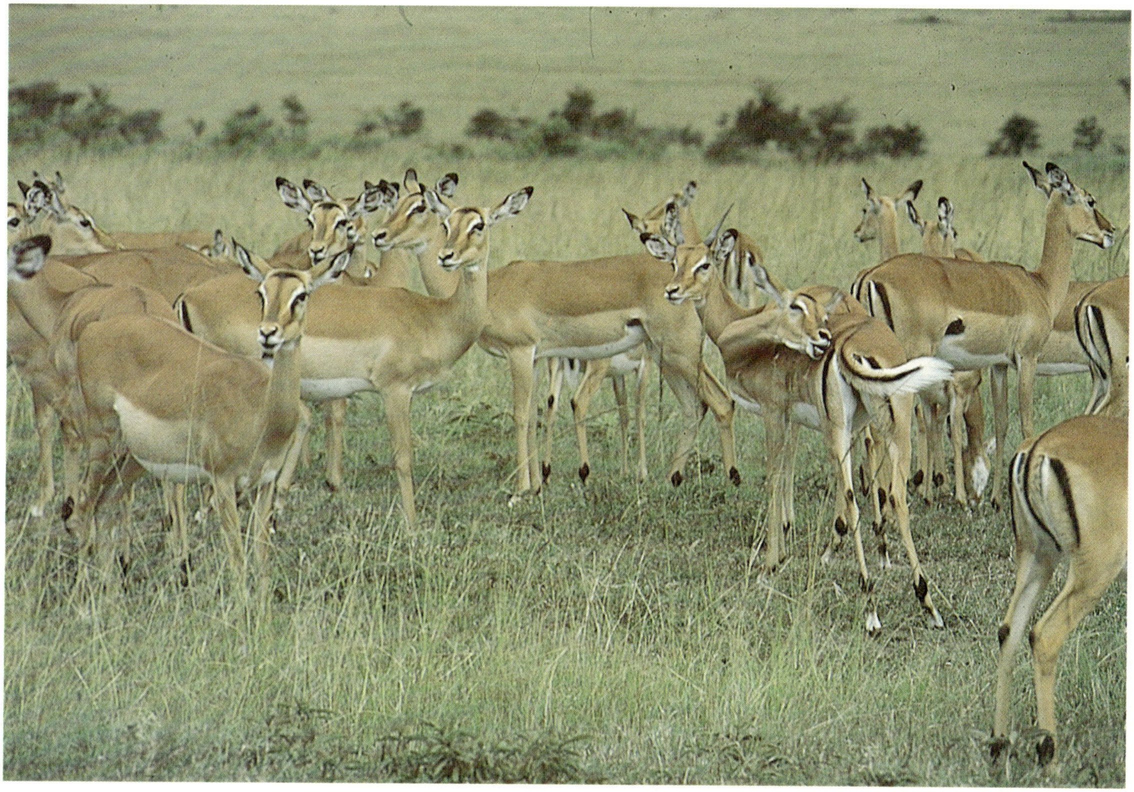

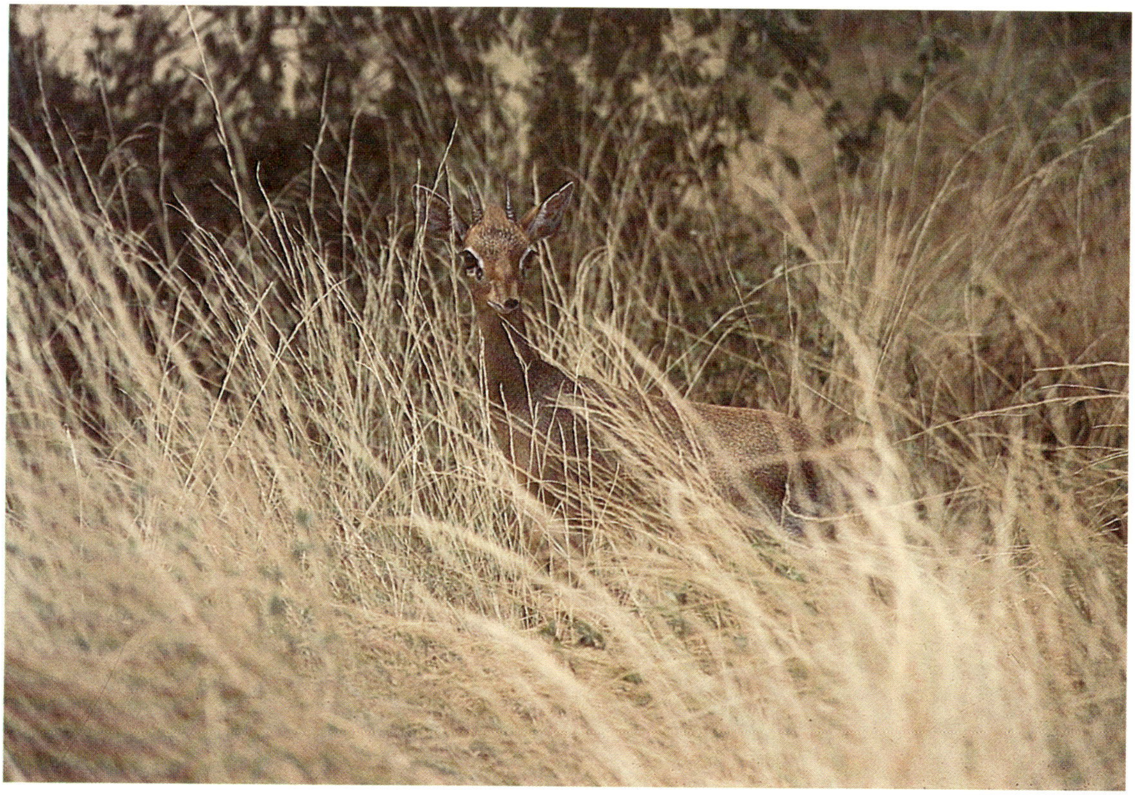

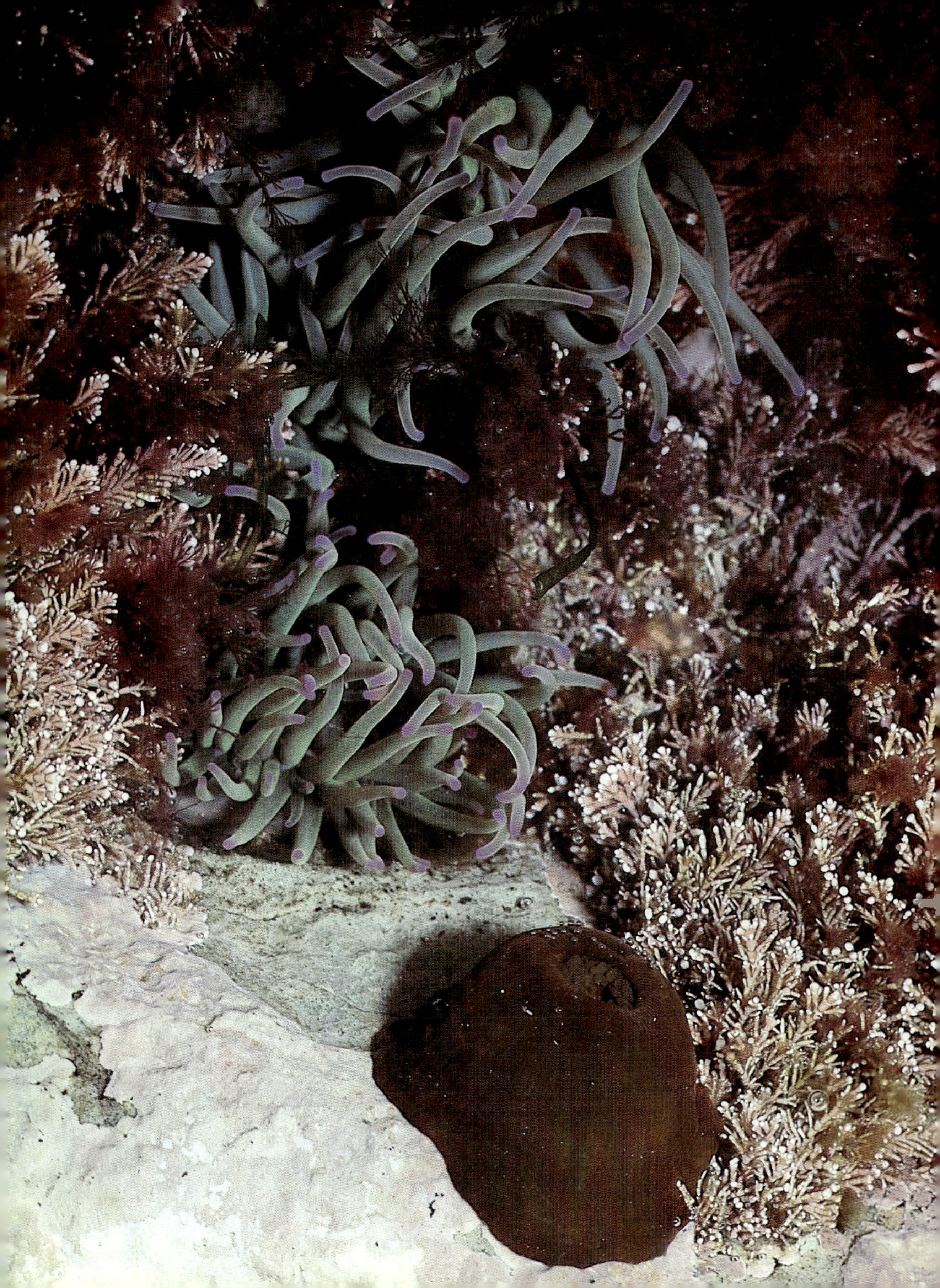

10 The Seashore

Many people reading this book will seldom have access to the seashore and even when a visit is possible, photography of littoral organisms may have to take second place to more typical holiday pursuits. For this reason and also because the majority of marine creatures are seldom exposed above water for long enough to take pictures without specialist equipment, I am keeping this chapter short.

Sandy and muddy shores

In temperate countries these types of shore offer few opportunities for portraying living organisms in their natural habitat. Interesting objects such as shells and the egg-cases of dogfish can be photographed *in situ* along with other flotsam washed-up along the strand-line on sandy beaches. These can be photographed very easily using available light and if necessary a tripod.

In the tropics sandy and muddy shores can be very rich in wildlife, especially if there are large areas of mangrove trees, where crabs of various kinds often occur in large numbers. The stilt-roots of mangroves may form an impenetrable forest on flatter tropical shores, which usually teem with a great variety of life. Mangrove crabs climb up the curved roots, to which are attached various barnacles and shells. As the tide recedes and exposes the wet mud beneath the trees, hoards of fiddler crabs emerge from their burrows to feed on the gleaming mud. Fiddler crabs often occur in thousands with their burrows spaced out only a few inches apart. Photographing these crabs can be a very frustrating occupation. The best approach is to squat facing a burrow with your telephoto or zoom lens focused on a spot a few inches to one side (they always come out at the same spot) and a little above the muddy surfaces. Have your flash unit charged (or light-reading taken if you are in a sunny spot). As soon as the crab sidles out of its burrow and starts to feed simply squeeze the shutter. Fiddler crabs seem to be even more sensitive than most insects to the minutest movements. I have seen them dart back into their burrows in alarm as they detected the slight movement of my finger as it depressed the shutter. At other times they continue to feed as you take a series of pictures. You must ensure that you wind on with extra caution. Unfortunately what usually seems to happen to me is that after a long sweaty wait in an awkward position under the hot tropical sun there are thousands of fiddlers feeding all around me just out of range, while within a 3ft radius of my motionless uncomfortable form there is a circle of bare mud totally innocent of the slightest sign of any crabs.

Male fiddler crabs have one claw greatly enlarged for use in fighting other males and securing a mate. The colour of the claw varies from species to species and is often bright pink or orange. Some species wave this huge claw in a strange circular motion while using their other tiny claw to stuff their mouthparts with food. Some fiddlers are extremely beautiful. In Borneo I saw thousands of brilliant sky-blue ones, all alas completely inaccessible as I was on a boat, the local equivalent of a bus, and could not stop it to photograph crabs. Sandflies can be a real nuisance on tropical shores, especially under mangroves, mainly attacking the wrists and ankles, so smear plenty of insect-repellent on exposed areas of skin.

Muddy tropical shores are also home to numerous other fascinating crabs, such as the manhole crab in Malaysia. As the tide comes in this crab scoops out a circular flattened disc of mud with its claw and then retreats into its burrow, pulling down the disc of mud in a neatly-fitting lid behind it. On some tropical shores large mudskipper fish, up to 1ft long, may be common. These fish can stay out of water and can be found sitting high up on mangrove roots as well as resting on the surface of the mud.

Muddy shores in temperate lands lack these exciting tropical animals and usually present a very drab and uninviting sea of bare mud. All the animals, such as lugworms are burrowing away invisibly beneath your feet, so that photography of their cast faeces is the only approach possible without digging them out for an unnatural picture.

Photography on muddy shores can be a very messy business. In Malaysia two huge 'overshoes' of glutinous mud soon formed around my canvas shoes. This mud is of course saline and has a knack of transferring itself all over your clothes and onto your camera equipment, so always carry a clean rag for wiping it off cameras and lenses. Tripods are at the greatest risk in this habitat, so either hand-hold everything or else tie some plastic bags around the feet of the camera and well up the legs to protect them. Sandy shores have their own problems, for sand always manages to insinuate its way into the insides of the

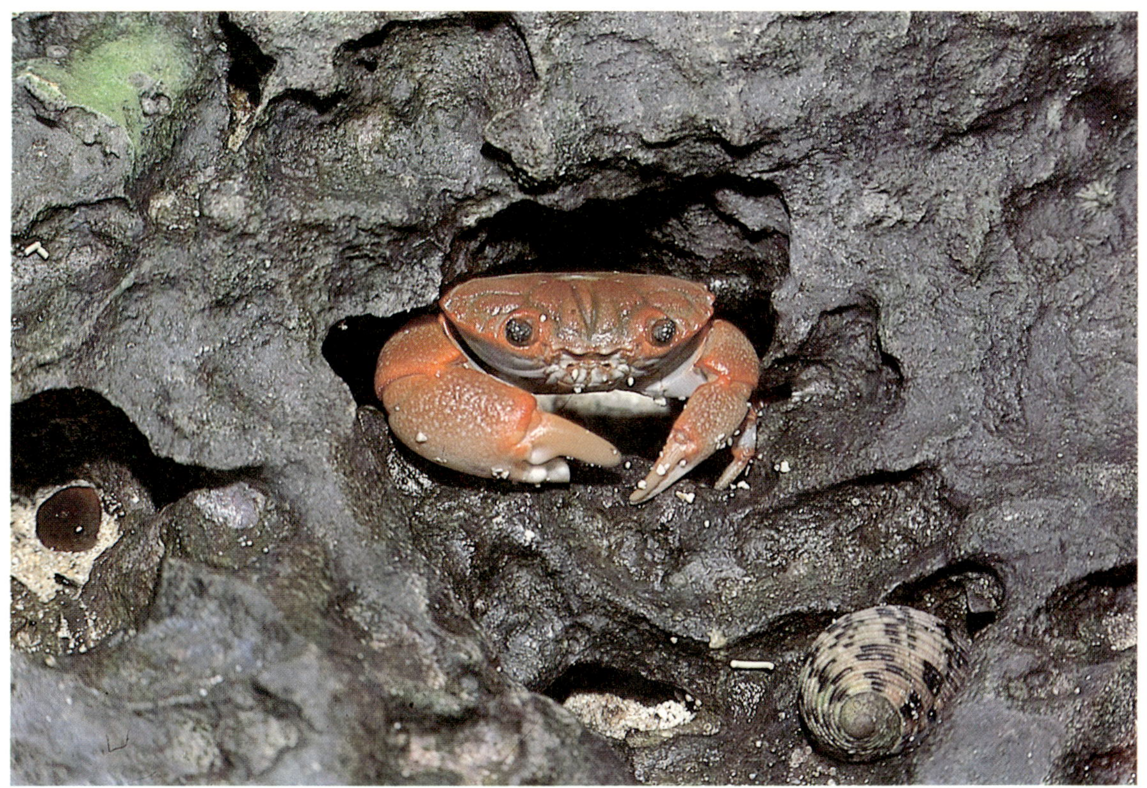

A Xanthid Crab photographed on the Kenyan coast, where they could be spotted peeping out of the pock-marked coral cliffs. This crab is about 2½ in wide; flash.

camera and inside the lens-barrel so that it makes horrible scrunching noises when you focus. If possible never take expensive SLRs onto sandy beaches in windy weather and never handle a camera if you have sand on your hands, something which is difficult to ensure as sand will stick even to a slight film of sweat on the palms. Be extra careful when reloading film, as a single grain of sand pressed against the emulsion will cause an ugly tram-line.

Rocky shores
These are much the best places for photographing littoral organisms, as they support the richest variety of life and lack the problems associated with photography in mud and sand. The best time to visit a rocky shore is during a spring tide, as at this time the lower shore will be exposed and you will have a rare opportunity to see and photograph marine life which is usually submerged. If you intend to visit the coast for photography, try to obtain local tide-tables so that you can ascertain beforehand the state of the tides and at what times of day they are at their lowest point. However, most rocky shores will have something of interest if there are rock pools. A rich assortment of life can usually be found in these natural aquaria.

On most rocky shores the most conspicuous and obvious living objects will be seaweeds. Large masses of brown seaweeds such as Bladder Wrack (*Fucus vesiculosus*) and Serrated Wrack (*F. serratus*) may cover boulders which are exposed at low tide. These large seaweeds are best photographed by available light, as flash usually causes unacceptably intense highlights. A bright overcast day is the best time for photographing seaweeds out of water and a tripod can be used to obtain maximum depth of field using a slow shutter speed and small aperture. Seaweeds often show a definite zonation on the shore. Using a wide-angle lens it is possible to show how one species succeeds another as they advance up the shore. As well as showing complete plants clothing the rocks, go in for close-ups of interesting details, such as the bladders on certain wracks.

On most rocky shores there will be huge numbers of barnacles encrusting the rocks, as well as molluscs such as Limpets (*Patella* spp) and Periwinkles (*Littorina* spp). These can be shown occuring naturally in groups, as well as individually in close-up. Available light is best for all these shelled animals on the rocks, as it enhances the striations and general sculpturing on the shell. Try to choose subjects which are in open spots so that natural sunlight can be used, if necessary with a tripod, although some molluscs prefer shady spots and you will then need flash. The shaded undersides of boulders or overhanging rocks often harbour encrusting animals such as sponges. In Kenya beautiful pink or blue sponges were common in such spots, where I photographed them using grazed flash.

Rocky shores are also rich in certain kinds of crab. Those in temperate areas are often rather small and rare and should be looked for jammed in crevices in the rock or under boulders and large seaweeds. In the tropics the situation is often very different. In Kenya as night fell the coral rocks became covered with hoards of striped crabs busily feeding, their feet making an audible rustling sound as they skittered across rocks in the growing darkness. During the day thousands of these crabs could be found under the overhanging cliffs. I managed to get some pictures using the zoom and flash and even some close-ups from 2 in with the 55mm.

Rock pools

The best place to look for a large variety of life is definitely in rock pools, for their inhabitants are living in a relatively normal marine environment and can be photographed going about their natural activities. In the tropics shallower pools exposed for long periods high on the shore become too hot for much life to survive, but this is less of a problem in colder temperate areas and in deeper pools. If the animals are to be photographed *in situ*, deep pools are unsuitable as the depth of water makes it impossible to focus on most of the occupants, unless you are equipped with an underwater camera such as a Nikonos and intend to wade into the pool. Most people, however, will want to take their pictures from above the pool through the air/water interface, and for this purpose select a pool which is not much deeper than about 9 in. These may still hold a rich variety of life, from lovely pink coralline seaweeds thickly decorating the edges, to pale green snakelocks anemones lazily waving their tentacles along the sides and on the bottom.

Once you have selected a pool which is of suitable depth and is filled with a rich variety of life you will have to solve the problems associated with taking pictures through water. First check that the surface is not covered in an oily film which would ruin your picture. Remove any objects floating on the surface which may appear in the picture-area. If you wish to use available light you will have to choose a well-lit pool, although this can create its own problems, for sunny pools may be filled with oxygen bubbles created by seaweeds.

Having satisfied yourself that your pool is a good choice, walk around it viewing the surface through the viewfinder. Surface-reflections should be obvious, even if they only manifest themselves as a slight shimmering. There should be at least one angle lacking reflections, so this is the place to start. Ripples caused by wind can be a real headache and on occasion may make photography impossible unless you want to show how your subject lives below the wind-rippled surface of a pool.

Eliminating the air/water interface is obviously the best solution. Some people solve this by making a water-tight box into which the camera is fitted with the lens focused through a piece of plain glass. This is rather a clumsy contraption and displaces rather a lot of water when dumped into a small shallow pool, where it complicates the photography of wary small fish and shrimps. Another solution, which I have used successfully, is to fit a circular piece of glass into a plastic flowerpot whose bottom has been removed. This is then glued to a filter-holder and screwed onto the lens. The front of the pot up to a depth of around 2 in can then be carefully eased into the water, eliminating both reflections and ripples. The main drawback is the care needed to ensure that you do not go too far and risk wetting the lens-barrel. When using this device it is best to have a companion around who can warn you when water and camera are getting too close for comfort.

The best results in rock pools are probably obtained with flash, giving plenty of depth of field for subjects such as snakelocks anemones and freezing the motion of active subjects such as small fish. It also helps to eliminate the problems of reflections, as you can shade the surface with your own body. With the flash pointing at a 45° angle to the water surface and a hand-held (or tripod-mounted) camera, photographing many aquatic organisms in rock pools can be as simple as taking pictures of plants or fungi on land.

The massed growths of seaweeds and anemones around the sides of many rock pools look very spectacular to the naked eye but is unfortunately often a muddled disappointment on a slide. Close-ups of single organisms are often much more satisfactory.

Never handle your equipment with salt water on your hands, so always take a towel with you. Do not rest equipment on wet rocks while you have a smoke or something to eat. Always keep a haze filter on your lens to protect it from salt spray. If you drop equipment into seawater you must transfer it immediately to fresh water. If this is impossible the equipment will be a certain write-off.

Aquaria

Most of the best published photographs showing small marine animals such as seaslugs and starfish are taken in aquaria, although frequently the captions do not tell you this. An aquarium is vital for obtaining really high-quality close-ups of both marine and freshwater organisms, and is probably the most valuable branch of all indoor nature photography.

If you plan much tank photography it will pay you to build a tank specifically for this purpose. Sheets of glass can be purchased from dealers in aquaria and glued together to form a watertight seal. The back of the tank should be longer than the front to reduce the likelihood of the corners being in the picture. Several different sizes of tank can be made to suit both large and small subjects. A sheet of glass inserted an inch or so from the front will be useful to confine active subjects for photography.

Making up a marine aquarium requires a great deal of skill if a natural-looking effect is to be obtained. I do not condone the collecting of marine organisms for photography later at home, possibly many miles distant, and prefer to see a portable tank in use. These can be taken to the coast and used on the spot. Fill them with clear seawater, leaving it for some time to settle. Lighting can either be by available light or flash. Most people seem to prefer flash, directing one unit at the front of the

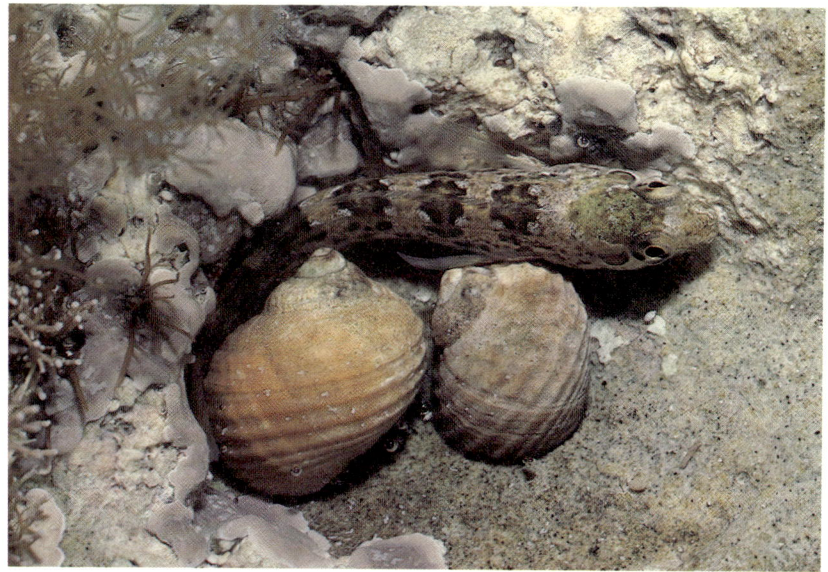

Blennius pholis, Shanny fish, and two *Littorina* species, Periwinkles, in a rock-pool in Dorset, England. Photographed through the water from above, in about 2 in of water, single hand-held flash.

tank and another from overhead or from the rear. It is usual to mask the camera with a large sheet of black cardboard with the lens sticking through. Backgrounds of various colours are inserted into the water in front of the rear wall of the tank. At the end of a day's shooting all the subjects can be released back to their natural habitat.

Freshwater life is usually rather drab compared with marine organisms, and it requires much imagination to produce interesting and attractive pictures. It is simple to maintain a permanent collection of freshwater creatures so that complete lifecycles can be photographed. Filter the water before commencing photography, and remember to stand tap water for 24 hrs before using it. For smaller creatures such as insect larvae, some people first boil the water to remove all the dissolved gases, giving very clear results. As oxygen is one of the gases removed, you must only keep the animal in the water for short periods, otherwise it may drown.

Setting up a freshwater aquarium requires a certain amount of knowledge of the natural environment and of the subjects. Most dragonfly larvae, for example, ambush their prey from among weeds, so it would not be correct to photograph these on a bare sandy bottom in a tank devoid of weed.

Most people seem to use a tripod-mounted camera, which is fine for most subjects but rather restricts flexibility when photographing active subjects such as swimming fish. I have used a hand-held camera and tracked fish in the same way as I track running insects, and this gives excellent results, permitting many pictures to be taken in a very short time.

Appendix: Ethics

After the discovery of some rare orchid or exciting animal, it is extremely easy to become carried away by the desire to secure pictures as quickly as possible. In these circumstances the welfare of the subject may be ignored. All wildlife photographers should try to remember that the well-being of their subjects may be dependent on their own behaviour when taking photographs. Careless unthinking attitudes can easily lead to loss of individual plants or animals and the degradation of their habitat.

Most bird photographers accept that the welfare of the birds is more important than the pictures. If an individual bird shows itself unable to adapt to the photographer's presence, then another nest is found and used instead. Unfortunately there are some exceptions and this may bring into disrepute wildlife photography in general and bird photography in particular. Trampling without permission across private property to obtain views and pictures of rare birds of passage can also make wildlife photographers locally unpopular.

Even rare plants may suffer from the over ardent attentions of photographers. In some places photographers attracted to a particularly fine specimen have often trampled seedling plants for yards around, flattening the whole area. This kind of behaviour is unforgivable and can so easily be avoided by carefully searching the area around the selected plants and placing handkerchiefs or hats over seedlings. Failure to act responsibly, especially on nature reserves, may lead to a 'no photographs' rule, which penalises everyone. Photography of any kind can lead to damage of delicate habitats such as bogs. Before venturing onto such an area, always ask yourself how you can minimise any damage and whether you really need to be taking pictures there at all. All wildlife can be harmed by human stupidity and nature photographers should be aware of their responsibilities to their subjects and act accordingly. Causing a rare bird to desert its nest or destroying a rare plant by trampling can never be justified by the pictures which result.

Index